# Grand-Guignol

The Théâtre du Grand-Guignol in Paris (1897–1962) achieved a legendary reputation as the 'Theatre of Horror', a venue displaying such explicit violence and blood-curdling terror that a resident doctor was employed to treat the numerous spectators who fainted each night. Indeed, *grand guignol* has entered the English language to describe any display of sensational horror.

The first part of this book, 'An Introduction to the Grand-Guignol', reconsiders the importance and influence of the Grand-Guignol within its social, cultural and historical contexts. It is the first attempt at a major evaluation of the genre as performance: since the theatre closed its doors forty years ago, its plays have been generally overlooked by critics and theatre historians. The authors give full consideration to practical applications and to the challenges presented to the actor and director.

The second part of the book, 'Ten Plays of the Grand-Guignol', provides outstanding new translations of a selection of Grand-Guignol plays. The presentation of these plays in English is an invitation to theatres to revive them as well as an implicit demand for a total reappraisal of the Grand-Guignol genre, not least for the unexpected inclusion of two very funny comedies.

**Richard J. Hand** and **Michael Wilson** are Principal Lecturers in Drama at the University of Glamorgan.

## Exeter Performance Studies

*Exeter Performance Studies* aims to publish the best new scholarship from a variety of sources, presenting established authors alongside innovative work from new scholars. The list explores critically the relationship between theatre and history, relating performance studies to broader political, social and cultural contexts. It also includes titles which offer access to previously unavailable material.

*Series editors:* Peter Thomson, Professor of Drama at the University of Exeter; Graham Ley, Lecturer in Drama at the University of Exeter; Steve Nicholson, Head of Theatre Studies and Principal Lecturer at the University of Huddersfield.

The façade of Théâtre 347 (formerly the Théâtre du Grand-Guignol), cité Chaptal, Paris, at the time of writing this book (Collection of Hand and Wilson)

# Grand-Guignol

## The French Theatre of Horror

Richard J. Hand

*and*

Michael Wilson

UNIVERSITY
*of*
EXETER
PRESS

First published in 2002 by
University of Exeter Press
Reed Hall, Streatham Drive
Exeter, Devon EX4 4QR
UK
*www.ex.ac.uk/uep/*

Reprinted 2003

**British Library Cataloguing in Publication Data**
A catalogue record of this book is available
from the British Library


Paperback ISBN 0 85989 696 X
Hardback ISBN 0 85989 695 1




Typeset in Sabon 10/12pt by Exe Valley Dataset Ltd, Exeter

Printed in Great Britain
by Antony Rowe Ltd, Chippenham

To Sadiyah, Shahrazad, Jayne, Phillip,
Gemma and Hannah

# Contents

# Illustrations

# Preface

The phrase 'grand-guignol' has entered the language as a general term for the display of grotesque violence within performance media, but it originates in a specific theatre down an obscure alley in Paris. The Grand-Guignol[1] was a remarkable theatre. For more than six decades it thrilled its audiences with a peculiar blend of horrific violence, the erotic and fast-paced comedy. In its time it achieved international notoriety and became one of the most successful tourist attractions in the French capital.

It is, therefore, all the more extraordinary that, both in its lifetime and since its demise, the Grand-Guignol has been virtually ignored by academics and today has the status of one of the world's great forgotten theatres. It is not difficult to lay the blame for this neglect at the door of institutional conservatism and general disdain in the past for the serious study of popular theatre in academic circles. For many years the Grand-Guignol was simply deemed unworthy of serious consideration and the very recipe for its success with the public was sufficient to secure its dismissal by theatre historians. It is, therefore, to be welcomed that recent years have witnessed a growing interest in popular culture; the horror genre, in its many forms, has now entered the arena of scholarly debate. This book has been prepared in that context and, partly at least, in response to the lack of material available on the Grand-Guignol, particularly to the English-speaking reader.

The Grand-Guignol emerged at a crucial and exciting time for theatre. It was conceived in the nineteenth century, directly from the ground-breaking work of André Antoine and his fellow naturalist radicals at the Théâtre Libre. In fact, it grew up to become a child of the twentieth century, emerging as a complex and seemingly contradictory mixture of theatrical traditions and genres characterized by its use of both horror and comedy plays, incorporating melodrama and naturalism, and going on to reflect the influence of Expressionism and film. Yet at its heart it always remained a *popular* theatre and, more crucially, a *modern*

---

[1] 'Grand-Guignol' appears in both its hyphenated and non-hyphenated form in equal measure in previously published material. However, the current trend amongst French scholars would appear to favour the hyphenated form. This is certainly the case in Agnès Pierron's substantial collection of Grand-Guignol plays (Pierron 1995) and follows the advice given to us by Professor Claude Schumacher. In this book we have, therefore, used the hyphenated form unless, of course, quoting from sources which use the alternative.

theatre. If the dawn of the twentieth century was a critical period in the development of European theatre, then the same can be said for the horror genre itself. As Paul Wells states:

> As the nineteenth century passed into the twentieth, this prevailing moral and ethical tension between the individual and the socio-political order was profoundly affected by some of the most significant shifts in social and cultural life. This effectively re-configured the notion of evil in the horror text . . . in a way that moved beyond issues of fantasy and ideology and into the realms of material existence and an overt challenge to established cultural value systems.
>
> (Wells 2000, 3)

The Grand-Guignol only became *what* it did because it emerged *when* it did and *where* it did. When talking of a 'Theatre of Horror' one might imagine the monster-iconography and Gothic extravaganzas (ironic or otherwise) on display in Richard O'Brien's *The Rocky Horror Show* (1975), Andrew Lloyd-Webber's *Phantom of the Opera* (1986), and even Anne Rice's *Interview with the Vampire* (1976). But as a realist form that never strays far from a grounding in Zola-inspired naturalism, '*Grand Guignol* requires sadists rather than monsters' (Carroll 1990, 15). Although the Grand-Guignol steers well clear of all things super-natural, it pushes the human subject into monstrosity, extrapolating, as it were, *la bête humaine* into *le monstre humain*. André de Lorde sums up this aspect of the Grand-Guignol when he writes in the preface to *La Galerie des monstres* (1928), 'we have a monster within us—a potential monster' (quoted in Pierron 1995, 1339).[2] The psychological motivation of the Grand-Guignol protagonist/antagonist—in the comedies as much as the horror plays—is dictated by primal instincts, or unpredictable mania, the plots obsessed with death, sex and insanity and exacerbated or compounded by grotesque coincidence or haunting irony.

Aside from a few books on the subject, the Grand-Guignol's most substantial surviving legacy is the collection of scripts, housed at the Bibliothèque de l'Arsenal, fifty-five of which are contained in Agnès Pierron's *Le Grand-Guignol* (1995). There also exists a number of photographic stills, documentary footage, press cuttings, programme notes and eye-witness accounts. The most useful of these are the memoirs of Paula Maxa, the most celebrated Grand-Guignol actor (Pierron 1995, 1381–95); what she is able to tell us about performing at

---

[2] All translations are by the authors, unless otherwise indicated. References are to the original French.

the rue Chaptal is invaluable, in spite of her subjectivity and desire to create her own mythology. Apart from this we have very little to tell us about the nature of performance in relation to Grand-Guignol and we are left to our own hypothesizing. To this end we have established a Grand-Guignol Laboratory at the University of Glamorgan to investigate the performative nature of the form. Using student actors we have attempted to learn more about Grand-Guignol performance through the practical exploration of scripts and themes in the drama studio and many of the conclusions contained in this book are informed by that work. We would agree with Mel Gordon (1997, 40) that the Grand-Guignol greatly influenced subsequent horror films, even though it was, ironically, the cinema that contributed largely to the theatre's demise. In the Grand-Guignol Laboratory we have found films particularly beneficial as an entry point into our speculative study towards understanding performance practice at the Grand-Guignol. At the same time it would be a grave mistake to make assumptions about the Grand-Guignol based solely on cinematic evidence. Cinema and theatre are different forms and so we have always trodden with great care in this respect. It is a difference recognized by Maxa herself when she says:

> In the cinema you have a series of images. Everything happens very quickly. But to see people in the flesh suffering and dying at the slow pace required by live performance, that is much more effective. It's a different thing altogether.
>
> (in Pierron 1995, 1392)

This book is divided into two parts. The first part is a discussion of the Grand-Guignol, including an historical outline of the theatre's sixty-five-year existence, and an examination of key aspects and issues pertaining to the genre: location, venue, performance, technical considerations and audience. The second part, and the bulk of this book, is a collection of translations of plays performed at the Grand-Guignol. To date only a small number of English translations of Grand-Guignol plays have been available. Gordon has published three in the various editions of his book (de Lorde and Binet's *L'Horrible Expérience* and de Lorde's *Le Système du Docteur Goudron et du Professeur Plume* in the first edition, whereas the former was replaced by de Lorde and Binet's *Un crime dans une maison de fous* in the revised edition). Deák (1974) also includes a version of *Goudron et Plume* (ibid. 44–54) as an appendix to his article and Gerould (1984) does the same with translations of Méténier's *La Brême* (Gerould 1984, 20–23) and *Le Loupiot* (ibid. 24–27). A number of translations that were presented in London during 1920–22 are available in the Lord Chamberlain's Collections at the British Library.

Whilst all of the plays included here premiered prior to 1930, some of them were reprised at later dates and we have selected them for their importance within the Grand-Guignol repertoire as well as for the representation of the genre that they provide as a collection. We have included comedies as well as horror plays, although the emphasis is on horror, and we have chosen plays that deal with many of the key themes contained within the broad Grand-Guignol repertoire, such as madness, claustrophobia, infection, technophobia, exoticism, eroticism, infidelity, mutilation, revenge and so on. In addition each play is preceded by a preface that not only contextualizes the play historically, but also analyses it in relation to a theoretical consideration of the genre.

Practical exploration of the Grand-Guignol in performance is at an early stage. This volume's aim is to make a contribution to the nascent interest in the French 'Theatre of Horror'.

RJH and MW
*April 2002*

## Acknowledgements

We would like to offer our sincere thanks to the following individuals and institutions:

Simon Baker, Paulo Biscaia Filho, David Cottis, Genevieve Davey, Kathryn Davies, Al Feldstein, Sadiyah Hand, Anna Henderson, Graham Ley, Steve Nicholson, Claude Schumacher, Mike Tarnower, Peter Thomson, Jayne Tucker

Bibliothèque de l'Arsenal
British Film Institute National Library
British Library
William M. Gaines Estate
School of Humanities and Social Sciences Research Committee and
Teaching and Learning Committee, University of Glamorgan
Past and present members of the Grand-Guignol Laboratory
Staff at Pixies Holt Residential Centre, Dartmoor
Colleagues in Theatre and Media Drama at the University of Glamorgan
Theatre Museum

We would also like to thank the Arts and Humanities Research Board for a grant to support the writing of this book.

Part One

# An Introduction to the Grand-Guignol

# 1

# An Historical Outline of the Grand-Guignol

Hidden amongst the decadence and sleaze of Pigalle with its roughnecks and whores, in the shadows of a quiet, cobbled alleyway, stands a little theatre. The spectators take up their seats in the auditorium eager for the show to begin, if only to escape the eerie mood of their surroundings. At last the curtain rises . . . But this is no ordinary theatre, this is the Théâtre du Grand-Guignol: A prostitute is trapped in a bedroom with a psychopathic killer . . . A doctor replaces medicine with poison and injects his unsuspecting patient . . . A man embraces his daughter before blowing out her brains . . . Another father strangles his son to death . . . A woman's face smokes and melts as it is covered in vitriol . . . A man amputates his own hand with an axe . . . A woman is skinned alive while another watches in sexual ecstasy . . . Members of the audience begin to lose consciousness while a desperate house-doctor attempts to revive them . . . Our innocent spectators feel light-headed, morally outraged and yet guiltily stimulated as they stagger out of the theatre to join other people vomiting in the alleyway to the sounds of violent sex emanating from the darkest corners of the street . . .

Such is the sensationalistic myth of the Grand-Guignol, an extreme and unique mixture of the horrific and the erotic, of the graphic and the morally dubious, of *sang, sperme et sueur* (blood, sperm and sweat). Although an examination of the facts will prove the Grand-Guignol to be less colourful than its reputation, the legend has a basis in truth: all the horrific stage episodes outlined above—and more besides—occur in the plays contained in this volume.

## Beginnings

When André Antoine founded the Théâtre Libre in 1887, one of his collaborators was a certain Oscar Méténier. Méténier, formerly a police secretary, provided Antoine with numerous *comédies rosses* (short dramatic pieces which looked at the lives and language of the Parisian underclass) as part of the theatre's naturalistic and experimental multi-play programmes. Antoine, of course, is one of the giants of modern theatre, above all in the contribution he made to the development of stage naturalism and the role of the director. However, he was far too eclectic a director, actor and producer to be labelled exclusively 'naturalistic'; eventually he grew tired of the *rosse* genre and he and Méténier moved in different directions (Gordon 1997, 13). After the Théâtre Libre collapsed in bankruptcy in 1893, Méténier continued his investigations into the *comédie rosse* and naturalism and he opened the Grand-Guignol in 1897 with the Théâtre Libre model in mind.

The plays of his own which Méténier staged during the initial seasons are good examples of pieces expressing naturalist concerns. *La Brême* (translated by Daniel Gerould as *Meat-Ticket* in Gerould 1984, 20–3 —the title is a reference to the slang term used for the prostitute's identity card issued by the police), for example, which contributed to the Grand-Guignol's opening programme, concerns a middle-aged couple discussing their daughter's future with a friend at the time of her first communion. After much discussion of moral values, the daughter enters to declare that, upon the parish priest's advice to never abandon her parents, she intends to follow her sister into prostitution so as to make a financial contribution to the household, a selfless act for which she is congratulated by one and all. Shocking as some of these plays may have been to audiences of the time, 'Méténier's miniature dramas expose the fraud of bourgeois morality when foisted on the poor' (Gerould 1984, 18) whilst the working classes 'parody the values of their supposed betters by adapting the precepts taught by the church and state to their own lowly circumstances' (ibid. 18–19). Méténier also included his *En famille* in the Grand-Guignol programme of April 1898, a play which had caused such moral indignation and outrage when first presented at the Théâtre Libre. Méténier clearly established the Grand-Guignol as a theatre that challenged moral orthodoxy and would continue the *succès de scandale* of naturalism.

It appears that the Grand-Guignol proved a success from its opening and the reason why Oscar Méténier handed ownership of the Théâtre du Grand-Guignol to Max Maurey after only two years at the helm is a matter that remains unclear. Whilst Gordon, Callahan and Homrighous maintain, rather unsatisfactorily, that he simply vanished (Gordon 1988, 17; Callahan 1991, 167; Homrighous 1963, 7), Pierron suggests more credibly that Méténier's decision was motivated by ill health (Pierron 1995, VI), although he was a relatively young man and destined to live for another fourteen years. Even the exact date of the takeover is shrouded in ambiguity.[1]

---

[1] Whilst Pierron (1995, VII) and Deák (1974, 36) maintain that Maurey's stewardship dates from 1898, in Pierron's 'Calendrier des Spectacles' Maurey does not seem to produce his first season until October 1899 and Méténier was still in charge until February of that same year (Pierron 1995, 1404).

Whatever the exact truth, Méténier was handing over a success and he must have felt assured that his enterprise was in safe hands. Yet the theatre that Max Maurey inherited was not a theatre of horror *per se*, but a successful house of naturalism, dedicated to the true-to-life representation of a society dehumanized by capitalism and bourgeois morality. Although Méténier founded and named the theatre, critics agree that it is really after his departure that his successor, Maurey, identified the potential success of the theatre and developed it away from being a Théâtre Libre imitation into being its own unique, successful—and ultimately legendary—venue and genre. During Maurey's fifteen (or sixteen) year reign, the Grand-Guignol became established as a popular theatre with its distinctive programming, acting and production style, with a loyal team of actors, writers and audience members.

It would be wrong to think that these changes occurred all of a sudden and that Maurey set off in the opposite direction to Méténier. In fact, rather the opposite is true, for Maurey, in order to create his 'Theatre of Horror', simply identified characteristics within Méténier's enterprise and moved them up the production agenda. Plays such as *La Brême* and *En famille* with their vicious and 'shocking' condemnations of bourgeois morality would not look out of place within the Grand-Guignol programme under Maurey, although they are clearly plays that emerge from the naturalist tradition of the Théâtre Libre.

The fact that Méténier's naturalist experiment was able to be developed so seamlessly into Maurey's popular *théâtre de la peur* merely shows how this 'serious, pseudo-scientific dramatic form, could be exploited for sheer thrills and entertainment' (Gerould, 1984, 18). Thrill and sensation were also integral elements of the *comédie rosse* genre and the opening year of the Grand-Guignol produced thrilling and sensationalist plays by Méténier such as *Mademoiselle Fifi* (an adaptation of a Maupassant short story) and *Lui!*[2] Both plays deal with prostitution and feature on-stage (*Mademoiselle Fifi*) and off-stage (*Lui!*) murder. As much as they can be primarily viewed as naturalistic works, both plays establish what became the classic formula of the Grand-Guignol play: a combination, broadly speaking, of the erotic and the violent. In addition,

---

[2] In referring to plays performed at the Grand-Guignol, we have always used the original French title, except when making specific reference to a translation or an English language production. Hence, *Lui!* refers to Méténier's play which was produced at the Grand-Guignol in 1897, whereas *Jack* refers to the translation of that play which appears later in this volume. Whilst it is usual in French for each word in the title of a play to begin in the upper case until the first noun is reached, we have noticed inconsistencies in this usage. We have referred to Pierron's 'Calendrier des Spectacles' (1995, 1403–24) for guidance on specific plays. For this reason, for example, *La Dernière torture* becomes *La Dernière Torture*.

each evening in the opening seasons presented a selection of plays in a manner which became the Grand-Guignol's trademark: *la douche écossaise*, a 'hot and cold shower' of dramatic pieces interspersed with comedies.

Camillo Antona-Traversi distinctly labels Antoine and Maurey as emanating from the same naturalist tradition (Antona-Traversi 1933, 65) and, although he may have had his own personal reasons for doing this,[3] Maurey lost no time in acquainting himself with the key figures of the Montmartre artistic community, such as Antoine and, most importantly, the playwright and friend of Oscar Méténier, André de Lorde. As Frantisek Deák asserts, initially 'Maurey continued to present naturalist plays' (Deák 1974, 36), such as *Lui!* in January 1902 and a number of comedies from the pen of Georges Courteline, another favourite from the days of Antoine's Théâtre Libre. Nevertheless, the Grand-Guignol did develop significantly during the first few years of the new century and Maurey is generally credited with establishing the Grand-Guignol in five key areas, namely performance style, production style (especially in the development of stage trickery and special effects), programming, the importance of the playwright and the establishment of the Grand-Guignol as the undisputed 'Theatre of Horror'.

At the same time, every one of these developments had been previously signposted by Méténier and it was Maurey's legendary skills as an impresario and publicist which allowed him to recognize certain aspects of Méténier's naturalist experiment as having popular and commercial viability. In 1903 Jacques des Gachon praised Maurey as being a man 'who had very clear ideas' (quoted in Pierron 1995, VII), comparing him to Antoine himself. It was indeed fortunate that, so early in its life, the Théâtre du Grand-Guignol acquired a director with such financial acumen and artistic vision.

## Performance Style

If Méténier's Grand-Guignol grew out of naturalist experimentation in the 1880s and 1890s, then it was also never entirely divorced from the great *popular* theatrical development of the nineteenth century, melodrama. Montmartre was home to the 'blood and thunder' theatres of the *boulevard du crime*, and the Grand-Guignol would, in its own time,

---

[3] Antona-Traversi was, for a while, the secretary to Camille Choisy, the third owner of the Grand-Guignol. In 1928 Choisy left the theatre after falling out with his partner Jack Jouvin, and the ever-loyal Antona-Traversi published his *L'Histoire du Grand-Guignol* (1933) as a tribute to his former boss and as an attack on Jouvin, whom he saw as the usurper of the Grand-Guignol tradition.

*Figure 1.* An example of the dramatic and gory illustrations typically used to accompany *fait divers* ('Un Crime Monstrueux commis par deux enfants', *Le Petit Journal*, 26 December 1909, 416) (Collection of Hand and Wilson)

become 'le théâtre de Montmartre' (Sabatier 1998, 141). Implicit in Sabatier's statement must be an acknowledgement that the Grand-Guignol remained inside, rather than outside, the area's melodramatic traditions.

Not unlike the great melodramas of the day, Méténier's *comédies rosses* drew their inspiration from, among other things, the *fait divers* of the Parisian popular press. These were short items of news (usually involving violent crime), gory and colourful illustrations of which often graced the front and back pages of *Le Petit Journal* and *Le Petit Parisien*. Here were documentary illustrations of vitriol attacks on former lovers (see front cover) and brutal murders by delinquent youths (fig. 1), which provided raw material for both forms. When Maurey took over and looked to develop the Grand-Guignol as a theatre of horror, he undoubtedly recognized the popular vein of melodrama that lay embedded within the material and sought to exploit it. Naturalism and melodrama used the same material in completely different ways. Whereas melodrama produced plays of sentimental and sermonising morality in a world where the righteous who suffered misery and poverty were rewarded in Heaven, naturalism was a far more radical doctrine, in which bourgeois society was blamed for the brutalization of humankind.

Mary Homrighous argues that the Grand-Guignol emanates from three separate traditions: naturalism, melodrama and the well-made play (1963, 25). Although these may be the key traditions amalgamated into the Grand-Guignol, it is worth noting how eclectic the theatre was and would always attempt to be. For instance, Symbolism too can be seen as bearing an influence. Indeed, the first successful attempt at a dramatized *fait divers* was *Intérieur* (1894) by Maurice Maeterlinck, the most celebrated of the Symbolist dramatists (Homrighous 1963, 23). As Claude Schumacher argues:

> [Maeterlinck's] theatre is a theatre of fear and a theatre of waiting —not the coward's obscene fear which expresses itself in histrionics, but hidden, internal and unutterable fear, which gnaws away at the soul and which stems from forces over which we have no control. Such waiting and such fear will only cease at the moment of death; life must be lived until then.
>
> (Schumacher 1984, 16)

The Grand-Guignol was even more famous as being a theatre of fear, and although there is very little 'waiting' in the exacerbated horrors of the Grand-Guignol, it displays a world governed by a similarly deep and unutterable fear, whilst resorting to the 'obscene' histrionics associated with melodrama.

Under Maurey, the performance style moved away from naturalism towards a more melodramatic approach, although the naturalist legacy (and maybe a touch of Maeterlinck's Symbolism) was never completely lost. By the beginning of the twentieth century, naturalism was practically a spent force as part of the artistic avant garde, whereas melodrama proved itself to be far more robust. Although the days of the great melodrama theatres were all but over, melodramatic styles of acting had found a new home in the silent film industry and were soon to influence the techniques of the Expressionists. It was under Maurey's stewardship, in 1909,[4] that the Grand-Guignol first began its uneasy relationship with the cinema industry with the production of a film version of de Lorde's adaptation of Poe's *Le Système du Docteur Goudron et du Professeur Plume* (Robert Saidreau 1909) with Henri Gouget, who had played the role of Goudron in the 1903 premiere at the rue Chaptal and was a key member of the resident company during this period (Pierron 1995, 1430). Maurey, it could be argued, was simply making the move towards a more popular style in keeping with the times. As the distinctive house performance style of the Grand-Guignol, melodrama tempered with naturalism, developed, it is in the production values of the time that the legacy of Antoine and Zola can be most readily perceived.

## Production Style

As Maurey rebranded the Grand-Guignol as the 'Theatre of Horror', much time, effort and expense was invested in creating effects that were as realistic as possible: whilst a victim may die a melodramatic death, the means by which they met that death were as naturalistic as possible. A key figure in this was Paul Ratineau. It is Ratineau who usually receives the greatest credit for developing the repertoire of stage trickery, special effects and sleight-of-hand sequences, which made the audiences at the rue Chaptal gasp and faint. It is testament to his technical skill and creativity that he was able to develop devices and props that were undetectable to audiences in this small and intimate theatre space. This was achieved, in part, through the ingenious use of stage lighting and shadows, and a great deal of credit must also go to the virtuosity and artistry of the actors themselves in successfully executing the special effects.

François Rivière and Gabrielle Wittkop (1979, 84) identify Ratineau as the third personality, along with Maurey and de Lorde, in the team that was responsible for developing the form in the first decade of the

---

[4] In the same year D.W. Griffith produced *The Lonely Villa*, starring Mary Pickford and Mack Sennett, a version of André de Lorde and Charles Foleÿ's Grand-Guignol classic, *Au téléphone*.

twentieth century. Effectively Ratineau took on the role of stage manager, where he was able to put his skills and knowledge to good use. According to Henri-René Lenormand—who made his playwrighting debut at the Grand-Guignol with *La Folie blanche* (1905), but never contributed more than a few plays to the repertoire—in his book, *Confessions d'un auteur dramatiques* (1949):

> He knew more than anyone else in Paris about the technique of horror effects. He was an expert in stage weaponry, blood stains, acid burns, pestilent ulcers and severed heads, and he had the composure of a highly experienced stage manager, a wicked Montmartrean sense of humour and a memory which contained, in astonishing detail, everything about the theatre of fear.
>
> (quoted in Rivière and Wittkop 1979, 84)

It is worth mentioning that first and foremost Ratineau was an actor, notching up probably the longest continuous career on the Grand-Guignol stage as a performer in mainly supporting roles. It was a career that lasted well over quarter of a century and spanned the directorships of Maurey, Choisy and Jouvin. Amongst his multitude of credits are appearances in the premiere of de Lorde's *Le Système du Docteur Goudron et du Professeur Plume* alongside Gouget in April 1903, de Lorde and Morel's *La Dernière Torture* in December 1904 (again alongside Gouget), and as the Englishman John Matthews in Héros and Abric's *La Veuve* in March 1906. By 1924 he was playing alongside Maxa in André-Paul Antoine's *La Nuit tragique de Raspoutine* (later renamed *La dernière nuit de Raspoutine*)[5] and he can even be seen playing the role of Hippolyte in the 1930 production of Jean Sartène's *La Griffe*, once more with his old colleague, the veteran Henri Gouget, who made a brief reappearance on the stage at the rue Chaptal under the direction of Jack Jouvin. Arguably, Ratineau's success as a stage manager can be largely attributed to his ability to apply an actor's perspective to the development of special effects. This was a form which relied as much on the artistry of the actor to successfully carry out the tricks on stage, in front of an intimate audience, as it did on the ingenuity of the effects themselves.

## Programming

We have already seen that it was Méténier who, from the very opening night with its programme of a prologue, two comedies and four dramas

---

[5] André-Paul Antoine (1892–1982) was the son of the founder of the Théâtre Libre.

or *comédies rosses*, introduced the concept of alternating different types of plays within a single evening's entertainment. However, *la douche écossaise* was not, as Rivière and Wittkop are at pains to point out, anything necessarily new; 'The system put in place by Méténier established the alternating of comedies and dark plays—this hot and cold shower, also represented by the famous masks which decorate Harlequin's cloak' (Rivière and Wittkop 1979, 76). Furthermore, as a programming structure, it is ideally suited to an evening of one-act plays, a dramatic form championed by Antoine at the Théâtre Libre.

Maurey's contribution was to recognize the importance of *la douche écossaise* to the effectiveness of a theatre of horror. Not only did it allow the theatre to take its audience on an emotional rollercoaster ride from erotic drama to sex farce and back again, but the horror plays were all the more successful for the comic relief provided by the comedies (and vice versa). The contrast between the styles exaggerated both the horror and the comedy and an evening was structured so that the increase and subsequent release of suspense was repeated, climaxing in the main horror at the end of the evening. In this sense, all the plays within an evening's programme should not simply be seen as a series of individual plays, but rather as equally important and interdependent components of the entire theatrical event. According to Pierron, 'From the rising of the curtain, the comedy prepares the ground for the horror' (1995, XIII). It is a technique of tension and release that has been put to good effect by a range of horror writers and film-makers, and Maurey consolidated the idea into the characteristic formula of the Grand-Guignol.

## The Making of a Myth

Under Maurey the Grand-Guignol grew into an immensely popular theatre, drawing its audiences from all echelons of society. This was achieved through a combination of a concretization of the form and the shameless use of publicity stunts to create a theatrical genre that became shrouded in its own mythology. The concept of performance had never been restricted purely to the stage as far as the Grand-Guignol was concerned. Méténier had already built around himself a reputation for shocking and offending critics and audience alike, not least by famously arriving at the Grand-Guignol dressed in black, flanked by two body-guards, and recounting to the audience, outside the theatre, the gruesome details of horrific crimes (Deák 1974, 36). He further sought to capitalize upon this by publishing a weekly journal, *Le Grand Guignol, Journal Hebdomadaire* in order to 'defend his position and also to publicise his reputation for scandal, contradiction, and a taste for the forbidden' (ibid.).

Maurey did not possess the public persona of Méténier, but must have recognized that the success of the latter's enterprise was, at least in part, due to his attempts at publicity. Maurey adopted another, and ultimately more successful, tack, promoting the Grand-Guignol as the unexpurgated 'Theatre of Horror' and creating a whole mythology around it. Maurey was not interested in experimental naturalism for its own sake, but wanted the Grand-Guignol to be seen as a popular, distinctive and profitable theatre, as much a genre in its own right as a theatre building. The other developments in performance, production and programming were all part of this, but Maurey recognized that his enterprise could only benefit from attention to the details of the whole theatrical experience.

When Maurey added a *médecin de service*, or house-doctor, to the permanent staff of the theatre to attend personally to members of the audience who were taken ill during the performance, it is more likely that this was a gimmick to publicize the anticipated horrors lurking inside the auditorium than a response to any real need to cope with an epidemic of faintings and vomitings. This suspicion is further confirmed by a cartoon by Abel Faivre, now famous in Grand-Guignol mythology. Published in *Journal* on 13 December 1904, it shows an anxious husband attending to his wife, who has fainted, calling for the help of the house-doctor. The scene takes place in the foyer of the theatre during a performance of *La Dernière Torture*, whilst a relaxed and nonchalant Max Maurey, hands in pockets, looks on and comments that the doctor himself is indisposed, having fainted like so many others (see Pierron 1995, XIV). Whether or not this is based on a true incident, as has been claimed, is open to debate, but Maurey did nothing (and quite the opposite, it would seem) to gainsay the story. A further example comes from a cartoon published in *Rire* from the same period,[6] which portrays a queue of audience members receiving a medical check-up from an aged doctor before being allowed admittance to the theatre. Maurey was so pleased with this piece of publicity that he took to reprinting it in the theatre programmes.

Maurey's great publicity success was to convince his audience—and some critics and commentators—that the Grand-Guignol was a theatre of physical violence where blood flowed by the bucketful (see Gordon 1997, 30) and the horror so intense that audiences would flee the auditorium or lose consciousness. He achieved this through a range of production techniques, alongside a mastery of public relations, whilst also shrouding everything in a kind of exotic secrecy, so creating a believable folklore around the Grand-Guignol.

---

[6] This cartoon is reprinted in Gordon 1997, 19, although no date of publication is offered. It is also referred to in Deák 1974, 37.

As with all such mythology, there is clearly an element of truth within it. It may be that Maurey's myth-making was so successful that it became a self-fulfilling prophecy, but it is clear that acts of extreme violence *were* simulated on the stage and that members of the audience did faint. In the same way that we might nowadays be bewildered by how our ancestors laughed at what seem the weak or incomprehensible jokes of music hall and variety comedians, we must exercise extreme caution when making judgements about staged acts of violence which might today seem tame and unconvincing. There is enough evidence to suggest that the audiences of the Grand-Guignol genuinely did attend the theatre to experience the thrill of fear. Nevertheless, this was not achieved through a frenzy of uncontrolled violence as the myth might suggest. Behind the myth and the cloak of secrecy created by Maurey lies a truth of greater artistry and subtlety.

## A Writers' Theatre

The third figure in the triangle, with Maurey and Ratineau, responsible for the creation of the theatre of horror, is the playwright André de Lorde, known as 'Le Prince de la Terreur'. De Lorde was not only the most prolific of all the Grand-Guignol writers, producing over 150 plays, novels and essays in his lifetime, but, from 1900 until his retirement in 1938, he was the writer most closely associated with the Grand-Guignol and his plays were still part of the repertoire well into the 1950s. Although it is his plays, above those of any other writer, that dominate the canon of Grand-Guignol classics, de Lorde's work was not exclusive to the Grand-Guignol, and he wrote for a number of other prestigious theatres, such as the Théâtre-Antoine, the Odéon and the Théâtre Sarah-Bernhardt. Nevertheless the 'Theatre of Horror' remained the spiritual home to the man who, in a remarkable testament to his contribution (which, in its turn, acknowledges the importance of writing to the Grand-Guignol as a whole), was even described as 'the inventor of the so-called "theatre of horror" or the "grand guignolesque"' (Sée 1933, 74). Even when criticizing the themes or morality of his plays, critics had to own, like Georges Bourdon in *Comoedia*, that 'nobody surpasses M. de Lorde in theatrical technique' (24 July 1921, 141).

Born André de Latour, comte de Lorde, in Toulouse on 11 July 1869 (Rivière and Wittkop 1979, 61) into a well-to-do family (his father was a doctor and his mother a pianist), de Lorde had, from an early age, a fascination with the macabre, which was merely fuelled by his father's somewhat unorthodox attempts to stifle it. Initially he trained as a lawyer and for a brief time practised at the bar in Paris and also worked in the Ministry of Finance, but his real passion was for the theatre. His

mother, having divorced his father, had remarried the famous actor
Mounet-Sully, who had encouraged the young de Lorde in his passion.
When he was appointed to the post of librarian at the Bibliothèque de
l'Arsenal[7] in 1892, a sinecure which he held for fifteen years, he began to
devote himself to a career as a writer.

De Lorde sent his manuscripts to Antoine for consideration (Pierron
1995, XXXVI) and soon became known within the theatre community.
He befriended Méténier and the two planned collaborative projects
together. However, it was under Maurey that de Lorde got his first
opportunity to write for the Grand-Guignol, making his debut in January
1900 with *Le Post-scriptum*, a comedy. Interestingly, many of his plays
were collaborations or adaptations. A number of his co-writers were
scientists, most notably Alfred Binet, inventor of the Binet Intelligence
Test, adding authentic detail to the plays. De Lorde's work included
adaptations of fiction, cinema and even historical events. This aspect of
his output reminds us that the Grand-Guignol would always be a
significant theatre of adaptation, giving rise to a number of fascinating
examples of this process.

Not surprisingly, with the services of a talent like de Lorde, the
writers of the Grand-Guignol under Maurey enjoyed a significant status,
and yet scripts were not treated as sacred. Maurey himself, who also
wrote a number of plays for the rue Chaptal, was renowned for taking a
particularly close interest in the development of the scripts in rehearsal.
Most illuminating in this respect is the playwright René Berton's account
of rehearsals at the Grand-Guignol under Maurey, quoted in full by
Antona-Traversi in his *L'Histoire du Grand-Guignol* (Antona-Traversi
1933, 30–36). According to Berton, Maurey would attend rehearsals
and, with an enviable eye for detail, become increasingly involved,
rewriting whole scenes and altering the way actors delivered lines, made
gestures or moved on the stage. This did not always endear Maurey to
his colleagues, and arguments regularly erupted during rehearsals,
including an incident when Severin-Mars, a leading actor, threatened
Maurey with a table. Gordon suggests that this tension was the basis of
the undoubted bounty of creativity that existed under Maurey's
stewardship, claiming that the 'atmosphere of barely restrained hostility
and frustration probably improved the evening's work' (Gordon 1997,
18). Berton has only admiration for Maurey: 'What made Max
Maurey's job easier was the spirit of discipline and commitment, the
flexibility and endurance of the actors under his direction' (Antona-
Traversi 1933, 35).

---

[7] The Bibliothèque de l'Arsenal is now, rather fittingly, home to the Grand-
Guignol archives in Paris.

Once again the creation of the Grand-Guignol as a writers' theatre was not an innovation of Maurey's. Méténier had also placed the playwright at the centre of the creative process. The differences between the two stem from the different agenda that they were trying to follow. Whilst Méténier was trying to create a theatre that dealt with social reality from a radical perspective, Maurey wanted to titillate and frighten. The Grand-Guignol writers often used the *faits divers* and other items of news for inspiration, but whilst Méténier's writers portrayed the bestial depths to which humanity had sunk under post-industrial capitalism, Maurey's team, led by de Lorde, sought to exploit contemporary fears. In this sense, the two regimes reflected two separate ages, divided by the turn of the century in which the obsessions of the nineteenth century gave way to the modernist concerns of *la belle époque*.

## La Belle Époque

Politically, the closing years of the nineteenth century were dominated by the infamous Dreyfus Affair (Mayeur and Rebérioux 1987, 179) which involved the brief imprisonment of Émile Zola and which dragged on from 1894 to 1900, resulting in the victory of the generally left-leaning Dreyfusards and the pardoning of Captain Dreyfus. At the same time, in 1898, French colonial ambition had been dealt a bitter blow following the stand-off with Britain and the withdrawal of troops from Fashoda. With the humiliation of defeat at the hands of the Prussians still fresh in the memory, French self-confidence was at decidedly low ebb (Hayes 1992, 24–25). All this was set to change as the old century drew to a close; the carbuncle of the old order was seemingly lanced with the end of the Dreyfus Affair and the election of a left-wing government in 1902 (Mayeur and Rebérioux 1987, 220–22). The separation of church and state followed shortly afterwards in 1905 (ibid., 227–32).

The period from the turn of the century to the outbreak of war in 1914 was a period of stability, growth and prosperity in France, and particularly Paris, which 'was the scene of creative thinking and invention unusually rich in quantity and quality' (Cronin 1989, 15). It is nevertheless important to qualify such a perception of *la belle époque*. The France of this epoch was hopelessly divided along class lines, exacerbated by the national and international political crises outlined above. In 1900, scarcely one in every forty boys received any formal education beyond the age of eleven and the education of girls was statistically insignificant. As Theodore Zeldin puts it, secondary education was 'a luxury, an investment, a status symbol' (quoted in Schumacher 1984, 3). In the light of such facts, it is easy to understand the vehemence of the attacks on bourgeois values and morality up to this point, whether in the novels of Zola or the plays of Méténier. Claude Schumacher reminds us:

> It is useful to remember that [the conventional image of *belle époque* France] as a country of song and dance, giddy with pleasure, belongs more to the world of myth than reality, and that the theatre in this period was an art form which of necessity could interest only a small minority of the population. In the troubled 1890s as well as during the years leading up to the First World War, the theatre catered to a middle-class audience looking for escapist entertainment.
>
> (Schumacher 1984, 5)

Schumacher illustrates bourgeois escapism with the massive success of Edmond Rostand's *Cyrano de Bergerac* in 1897–98 (the same year as the height of the Dreyfus Affair and the opening of the Grand-Guignol), a play which was hailed by critics as the ' "triple protest of idealism, poetry and French *clarté* (enlightenment)" against the prurience of naturalism' (Schumacher 1984, 15). An example like this throws the nihilism and naturalism of the Grand-Guignol into an interesting light. It reflects, perhaps, that even a theatre of horror is escapist or, more likely, that its success was with an audience that was, at this time, distinctively Montmartrean: working class or avant gardist. Either way, it is interesting that Max Maurey's directorship of the Grand-Guignol coincides with *la belle époque*. What was produced at the Grand-Guignol at this time (and subsequently became defining characteristics of it) reflected the moods, anxieties and preoccupations of Parisian society during this complex and critical period.

## The Golden Age of the Grand-Guignol

In August 1914 Europe embarked on a four-year war, fought largely in the fields of Northern France, which saw death and horror on a scale previously unimagined. Europe was to be changed forever, and within a year of the outbreak of war Maurey had withdrawn from the enterprise and handed over directorship of the theatre to Camille Choisy and his partner Charles Zibell. In her memoirs Paula Maxa suggests that the reason for Maurey's departure was a fear that, after the real-life horrors of the war, his audience would have no further appetite for the horrors of the stage (see Pierron 1995, 1383). Perhaps Maurey, privately a man of high morals and a deep sensitivity, lost that appetite himself.

It is still easy to underestimate Maurey's contribution to the Grand-Guignol form, not least because Choisy's stewardship is often described as the period in which it 'reached its artistic apogee' (Gordon 1997, 24). It is true certainly that the post-war period saw the Grand-Guignol, in the words of Maxa, become 'the most fashionable theatre in Paris' (in Pierron 1995, 1383) and one of the three main theatrical tourist attractions alongside the Comédie Française and the Folies Bergères (ibid.), but Choisy, as able and gifted as he was, was merely building on the foundations provided by his predecessors. If Méténier and Maurey were the architects of the Grand-Guignol, then Choisy was the master decorator (see Pierron, 1995, VII).

Maurey had expected the Grand-Guignol's demise after the 1914–18 war. According to Gordon, André Antoine also felt the Grand-Guignol's novelty was over, a sentiment echoed by many contemporary reviewers (Gordon 1997, 24). Fernand Gregh, in 1921, highlights what he sees as the redundant form and technique of the genre:

> I already said last year that the so-called Grand-Guignol genre seems to me to be exhausted; I say it again after yesterday evening's show. The alternating of hot and cold, terror and mad laughter, has given us all that it can; in spite of the talents of the writers, something else is needed. (. . . We) no longer shudder like we used to. We have been shown too much in the small dark auditorium at the rue Chaptal, its walls dripping with artificial anguish and theatrical fear, and we have had our fill of it.
>
> (*Comoedia*, 24 April 1921, 57)

However, Gregh, Maurey and Antoine could not have been more wrong as the Grand-Guignol entered its 'golden age'. Maybe part of the reason for its continued, if unexpected, success was the form's ability to evolve. In 1925, for example, we see de Lorde and Henri Bauche's *Le Cabinet du Dr Caligari*, a stage adaptation of Robert Wiene's 1919 masterpiece of German Expressionist cinema. The production was revived several times, including after the Second World War. Such developments enabled the Grand-Guignol to preserve the defining features of the genre which had developed during *la belle époque*, whilst embracing and rejuvenating itself with the innovations of Expressionism, and they reflect the success of Camille Choisy's management.

Choisy was a man of the theatre who had for years made an unremarkable career as an actor in second-rate melodramas, but was clearly suited to lead the Grand-Guignol into a new era. Charles Zibell provided the continuing financial capital for the project, but beyond that he took little interest in the enterprise and was content to leave the day-to-day management of the theatre and the artistic decisions to his partner.

As with Maurey, Choisy cannot claim the entire credit for himself as he was ably assisted by a highly skilled team of actors and writers, retaining the services of de Lorde and Ratineau, who also took on directorial responsibilities. Nevertheless, Choisy certainly deserves recognition for nurturing the talent of the two most influential performers to grace the stage at the rue Chaptal.

## Maxa and Paulais

During the 1920s the Grand-Guignol was dominated by L. Paulais[8] and Paula Maxa, the greatest exponents of the craft of the Grand-Guignol performer. Paulais was known as 'le Mounet-Sully du Grand-Guignol' (Antona-Traversi 1933, 75) and is credited with the creation of many memorable roles. If the Choisy era marked the final stage of transition from nineteenth-century naturalism towards a performance style more influenced by the heightened emotions of melodrama (given a greater impetus during this time by the advent of Expressionism in Germany and the emerging dominance of cinema), as is argued by Gordon when he claims that, 'instead of the single-minded, Antoine-like naturalism in the creation of character and action, a more colorful and complicated behavior was expected from the players under Choisy' (Gordon 1997, 24), then Paulais played no small part in these developments. The existing photographs of Paulais show him demonstrating a full range of stylized gestures and facial expressions, with a stiff posture, wide eyes and flared nostrils, all accentuated by the skilful application of make-up.

Paulais's name, however, is forever linked with that of Paula Maxa, his leading lady and the most celebrated of all Grand-Guignol actors. She first appeared at the rue Chaptal in 1917 in Jean Bernac's *Le Poison noir* (Pierron 1995, XLII)[9] and had left by the end of the following decade; during this period her name became synonymous with Grand-Guignol performance, earning her the enviable nicknames of *la Sarah Bernhardt de l'impasse Chaptal* (Pierron 1995, 1381) and *la princesse de l'horreur* (Antona-Traversi 1933, 78).

There may be some hyperbole at play when Gordon claims that Maxa was murdered on stage more than 10,000 times (Gordon 1997, 26),[10]

---

[8] Interestingly, Maxa refers to Paulais's forename as Georges (Pierron 1995, 1384).

[9] In her memoirs, Maxa herself claims that her first appearance at the Grand-Guignol was in Charles Méré's *La Nuit au bouge* (Pierron 1995, 1384), although, according to Pierron, this did not play until November 1919 (Pierron 1995, 1412).

[10] See also Antona-Traversi (1933, 79), who estimates that Maxa cried 'Au secours!' 983 times, 'On m'assassine!' 1,263 times and 'Au viol!' 1,804½ times!

but it does give an indication of her importance to the Grand-Guignol at this time and it earned her the title of 'the most assassinated woman in the world' (quoted in Pierron 1995, 1381). A columnist of the time wrote in admiration:

> All the humiliations that this charming artist has endured during her short, but already glorious, career cannot be ignored. Cut into ninety-three pieces by an invisible Spanish dagger, stitched back together in two seconds by a Samaritan; flattened by a steamroller; disembowelled by a slaughterman who steals her intestines; shot by firing squad, quartered, burned alive, devoured by a puma, crucified, shot with a pistol, stabbed, raped and still she stays happy and smiling.
>
> (Quoted, but unaccredited and undated in
> Antona-Traversi, 78–79)

It was clearly a testimony that flattered the actress, as she later embellished it for inclusion in her own memoirs (see Pierron 1995, 1381).

Choisy's stewardship effectively ended in 1926 when Zibell, facing financial ruin, sold his share to Jack Jouvin. Jouvin had no intention of playing the sleeping partner and attempted to assume control of the theatre. There followed a brief but seemingly acrimonious relationship between the two new partners, at the end of which Choisy left the Grand-Guignol in 1928 to set up 'Le Théâtre du Rire et de l'Épouvante' at the Théâtre Saint-Georges. Maxa claims this was a success (Pierron 1995, 1394), but it appears to have been a short-lived enterprise.[11]

Maxa herself was contractually obliged to remain at the Grand-Guignol, but as soon as Jouvin was assured of victory in his battle with Choisy, she too was unceremoniously released, according to her own version of events, for having too popular a following. Jouvin, it seemed, wanted a more anonymous company (ibid.). Maxa established her own experiment called 'Le théâtre de la Vice et de la Vertu' in 1933, but once again the name of the Grand-Guignol alone was enough to secure its supremacy over any rivals, and shortly afterwards, the rift between her and Jouvin presumably healed, she returned to the rue Chaptal. It was one of a number of times she was to play at the Grand-Guignol over the

---

[11] Choisy's venture, seems to have caused Jouvin some concern, however, if we are to believe Antona-Traversi's partisan account of events. In April 1928 Jouvin went so far as to publish an open letter in *Le Figaro* claiming the authenticity of his own theatre over Choisy's. It is quoted in full in Antona-Traversi (86) and suggests that Jouvin perceived Choisy's theatre as a genuine threat.

next twenty years, but she never regained her former cult status. Her trademark bloodcurdling scream, it is claimed, had permanently damaged her voice (Gordon 1997, 30).

## The Grand-Guignol Abroad

In spite of its popularity and international notoriety, the Grand-Guignol remained a peculiarly French, and specifically Parisian, form. Nevertheless a number of attempts were made to export the Grand-Guignol, mainly during the Choisy period, either through the tours of the Parisian company or through independent attempts to copy the Grand-Guignol formula in other countries.

Maurey himself had taken the company touring outside of Paris and, in 1908, even to London, but with limited success. Choisy organized a much more ambitious series of tours in the 1920s, which are well-documented in both Pierron (1995, LII-LVII) and Gordon (1997, 35–40). One such tour was to New York in 1923, where critical reception was fairly harsh. The *New York Times* bewailed the decline of drama since the Greeks and their *off-stage* horrors, while *Variety* described the visiting productions as being 'unqualified dirt, unsubtle, coarse, vulgar, obscene and foul' (quoted in Skal 1993, 60). The Grand-Guignol of the rue Chaptal was so inextricably linked to Paris, to Montmartre, to the theatre building itself, as well as the unique experience that the whole theatrical event provided, that it only really enjoyed any success as a form abroad when local impresarios attempted to set up their own permanent companies in the style of the Parisian theatre, reinventing it anew for a different cultural context. The most interesting of these experiments is that which took place in London between 1920 and 1922,[12] involving the producer Jose Levy and the already established theatrical dynasty of the Thorndike-Cassons, if only because of the popularity it enjoyed during its all-too-brief lifespan.[13]

---

[12] An Italian Grand-Guignol, based in Rome, also enjoyed some success during the inter-war period, although an attempt to establish a permanent Grand-Guignol in New York never took off.

[13] London's Grand-Guignol ran for a period of two years producing programmes of original work from writers including H.F. Maltby and Noel Coward, and translations of plays from the French. It had a precarious relationship with the Lord Chamberlain, the official censor, which finally came unstuck after a production of *The Old Women* by André de Lorde and Alfred Binet (this was interestingly the world premiere of the classic play which was later produced at the rue Chaptal as *Un crime dans une maison de fous*). Up until that point the on-stage horrors had been restricted to poisonings, strangulations and the like and, realizing that no licence would be granted to the Little Theatre for a

## Decline and Fall

It would be unfair to lay the blame for the decline of the Grand-Guignol entirely at the door of Jack Jouvin. It is important to disentangle him from the partisan bad press he received at the hands of Antona-Traversi and Maxa, who were both ultimately loyal to Choisy, and although it is true that it was under Jouvin's stewardship that the Grand-Guignol began its slow and irreversible decline, Jouvin was without doubt having to operate under very different (and more difficult) circumstances. It is unclear whether the changes that Jouvin made to the artistic policy of the theatre contributed to its decline, were made in the attempt to arrest its decline in a changing context, or were merely coincidental to it, but Jouvin could not have taken over the Grand-Guignol at a more challenging time. Choisy was a hard act to follow and Jouvin, in the context of competition from his predecessor's 'Théâtre du Rire et de l'Épouvante', no doubt felt the need to assert his authority by placing his individual stamp upon the programmes offered by the Grand-Guignol.

Jouvin still retained many of the Grand-Guignol's old favourites in his programmes, including Level's *Le Baiser dans la nuit* (1930 and 1938), de Lorde's *Le Laboratoire des hallucinations* (1931 and 1933) and Autier and Cloquemin's *Gardiens de phare* (1933) to name but a few. He was also responsible for premiering a number of other plays which were destined to become classics of the genre, such as Aragny and Neilson's *Le Baiser de sang* (1929 and reprised in 1937) and Maurey, Hellem and d'Estoc's *Le Faiseur de monstres* (1929). According to Gordon, Jouvin all but abandoned de Lorde's plays, retaining only three in his programmes (Gordon 1997, 28), although a closer examination of Pierron's 'Calendrier des Spectacles' (1995, 1403–24) reveals that Jouvin actually staged on average one de Lorde play every year during his eleven-year reign at the rue Chaptal. Although this is a divergence from the thirty-one productions of de Lorde plays staged by Choisy in thirteen years (including the brief period of Choisy-Jouvin collaboration), it does not quite confirm the haemorrhaging of the old policies implied by Gordon, especially when set alongside Maurey's very similar record of nineteen productions in sixteen years. Further-

---

play which contained an eye-gouging, Casson persuaded a friend of his, a rural vicar, to apply for the licence in the name of an amateur drama group. As a result the play was not scrutinized and the licence was granted. By the time the Lord Chamberlain realized that he had been tricked, it was too late and the play was staged at the Little Theatre. Victory was hollow, however, and the censor applied intolerable pressure on Levy from that point on. Within a year this popular and successful enterprise had been abandoned and, although numerous attempts at a revival were made, all were short-lived.

more, Jouvin's programmes reveal a healthy sprinkling of plays by established Grand-Guignol writers such as Level, Méré, Duvernois and Berton.

Gordon identifies a preference under the Jouvin regime for plays which replaced physical violence with psychological and sexual menace (Gordon 1997, 28), and Rivière and Wittkop suggest that 'Jouvin decided to modify slightly the tradition . . . and to spice up the alternating of terror and laughter with a certain seductive eroticism' (Rivière and Wittkop 1979, 91). Maxa claims that the Grand-Guignol began its decline because of Jouvin's insistence on retaining control over all aspects of production, rather than any lack of ability or abandonment of traditional Grand-Guignol values on his part, stating 'Jouvin was not a bad director, he put on some good shows, but he wanted to do everything himself, especially the writing of all the plays, which created a great monotony' (Pierron 1995, 1394). Certainly Jouvin's programmes reveal an extraordinary number of plays accredited to his own name or one of his many pseudonyms. Perhaps Jouvin, competent as he might have been, just did not have the flare and imagination of his predecessors.

Rivière and Wittkop offer a more credible explanation when they point to the release of James Whale's film *Frankenstein* in 1931 (Rivière and Wittkop 1979, 98). During the silent era the Grand-Guignol had enjoyed a fruitful relationship with the cinema, but the advent of talkies and a new genre of horror film in the 1930s, which made stars of Karloff and Lugosi, ushered in a new era. Cinema achieved hitherto unknown heights of realism and became the entertainment of choice for an increasing proportion of society. It entered a problematic relationship with the Grand-Guignol and one that was a mere foretaste of what lay in store. Rivière and Wittkop also suggest that the Grand-Guignol at this time had lost 'its freshness and credibility' and that its audience was becoming less susceptible to its charms (Rivière and Wittkop 1979, 98). It is a debate that is consistently played out by the critics in contemporary reviews of the Grand-Guignol plays. Behind this lurks the historical context in which Jouvin took control of the Grand-Guignol. With the exception of the period covering the First World War, France had enjoyed a period of relative stability and prosperity. Maurey had been running the theatre during the halcyon days of *la belle époque* and in the post-war years of Choisy's directorship, France had regained a certain self-confidence following the Treaty of Versailles which restored both territories and national pride previously relinquished in the aftermath of the Franco-Prussian War of 1871. However, by the 1930s Mussolini was in power in Italy and the dark shadow of fascism hung over the rest of Europe. In 1933 Hitler became Chancellor of Germany and within weeks had given the world a taste of what was to come as he began to reverse the effects of Versailles with a policy of remilitarization and reoccupation of the Saarland. By 1936 the fascist threat had spread to Spain and civil war erupted. Gone were the optimism and good times of the 1920s, to be replaced by an air of pessimism and foreboding. Although we must be careful not to overplay the decline of the Grand-Guignol during this period—it still enjoyed a significant popularity and success—it could be argued that it no longer captured the *Zeitgeist* in quite the way it had previously done. Perhaps if it was not for Jouvin the genre would have declined more rapidly, as any failures were not due to lack of effort on Jouvin's part. When he relinquished ownership of the theatre in 1938, he had, according to Maxa, exhausted himself in the process (Pierron 1995, 1394).

Jouvin's final programme played in July 1938, but it was not until February of the following year that Eva Berkson, an Englishwoman, staged her first season. In the meantime the theatre was briefly under the control of Clara Bizou, who (according to Maxa) merely staged comedies for her own benefit (Pierron 1995, 1394). Berkson was in charge for little more than a year before the fall of Paris forced her to flee to England. As a result, Choisy returned once more to the Grand-Guignol, along with Maxa, and introduced programmes packed with de Lorde and Méténier classics. Following the liberation in 1944 the Grand-Guignol closed down until Berkson returned in 1946 to reclaim her theatre. The genre was now set into a pattern of decline which only seemed to accelerate with time, and not even the legendary expertise of Paul Ratineau, who had begun his career at the Grand-Guignol forty-five years previously and who returned to direct three seasons in 1946 and 1947, could halt the downward path. In 1951 Berkson brought in Charles Nonon as an adminstrator and retired the following year, fleeing to England again, according to Maxa, this time to escape spiralling debts (Pierron 1995, 1395).

There followed a series of owners and directors including Maurey's sons Denis and Marcel,[14] Raymonde Machard and Christiane Wiegant, each trying in vain a range of solutions from revivals of old standards to new writings and adaptations, including a high-profile and full-length adaptation of James Hadley Chase's *No Orchids for Miss Blandish* in 1950.[15] By this time, the name of the Grand-Guignol was not so much legend as a curse. The form had lost its connection with its audience and the stylized performances and the plays themselves seemed out of touch with the post-war mood. We find reviewers in the

---

[14] Or Michel, according to Gordon (1997, 33).

[15] One of the few occasions on which there was no *douche écossaise* at the Grand-Guignol.

1950s begging the Grand-Guignol to lose the old (and now irrelevant) warhorses of the repertoire. 'R.R.', discussing the crisis facing the Grand-Guignol, complains that 'The Grand-Guignol method has not been overhauled for fifty years . . .' (*L'Homme libre*, 30 May 1952, 7) and optimistically asserts that the Grand-Guignol should find some new writers to revitalize the genre. This was easier said than done, and the new writers it recruited were not given an easy ride. When Frédéric Dard's *Les Salauds vont en enfer* was premiered in 1954 several critics were shocked by its coarse language. Guy Verdot likens Dard's 'brutality of language' to Jean Genet's, but with a crucial difference: 'with Genet there is always poetry'('Le Théâtre' column in *France Tireur*, 28 April 1954, 16).

The final few years of the Grand-Guignol were dominated by the figure of Eddy Ghilain, actor, writer and director. Between 1956 and 1961, over nine seasons, twenty-two productions of his plays were staged and in 1960 all the plays at the theatre were written and directed by Ghilain, an indication of his energy and commitment to the genre and the increasing desperation of the theatre's management. That is not to deny any credit to Ghilain, who was responsible for some notable pieces, such as *Les Coupeurs de têtes* (1960), *La Loterie de la mort* (with Pierre Larroque, 1957) and *Les Blousons sanglants* (1961). Rivière and Wittkop honour him as 'the last master-purveyor of the Grand-Guignol' (Rivière and Wittkop 1979, 100), but Ghilain's significance resides in his attempts to rediscover and re-establish the Grand-Guignol genre after the failed efforts to transform the theatre into something other than the one and only 'Theatre of Horror'.

There has been much speculation as to the reasons for the decline of the Grand-Guignol. It has been suggested that, after the horrors of the Nazi genocide, there was no place for theatrical, stylized horror in a modern society. Pierron suggests that 'during the 1940s reality surpassed fiction' (Pierron 1995, XXXIII) and Anaïs Nin recalls a friend explaining that 'after the war and the concentration camps, what the theatre presented seemed to be laughable and infantile' (quoted in Pierron 1995, XXXIII). Charles Nonon goes further in an interview with *Time* magazine (30 November 1962) suggesting 'we could not compete with Buchenwald. Before the war everyone believed that what happened on the stage was purely imaginary, whereas now we know that it—and much more—is possible' (quoted in Pierron 1995, XXXIV). It would seem that Nonon alludes to some of the derogatory criticism the theatre received immediately after the war that cast a long shadow over its drawn-out demise. In a particularly damning review of the 1948 revival of *Le Laboratoire des hallucinations*, René Barjavel dismisses the play as being 'terribly out-of-date' in the light of recent changes in society caused by the experience of war:

Our mothers fainted at André de Lorde's plays. Our young cousins 'have a bit of a laugh' at them, as they say nowadays . . . our fathers allowed themselves to think that these horrible things only happened in the theatre . . . but recently . . . I am reminded of the local woman who, during an air raid, had the head of her neighbour land in her lap. I am reminded of Buchenwald, of Hiroshima, of Katyn. And of all the future Hiroshimas. It seems that the Grand-Guignol can be nothing more to us than a mere diversion.

(René Barjavel in *Carrefour*, 26 May 1948, 23)

Barjavel's argument is eloquent and convincing, and yet provides an incomplete answer, since the Grand-Guignol had begun its decline more than a decade before the discovery of the concentration camps, and the First World War had produced carnage on a scale never before witnessed in modern Europe and yet the form had prospered and became more popular in the years that followed.

More credible is the suggestion that the Grand-Guignol became a victim of cinema. The horrors of the war did not affect the popularity of horror films, but, as Pierron points out, the final decline of the Grand-Guignol 'coincides with the ascendancy of the Hammer film' (Pierron 1995, XXXIV). Cinema had already established that it could present horror more realistically than the theatre and so the Grand-Guignol retreated increasingly into its stylized conventions of performance. While the early Hammer movies drew on a Gothicism far from the 'real' horrors of the Grand-Guignol, movies like Alfred Hitchcock's *Psycho* (1960) and Michael Powell's *Peeping Tom* (1960), as well as home-grown films like Henri-Georges Clouzot's *Les Diaboliques* (1954) and Georges Franju's *Les Yeux sans visage* (1959), are all true descendants of the Grand-Guignol form: remorseless slices of *possible* horror but with all the advantages of editing and location shooting. A stage version of *Les Yeux sans visage* was attempted in 1962, but, with the advent of such horror films, the Grand-Guignol finally had nowhere to go, per-forming for the last time in November of that year with a sale of all props and scenery taking place on 5 January 1963.

Most probably it was a combination of all these factors that signed the death warrant for the Grand-Guignol. It was a form that had grown out of *la belle époque* at the beginning of the century and had thrived during the 1920s, but it ceased to sit easily with a post-1945 mood characterized either by soul-searching or by looking forward to a brighter future. The Grand-Guignol belonged to another age; it was an archaic museum piece to its 1950s and 1960s audience, with little relevance to the new era. Like so many other things during this time, it was abandoned as obsolete by a new generation and replaced with the more technologically sophisticated offerings of cinema and television.

# 2
# The Topography of Horror
## Location and venue

In the nineteenth and twentieth centuries there has been an inclination to interpret the French capital in terms of labyrinthine or subterranean metaphors. This is undoubtedly a habitual metaphor in the analysis of any modern city, but Paris is a special case. The location (city, district, street and *impasse*) of the Théâtre du Grand-Guignol, and even the very structure of the building, make it one of the most interesting specific performance venues in theatre history. At the same time we should not forget that there were several small theatres in Montmartre that produced—and even premiered—works of the Grand-Guignol *genre*, such as the Théâtre-Antoine, Théâtre Sarah-Bernhardt, Théâtre de l'Ambigu and the Théâtre des Deux-Masques. Nevertheless, there was only one *Théâtre* du Grand-Guignol, a venue indelibly linked with the genre it very quickly gave its name to: for, as we shall see, a performance at the Grand-Guignol began long before the curtain rose, and the constitution of its meaning owed a great deal to its geographical location and architecture.

## The Grand-Guignol *in situ*

When Maurice Magnier took over the lease of the former chapel and current studio of artist Georges Rochegrosse in 1896 to found the Théâtre-Salon, he can hardly have been aware of the appropriateness of the building's location for what it would eventually become. Magnier's choice of Montmartre for the location of his enterprise was not entirely without reason, as it was a neighbourhood already renowned for its small intimate playhouses and his vision of a theatre for one-act dramas was in keeping with the culture of Montmartre, including the nearby Théâtre Libre. As passionate as he was about theatre, however, Magnier was no businessman and when Méténier took over the bankrupt enterprise the following year, renaming it the Théâtre du Grand-Guignol and concentrating on the less palatable *comédies rosses* that had formed part of Antoine's earlier programming, not only was he arguably a truer inheritor of the radical Théâtre Libre tradition, but it was at this point that the theatre's location gained an additional significance.

In addition to its association with the *bas-fonds* and the sex industry, Montmartre was an area traditionally linked with radical thought and action (the 1871 Paris Commune, for instance, started in Montmartre). It was also associated with performance and spectacle, where separate traditions of live entertainment co-existed (including Pigalle's famous *maisons de tolérance*). It was an area of cabarets and the titillating thrills of another truly legendary venue, the Moulin-Rouge (which opened in 1889, eight years before the Grand-Guignol). With regard to more orthodox theatrical traditions, Montmartre was essentially the home of the 'blood and thunder' melodrama houses, the nineteenth-century popular theatres that attracted large working-class audiences with their plays of crime, murder and tragedy and overstated, histrionic acting conventions. For the radical naturalists such as Antoine, it was the natural location to set up their small, avant-garde theatres, well away from the cultural mainstream in the centre of the city. Montmartre, where the lowest strata of Parisian society mingled with members of the new generation of *bohèmes*—radical, avant-garde intellectuals, was a multifaceted home of spectacle and an understanding of the social and cultural environment of Montmartre is crucial to a full understanding of the Grand-Guignol.

For a theatre which came to embody the fusion of the two intrinsically different forms of melodrama and naturalism and which delved so shamelessly into the world of the *misérables* for its material and eroticism for its themes, the rue Chaptal would seem to be the ideal location. According to Guy Sabatier the Grand-Guignol 'stood for its locality, its inhabitants, its spirit' (1998, 141). This indicates that the Grand-Guignol soon became embedded into the fabric of its local community. As a theatre, it was embraced as an integral part of the locality in the same way as any bar or brothel on the rue Pigalle, and its success in bridging the gap between the two aspects of Montmartre life (intellectual and proletarian) is notable. What is more significant is that both Méténier and Maurey used this to their advantage by extending the theatrical experience beyond the walls of the theatre building. The Grand-Guignol is perhaps unusual in its nineteenth- and early twentieth-century context for being a theatre for which the theatrical 'event' began before the audience entered the theatre, with a kind of pre-show game designed to create 'a vague sense of unease' (René Berton quoted in Antona-Traversi 1933, 31). Méténier's well-documented pre-show antics were clearly a part of this strategy, but several accounts of the journey to the Théâtre du Grand-Guignol certainly suggest that the theatrical experience began much earlier, as the spectator emerged from the anonymity of the Métro into the world of Montmartre. According to Deák, 'the trip through the dark narrow streets of old Montmartre was a part of the experience'

(Deák 1974, 43). The most evocative description in print is André Degaine's account and it provides a clear sense of the atmosphere of the journey to the theatre:

> Leaving the Métro at Pigalle, you had to walk down the rue Pigalle between the ranks of fishnet stockings and cigarette smoke, in the light of the neon signs and the sound of the music that emanated from the clubs lining both sides of the street. At the crossroads with the rue de Notre Dame de Lorette, the rue Fontaine and the rue Chaptal, you took a right turn down the rue Chaptal. The contrast was alarming; darkness and silence, a sad street, curiously barely lit, without any shops, deserted. You could hear the sound of your own footsteps on the pavement. Three hundred metres further along, invisibly, suddenly emerging on the right, the cité Chaptal, a narrow dead-end alley, about one hundred metres long, culminating in the barely lit façade of the theatre. Some inordinately tall trees, which are no longer there, reached for the sky above the roofs, amidst the sinister light of the street lamps.
>
> (Degaine 1998, 196)

Degaine's account is interesting in two respects. Firstly, although he is recounting his experiences in the late 1940s, it is a journey that can be repeated today with the feeling that nothing much has changed. One still emerges from the dark, characterless Métro station at Pigalle to the sudden bright lights of the highly visible sex industry on the place Pigalle. The rue Pigalle is still lined with rather more downmarket bars and strip joints, prostitutes languishing in the open doorways. The rue Chaptal remains a sudden contrast of silence and the cité Chaptal, with the still recognizable, yet forbidding, theatre building at the end, is still a surprise when it emerges, in spite of the small wall plaque which announces it. Although Pigalle has no doubt undergone some changes since Degaine made the journey, there is still enough of the atmospheric seediness to make the journey a worthwhile one for anybody interested in the Grand-Guignol. As Paula Maxa recalled in her memoirs, a trip to the rue Chaptal was shrouded in an 'atmosphere of dread before arriving—to make even the bravest think twice' (in Pierron 1995, 1381).

Crucial to the Grand-Guignol form, both inside and outside the theatre building itself, was the sense of anticipation. This sense that *something* was going to happen was embedded into the journey to the rue Chaptal itself, ensuring that 'before entering, you were already frightened . . .' (Paula Maxa, in Pierron 1995, 1381). Such a sense of danger and fear results in disorientation. Peche, frequently an audience member during the 1950s and 1960s, recalls: 'When you arrived in the rue Chaptal it was dark . . . It felt as if Paris life had been left far behind. I was a bit scared and checked to see if anyone was following me' (quoted in Jones 1997, 109). As her account reveals, even 'Paris life' itself seems to disappear when one arrives in the macabre rue Chaptal. Christopher Prendergast's account of the 'city as labyrinth, in which one gropes like a blind person, without the aid of an Ariadne's thread . . .' (Prendergast 1992, 208) was never more apt than when applied to such eyewitness accounts of the enigmatic arrival at the lair of that urban Minotaur: the Grand-Guignol.

To return to Degaine, it is also significant that he is travelling *to* Montmartre. Degaine is not himself a resident of Pigalle, but a visitor to it. There is the implication here, as in Peche's description, that Montmartre/ Pigalle is no longer 'Paris' but something unto itself. For a theatre that came so strongly to represent its locality, the Grand-Guignol is able to draw its audience from all over (we should not forget the Grand-Guignol's place for many years on the foreign tourist trail) and uses this to enhance the experience. It is significant that Degaine begins his account with his emergence from the Métro. The journey is a vital ingredient in the theatrical experience, but that journey does not begin when he leaves his apartment. It rather begins (and presumably ends, if the return journey also has a role to play in the event) with Pigalle. It is actually *the journey through Pigalle* that is the important factor, not so much the journey in its own right. Pigalle can be seen as a central player in the pre-show game and it is one of the most prolific actors in the Grand-Guignol drama. If an audience is to shudder at the onstage horrors, then the preparations must be made earlier and the sinister and pregnant atmosphere of the streets of Pigalle was the warm-up act for Paulais and Maxa.

## Entering the Grand-Guignol

Robert Hossein (a theatre director and Grand-Guignol actor in the 1950s) recalls arriving at the theatre in the following terms: 'Suddenly, you were in this cobblestoned alleyway . . . A mysterious alleyway. If you didn't know the area and the street, you'd miss it. At the end of the street was this theatre, an old wooden chapel' (quoted in Jones 1997, 109–10).[1] This statement establishes the ambivalent nature of the Grand-Guignol. The Théâtre du Grand-Guignol was not a purpose-built theatre, but very significantly, a *converted* space. The building was originally erected in the

---

[1] Hossein is presumably referring to the interior of the theatre/chapel when he describes it as 'wooden' as the exterior was, and is, clearly stone-built.

late eighteenth century as a Jansenist chapel, which was part of a convent. It was sacked and gutted during the 1791 Reign of Terror (Gordon 1997, 14) and after that was variously a blacksmith's workshop, a church again, and an artist's studio before becoming the Théâtre-Salon and the Théâtre du Grand-Guignol. Before the theatre was even inaugurated, the building itself was associated with controversy and scandal. Aside from its misfortunes during the Reign of Terror, Homrighous informs us that 'Henri Didon, a Dominican priest preached there his unorthodox views on the indissolubility of marriage in 1879. His sermons were reported widely in the press and the following year he was banned from preaching by the church authorities' (Homrighous 1963, 2).

The Grand-Guignol must have been thankful in retrospect that Maurice Magnier's conversion of the chapel into a theatre was so minimal: the space retained two giant carved angels in the rafters who would look down at the audience for the duration of the theatre's existence. The *Ecco* (Gianni Proia 1965) documentary footage of a Grand-Guignol performance also reveals religious murals clearly visible in the auditorium. As Pierron writes, 'the ground floor boxes have grills on them, which gives them the appearance of confessionals' (1995, IX). Peche describes the ever-present smell of candle wax and incense impregnating the walls: 'Inside, there was a certain atmosphere and smell . . . Being an old chapel, maybe the smell was incense or maybe wax—I don't know. It felt like plunging into a tomb. But the point was, it created a spooky atmosphere.'[2] Even the dilapidated roof enhanced performances: according to Robert Hossein the 'rain sometimes leaked through the roof. The audience thought it was raining blood!' (Jones 1997, 110).

The fact that the Grand-Guignol presented a repertoire of plays that dealt with such taboo subjects as violent death and illicit sex, and that the performance space was established in what was instantly recognizable as a church must have enhanced and complicated the theatrical experience for the audience. Layers of complexity are always added to any performance when it is lured away from purpose-built theatres. Such theatrical experiences play around with the boundary between 'this is not *a* theatre' and 'this is not *theatre*', a particularly interesting concept in relation to the ostensibly extreme and shocking realism of the Grand-

---

[2] When reviewing the Grand-Guignol Laboratory's production of *A Night at the Grand-Guignol* in Edinburgh, Chris Campbell also picked up on the importance of the venue in creating an atmosphere, writing that 'because it is staged in the sepulchral St Columba's at the spookily appropriate time of midnight, you'll be hard pushed to find a show on the Fringe that complements its venue quite as well as this' (*The Scotsman*, 10 August 1999, 8).

Guignol form. Purpose-built theatres have often offered a false sense of security in their cultural role as temples of art. The fact that the Théâtre du Grand-Guignol was, ironically, a deconsecrated chapel located in the heart of Pigalle would have also served to problematize even further the audience's relationship with the comforts of bourgeois morality and religion.

## The Grand-Guignol stage

The Grand-Guignol had a small stage of approximately 7 by 7 metres. This was not unique in its Parisian context as such spatial dynamics were seen as ideal in the pioneering days of the naturalist theatre salons. Although Gordon recounts an anecdote from an unnamed critic that states that the Grand-Guignol 'was so cramped inside that a front-row spectator could shake hands with the actors as he stretched his feet into the prompter's box' (Gordon 1997, 14–16), this seems to derive from Homrighous's quotation of Jules Lemaître: 'You could shake hands with the actors across the footlights and stretch your legs out into the prompter's box' (quoted in Homrighous 1963, 4–5). Lemaître, however, is not talking about the Grand-Guignol specifically, but early naturalist theatres in general. Lemaître goes on to say that in this kind of theatre the 'stage was so small that only the most elementary scenic attempts were possible, and the audience was so close that illusion was an impossibility'. The important issue, regardless of whether the Grand-Guignol stage was an exception or the standard, is not the auditorium's *smallness*, but rather its *intimacy*. This is borne out by the seating plan for the theatre reproduced by Rivière and Wittkop (Rivière and Wittkop 1979, 96–97) which indicates that the stalls were arranged in six rows of between fifteen and twenty seats, the circle had three rows of between twenty and twenty-four seats, and there were about thirteen boxes. This ensured that no member of the audience felt far from the performers and vice versa.

This level of intimacy, familiar in naturalist theatre, exerted a major influence on the performance itself, producing a focus and intensity that came to characterize the style that evolved when the Grand-Guignol discovered its money-spinning role as the 'Theatre of Horror'. Moreover, the mood and material of the repertoire would have made it seem particularly claustrophobic. We need only think of some of the themes and processes closely associated with horror, such as morality, psychology and the erotic: what is an 'intimate' theatre one moment can become 'oppressive' the next. Of course, the shift in dynamic in this direction is not a shortcoming but rather a carefully manipulated aim.

The limitations of the stage area severely restricted the action that could take place and the scale of locations that could be used. In this volume, for example, we present plays set variously in bedrooms in brothels, the ramparts of besieged consulates, lighthouses, rooms in museums, sitting rooms, boats, opium dens, doctors' surgeries, operating theatres and so on. Most of these settings recur elsewhere in a repertoire that has other favourite locations such as cells in prisons and asylums, execution courtyards, carnival caravans and barber shops. The claustrophobic potential of all these locations is exploited to the full in the Grand-Guignol from *Lui!* onwards, and we find a repertoire that loves to confine its characters to an oppressive setting and ensnare its audience in an intimate auditorium. The audience, in due course, would witness a victim trapped in a tightly enclosed space with either his or her tormentor, a dangerous lunatic or merely under the knife of a surgeon. In the Grand-Guignol we recognize these claustrophobic locations to be the lair of the Minotaur or Medusa containing the greatest horror (or, in the comedies, humiliation) from which there is no place to hide. The Grand-Guignol did not have the complex cinematic devices available to it that Alfred Hitchcock did in making *Psycho* (1960), but it did, nevertheless, have abundant equivalents to the horrific, entrapped locations of the Bates Motel shower-room and Norman Bates's fruit-cellar. Some plays treat the claustrophobic dynamic with irony: in *La Dernière Torture*, for instance, the intimate space afforded by the consulate is presented as a haven against the encroaching menace beyond the walls. However, as the oppressive claustrophobia grows, the horror comes from within and we realize that the ultimate monster was not outside but within the safety of the walls from the beginning.

The Grand-Guignol stage was naturalistic inasmuch as it was strictly proscenium, which worked to its advantage in creating a 'four-walled' claustrophobia. In addition, the proscenium stage was invaluable for the effective execution of many of the special effects that the theatre developed. Whilst Jules Lemaître stated that illusion was impossible in such intimate theatres, the Grand-Guignol was a self-styled theatre of naturalism *in extremis*, and embraced this 'impossibility' with the consequence that the stage effects that it developed were, out of necessity, extremely convincing in verisimilitude and delivery.

# 3

# Acts of Horror
## Performing in the Grand-Guignol

Theatre is an ephemeral process. Paolo Biscaia Filho likens the theatre historian of the Grand-Guignol to a 'palaeontologist' (Biscaia Filho 1995, 1), and this is an apt description for the process of digging up the bones of this long-dead theatre. Like many other examples in theatre studies, most of them less macabre than the Grand-Guignol, when it comes to the analysis of a specific performance practice one has to embark on a process of deduction and guesswork. In studying the Grand-Guignol we are in many ways fortunate to be looking at a modern form of theatre that is documented by a large body of photographic stills, a few metres of documentary film, some eyewitness accounts and performers' testimony, theatre reviews, and many extant scripts and related writings by Grand-Guignol playwrights. The Grand-Guignol is probably a unique example of a *legendary* theatre, however, and many contemporaneous writings on it (especially by reviewers and by those personally connected to the Grand-Guignol) are full of myth-making hyperbole, innuendo and mystique. Furthermore, the Théâtre du Grand-Guignol's status during its existence means that it was regarded as too popular to be taken seriously as a theatrical methodology. When it comes to the detailed analysis of the spectators' experience and the actors' performance practice at the Grand-Guignol, we have to fill in the gaps with our imagination and use a mixture of hypothesis and practical experimentation.

In their excellent essay on 'Directing Grand Guignol' (www.aboutface. org), Marty Fluger and Dawn Williams of the Aboutface Theatre Company give an enlightening account of the processes involved when exploring Grand-Guignol through performance. They put great emphasis on 'the moment of violence', and we know from our own Laboratory work that this is not simply an important aspect of the form, but its most defining and unique feature. The use of the word 'violence', however, needs qualifying as it generally has a *physical* connotation and, although this is often an important feature of the Grand-Guignol repertoire, there are numerous examples where the onstage violence is *psychological*. It is for this reason that we prefer to talk of 'the moment of horror', as this can encompass physical violence without precluding psychological examples. Moreover, 'the moment of horror' can even be applied to comedy where the theme of *Schadenfreude* frequently appertains to mortifying experiences of sexual humiliation and embarrassment.

## Naturalistic and Melodramatic Acting Conventions

Grand-Guignol drama is essentially a form of stage realism (albeit, at times stylized), and this has an impact on the performance style an actor takes as well as the technical execution of 'horror' effects. Fluger and Williams define the curious dichotomy Grand-Guignol performers experience:

> [The] actors must contend with two primary opposing problems in order to pull off the moment of violence. They must completely inhabit the psychology and physicality of the violence as though it is real. At the same time, they must disengage from the moment, in a sense, in order to execute the technical demands of the stage violence (performing elaborate stage-fight choreography; bursting blood bags on cue; manipulating blood-rigged knives and other speciality props, etc.). While doing all this, each actor must maintain the arc of the play and remain aware of and open to the other actors on the stage.

The Grand-Guignol emerged out of naturalism and many early plays in the repertoire are fine examples of the genre. Certainly a naturalistic approach to the characters in a play is an obvious way forward for a performer, and many early performances were rooted in this method. Indeed, Fluger and Williams imply that what we would recognize as a naturalistic method is an option available for a Grand-Guignol performer:

> [A moment of violence] can be examined physically, emotionally, and in terms of relationship and status. The violence has a dramatic context for the actor. The actors can understand the series of events that has brought their characters to the loss of control, the violence. Because the actors have a strong feel for where the violence fits into the established movement, energy, and rhythm of the play, the violence will be organic to it, growing out of the overall structure.

Such an approach may seem obvious given the broadly realist nature of many Grand-Guignol scripts, but it is by no means the only one. Although this method may have its merits, Fluger and Williams highlight several problems with it, perhaps most significantly the fact that a moment of violence is so crucial in any given Grand-Guignol play that it cannot just be built into the organic flow of a piece, but must be rehearsed with all the care one would take with 'a number in a musical or a complex slapstick scene in a farce'. We have similarly found that more traditional Stanislavskian approaches to the actor and rehearsal are useful, but only up to a point. The Grand-Guignol is a form that seems to break away from conventional naturalism as often as it embraces it.

Although caution must be exercised when looking at photographic stills of performances (which might have been, after all, arranged for the aesthetic of the photographic studio more than the theatrical stage), there is much of interest in such examples. The small batch of photographs of Zacconi as Marex in *Au téléphone* (some are reproduced in Rivière and Wittkop (1979) and Gordon (1997) while *Clive Barker's A-Z of Horror* (1995) displays a fuller sequence of seven) show the character in the final scene of the play as he hears his wife and child being murdered at the end of the telephone. We see him become more and more distracted, his mouth increasingly agape, holding the receiver with ever-increasing tension with his right hand while, eventually, the fingertips of his left hand are pressed against his temple. Most interesting is what Zacconi does with his eyes which widen until they seem to bulge out of their sockets. In one of the most intense photographs Zacconi achieves the not inconsiderable feat of furrowing his brow while keeping his eyes wide open to the extent that his eyelids do not cover any part of his irises. What is particularly fascinating is the direction of the performer's gaze: the photographs show him looking down to the floor, looking stage right, and staring above. If this is a faithful reproduction of what Zacconi did on stage, it would seem that he did not look out at the audience. This would be in keeping with the principles of stage naturalism as it would have preserved the sanctity of the 'fourth wall'. There is a sound argument for protecting this wall, as not only does it contribute to the slice-of-life realism of the play, but it would also help to enhance the claustrophobia so important in the repertoire.

In contrast, the decision to break the fourth wall and make eye contact with the audience is an option that was exploited by the Grand-Guignol, as is seen in the Italian-made documentary *Ecco* (1965). This includes a clip from what is claimed to be 'the last performance of the Grand-Guignol' and, although it is unclear whether the performance was restaged specifically for the camera and later had edited-in shots of the audience and the auditorium,[1] its authenticity as a true reflection of Grand-Guignol performance at the time is convincing. The clip shows the lead actor, portraying Henri Landru, the notorious real-life 'Bluebeard', enacting one of the French serial killer's murders. Having lured a young woman into his home, they share a moment of convivial laughter before Landru hypnotizes her and lays her down on a table. Once she is unconscious, he lifts up her skirt and looks at her underwear, and then touches her breasts through her blouse. He takes a knife and makes an incision in her right forearm. The victim wakes up and screams, turning her contorted face into full view of the audience. Landru drugs her with chloroform and walks away from her, returning with a hacksaw. As the murderer raises the saw above the victim, he pauses a moment to look at the audience, with the merest hint of a smile, before proceeding with the amputation of the woman's arm, just below the elbow. Despite his clearly sadistic intentions and his appearance of a melodramatic villain (albeit closely modelled on actual pictures of Landru), the look he gives the audience is not the wild look of a stage lunatic, but rather a look of invitation, even collusion.

It is a performance decision which is heavily loaded with meaning, since, by a simple acknowledgement of the audience, the actor has not merely demolished the fourth wall, so beloved by naturalism, thus showing how far the form had developed from its naturalist roots sixty-five years earlier, but he has almost invited the audience onto the stage, if not physically, then spiritually (maybe even morally), to participate in what is ostensibly the reconstruction of a true-life murder. The audience become accessories to the act and, most crucially, willing witnesses. It is an acknowledgement by the actor that the violence on stage is not an abstract violence that exists in some fantastic realm far away from our everyday lives, but is an action by a de Lordean 'monstre virtuel', which we are all, at any given moment, but a step away from (whether as potential victims *or* potential killers). This serves to intensify the horror by suggesting that the audience itself is, at least partly, responsible for the violence enacted on stage. The *Ecco* gaze is a moment of Medusa-like petrifying horror, for as well as the concept of audience particip-ation, or even collaboration (not a word to be used lightly in post-war

---

[1] It seems most likely that specific scenes were restaged for the camera, perhaps in between actual performances. If the film was shot during an actual performance, it is hard to imagine how the camera(s) would have coped with the lighting inside the theatre and would not have been obtrusive to the audience. In addition, appropriate music and a red wash have been added to convey something of the atmosphere inside the auditorium, although the red wash may also have been added to approximate the theatrical lighting actually used, if harsher lights for the filming were necessary.

France), Landru's gaze can also function in the way that the omniscient eyes of the monster or killer do in so many examples of horror or thriller films: *we can be seen*. The difference between film and stage performance, however, is the immediacy of the latter form. We have found in our Laboratory and production work that the effect of a well-planned gaze at the audience can be electric. Horror theatre, as found in the Grand-Guignol, is an unusual form nowadays and audiences, accustomed to cinema, can be startled by the intense effect of being *looked at* in the flesh.

It is significant that, in Grand-Guignol, the theatrical device of direct address, effectively destroying the naturalistic fourth wall, is used to implicate the audience and so intensify the horror. It is at these moments that any pretence to naturalism is finally abandoned and the full force of stylized melodrama is brought to bear on the performance. In the Grand-Guignol Laboratory's production of *The Final Kiss* (1999) there was a moment when Henri, holding Jeanne in a headlock, raised his head slightly to the audience before removing the stopper from the bottle of vitriol with his teeth and, with the slightest smile, informed Jeanne what will happen to her while fixing his gaze on the audience. The next moment he has poured the vitriol over Jeanne's face and she is writhing in agony on the floor as the acid burns into her flesh. The audience is horrified by the assault but also by the petrifying gaze. We have found controlling a direct address to be a valuable strategy in performance practice, although it should never be over-used (except, occasionally, in comedy). We have used the calculated gaze for numerous moments of horror: whether it is the Grand-Guignol 'monster' before a moment of physical violence, or a 'victim' at the moment of revelation.

The *Ecco* footage is an extremely valuable artefact, as it gives us an insight into the Grand-Guignol's melodramatic performance style at the time of the theatre's demise. It indicates that the theatre never lost touch with its melodramatic influences. Although the stylized performance of the stage Landru in *Ecco* may seem far away from what we may believe to have been the early performance practice of the Grand-Guignol, Zacconi's histrionic posturing in the *Au téléphone* photographs looks melodramatic, even if his carefully directed gaze would seem to endorse naturalism.

Paula Maxa describes the atmosphere of a performance as being 'tense, nerves all on edge, the slightest thing could spark off laughter' (in Pierron 1995, 1393). This implies the fragility of the genre. She also says:

> Just a word or a phrase delivered a little too quickly, a little too harshly, could cause laughter. It required millimetre precision . . . If the atmosphere was broken, it had to be recaptured, which was at times very difficult and often impossible.
>
> (ibid.)

It is the specific skill of the Grand-Guignol actor to negotiate the precarious journey between horror and comedy. It is a journey which leads 'from bourgeois security to mortal danger, from the rational to the insane, from—in effect—Naturalism to Melodrama'. Furthermore it is a journey that is made all the more hazardous by the fact that the actor would shortly be required back on stage to participate in 'the rapid-fire innuendo and physical romps of Grand-Guignol comedy' (Hand and Wilson 2000, 269).

Grand-Guignol may have had its roots in melodrama, naturalism and the well-made play, but its continued eclecticism as a theatrical form that also incorporated the influence of Symbolism, Expressionism and cinema, goes some way to explain why this unique brand of popular theatre survived as long as it did. We would sooner adhere to this thesis than accept Walter Kendrick's argument that the Grand-Guignol 'looks more like the end of a tradition (i.e. melodrama) than the source of one (i.e. modern horror)'. Even if it was 'the death rattle of horrid melodrama' (Kendrick 1991, 203), that was but one aspect of the incarnation of a form that evolved and adapted throughout its sixty-five years.

## The Importance of Pace

One of the most important outcomes of the performance extract in *Ecco* is its relation to the *manipulation of time*. The moment of horror is deliberately staggered in order to squeeze every ounce of tension out of the scene. Fluger and Williams make the following observation:

> [There] is a tendency to rush through the violence and end the play, instead of playing the violence out fully. When this happens, the climax is perceived in performance as a brief anti-climax, despite the company's intentions. Only time to rest in the violence—to fully explore it, not only as it relates to the character, to the text, and even to the audience, but equally as it relates to the actor personally in the physical, emotional and psychological way—will allow the moment its real boldness, its real immediacy and its real terror.

Time and again we have encountered exactly the same problem. An eye-gouging, disembowelment, stabbing or throat-slitting needs to be performed slowly, with care and precision. If it is rushed the effect is lost in the mayhem and the audience resents being denied the right to relish the moment. Performers tend to rush the moment of horror for a number of reasons. If some stage effect is required, the performer may hurry through it out of anxiety (worrying that the audience may see how the effect is done). It can also be, in our experience, because of the influence of film, where performers (who have usually only experienced performance horror through movies) try the impossible task of emulating the effects that cinema achieves through montage and quick-fire editing. Another reason can be a general anxiety about enacting such physically or psychologically violent scenes. Any Grand-Guignol company requires a great deal of trust in its working environment and rehearsal process, perhaps more than in any other modern theatrical form. As Fluger and Williams put it, an atmosphere of trust is essential in order to make the performers 'feel safe in unmasking themselves, in opening themselves to the perversion of the moment, to go over the top, to make fools of themselves, knowing that they have the support of the company'.

The taboo territory of the Grand-Guignol has far-reaching implications for the performer, and the necessity to perform moments of horror, whether these are explicitly physical or involve the portrayal of terror or madness, can be most demanding. The presence of an audience only serves to exacerbate this, especially if we take into account the complicated erotic dimension to the form. Moreover, laughter is a very complex response in a Grand-Guignol performance. Obviously laughter during a comedy is highly desirable, but the kind of laughter that Maxa described in a horror play is totally destructive. This is not to say that laughter should be totally banished from a horror play in an ideal performance: a tell-tale nervous giggle is often a clear indication of the play's success in building up suspense and terror.

As we have seen, the melodramatic technique of direct address is one useful way of slowing down the action. Other methods include the manipulation of blocking so that a character can interrupt a movement in order to move away from the focus of action and then return to it a few moments later. We have also made use of careful rehearsal experimentation in which sections of physical action are slowed down, sometimes artificially to the point that they become momentarily slow motion or frozen (often very effective in the seconds before a blade, needle or vitriol makes contact). What is most important is that the performer learns to gauge, and trust, their manipulation of pace and time and comes to understand its potential effect on the audience. Paula Maxa provides a helpful analysis of this:

> The play was always performed slowly, as if we had difficulty saying certain words. The silences and the pauses are indispensable, because it is during these silences that the audience's imagination is at work. All in all it is something of a collaboration.
>
> (in Pierron 1995, 1392)

## Posture and Heightened Gesture in the Grand-Guignol

We have already mentioned Zacconi's use of posture and heightened gesture in the photographs of *Au téléphone*, and it is clear that this was not an isolated example. The Grand-Guignol—either as a late or post-melodramatic form—would seem to have used such techniques as a central feature of its practice. Although some publicity shots of Grand-Guignol present images that look naturalistic, many pictures and displays of the form reveal gestures and expressions that are heightened to the extreme.

In addition to his work as a dramatist André de Lorde wrote a practical guide for actors entitled *Pour Jouer la Comédie de Salon* (1908). In this work de Lorde provides some interesting guidelines for performance practice that, although not expressly about Grand-Guignol, are nevertheless worthy of consideration. De Lorde quotes Blaize's *L'Art de dire* regarding it as providing 'invaluable guidelines on how gestures give expression to emotions' (de Lorde 1908, 82). This systematic study provides many guidelines to body language such as:

THE FACE

The *eyes*.—Half-closed: malice, disdain. Lowered: great respect, shame. Wide open: amazement, anger, terror. ( . . . )
The *mouth*.—Half-open: surprise, joy. Wide open: astonishment ( . . .) Lower lip extended: disdain, sulkiness, ignorance. Lower jawbone extended: ferociousness. Chattering of teeth: mad terror.

THE HEAD

Forward: curiosity, ferociousness. Back: audacity, insolence, fear. To the side: pity, indolence. ( . . . ) Lowered: shame, fear. ( . . . )

THE BODY

With shame, and often with terror, the body is held in, the back is curved, the arms held tightly by the sides . . . with fear and with repulsion, the torso is held back.

(de Lorde 1908, 83–86)

Such classifications of body language are interesting in that they give possible clues to the stylization of the body in Grand-Guignol performance. At least one assumes that de Lorde had such body language in mind when he wrote his plays. The documentation we have already referred to would seem to support this, as would the photograph of M. Krauss as Lionel Bercier a few moments before he is murdered by his own brother in de Lorde and Binet's *L'Homme mystérieux* (*Monde Illustré*, number 2799, 1910, 32) (fig. 2): this distinctly melodramatic

*Figure 2.* The face of fear: M. Krauss as Lionel Bercier in André de Lorde and Alfred Binet's *L'Homme mystérieux* (*Monde Illustré,* number 2799, 1910, 32) (British Library)

image impressively captures a Grand-Guignol 'face of fear', complete with the textbook wide eyes and open mouth of terror.

## Enacting Death

In the short BBC documentary on Grand-Guignol (part of *Clive Barker's A-Z of Horror* BBC TV, 1995) some surviving veterans of the theatre—principally André Chanu, Mado Maurin and Bernard Charlan—give a fascinating insight into the performance practice of the form. When they recreate some of the death scenes, we witness trick daggers held in momentary tableau and at artificially heightened distances and angles above the head before being brought into contact with their victim. When the blade strikes, the face of the victim is contorted—eyes screwed up, mouth agape—in another frozen moment. In one example, André Chanu is stabbed in the upper chest: after the facial tableau, he slowly looks down at the wound and then equally slowly raises his eyes to stare outwards in disbelief with his mouth slightly open. Once again, we see a meticulous pacing that is enhanced by the careful manipulation of body language.

In our Laboratory research, the Grand-Guignol death scene is one facet of performance practice that has been constructively investigated through the use of film. In *Les Diaboliques* (Henri-Georges Clouzot 1954), the protracted and disturbing scene in which the sadistic Delassalle (Paul Meurisse) is drugged and 'drowned' by the confident Nicole (Simone Signoret) and the cowardly Christina (Vera Clouzot) is a masterful example of suspense, psychological motivation, pace and the claustrophobic environment. Also, in the same film, the death of Christina is an excellent Grand-Guignolesque moment. Having been frightened by strange noises, shadows and eerie events in the boarding school at night, she finds her way into a bathroom. She turns on a tap in the washbasin, taps her forehead with cold water, when suddenly, the object in the bath catches her eye. As her 'dead' husband rises from the water, Christina clutches her chest, shakes her head in disbelief, and opens her eyes extraordinarily wide. She slowly steps backwards to the bathroom door, one hand on her failing heart (fig. 3), and then slides down to the ground into a sitting

*Figure 3.* A Grand-Guignolesque moment of death: Christina (Vera Clouzot) frightened to death in *Les Diaboliques* (Henri-Georges Clouzot, 1954) (Collection of Hand and Wilson)

position, never taking her eyes away from the apparition. Her mouth now opens to emit a deep, mournful howl before she suddenly topples to the ground in a fast and grotesque spasm.

*Les Yeux sans visage* (Georges Franju 1959)—which was subsequently adapted for the Grand-Guignol repertoire—offers a similar death scene with the demise of Louise (Alida Valli). Christiane (Edith Scob), the tragically disfigured—and ever-masked—heroine, approaches Louise with a scalpel raised behind her head. She suddenly stabs Louise in the front of her neck, through the rows of pearls on the choker she always wears to conceal her surgical scar. Louise stares at Christiane in disbelief and slowly steps backwards to the surgery wall, her eyes always fixed on her killer. When she reaches the wall her eyes brim with tears and she slides down the wall to a sitting position (fig. 4). Her head suddenly sinks down while her body remains grotesquely upright. The deaths of Christina and Louise in these respective films are outstanding examples of the Grand-Guignol death scene: both are stylized, carefully paced

*Figure 4.* Another Grand-Guignolesque moment of death: Louise (Alida Valli) stabbed in the neck with a scalpel in *Les Yeux sans visage* (Georges Franju, 1959) (Collection of Hand and Wilson)

with a touch of the grotesque. Importantly, neither victim takes her eyes off her assailant and so the spectator watches the horror of death and also the horror of *witnessing*.

## The Centrality of the Witness

The concept of witnessing is crucial to a full understanding of how and where horror is located within the Grand-Guignol. When we talk about the concept of witness in terms of theatre, we are usually talking about the audience. The audience in the Grand-Guignol is certainly witness to the onstage horrors, but it is important to identify the exact nature of that witnessing, which is very much that of voyeur, the willing witness-collaborator in the act of violence. At that moment in the clip from *Ecco* when the actor pauses momentarily to engage eye contact with the audience, it becomes clear that the relationship is no longer one of performer and objective, dispassionate observer. That moment of acknowledgement implicates the audience in the action and so the relationship becomes almost one of pornographer and consumer of pornography. It is crucial, however, to distinguish between the 'audience as witness' and the 'character as witness'.

There are many instances in Grand-Guignol plays where the victim *is* the witness. This is evident in the film examples we have just given, where—pushed to an ingenious extreme in a film like *Peeping Tom* (Michael Powell 1960)—the ultimate horror is in the staring eyes of victims who consciously witness their own killer and, hence, their own demise. The horror can also be located around a *bystander*, who does not come to any physical harm but in the process of *witnessing* is taken to the ultimate horror. This idea of the centrality of the witness is clear in many plays where there is a distinct separation of the victim of physical horror and witness to it. For example, Philippe in *Sous la lumière rouge* is not the victim, as such, but the horror is located around him as witness, via the medium of the camera/photograph, which acquires a status beyond merely being a prop, becoming a 'weapon' in the unfolding drama, with which the character interacts. Charles Atamian's sketch in the first publication of the play (*Monde Illustré*, number 2831, 1911, 10) of Philippe as he looks at the photograph of the 'corpse' of Thérèse and realizes that she has been buried alive (fig. 5) is a fine demonstration of the centrality of the witness in the play's pivotal moment of horror.

It is not uncommon for the witness also to be the victim later on in the drama; for example, Jeanne in *Le Baiser dans la nuit*, who both witnesses Henri's horrific disfigurement through the vitriol attack she instigated and has to endure being told what will happen to her before

*Figure 5.* The centrality of the witness: Philippe in Maurice Level and Étienne Rey's *Sous la lumière rouge* (sketch by Charles Atamian in *Monde Illustré,* number 2831, 1911, 10) (British Library)

Henri wreaks his revenge. The same centrality of witness can even be detected in relation to those who actually commit the act of violence. Sometimes a killer is made to function as the witness in terms of staging. An example of this is in D.O. Widhopff's sketch of Raymond murdering Lionel in de Lorde and Binet's *L'Homme mystérieux* (*Monde Illustré*, number 2799, 1910, 31) (fig. 6). The sketch captures an image of highly stylized violence with Lionel on his knees, his back arched and his arms outstretched (rather than attempting to struggle with his psychotic brother!) while all the focus is on the strangling hands and maniacal face of the vengeful Raymond as he witnesses the crime he is himself committing as he slowly throttles his sibling. Two fascinating examples of killer-witnesses are D'Hémelin in *La Dernière Torture* and Bréhan in *Gardiens de phare*. In the first play it is not Denise who suffers, nor is it the case with Yvon in the second work. In both cases they plead with their fathers for salvation and their deaths would seem to be, at that moment, a welcome release from worse fates. The horror instead remains firmly with the filicides who are both the perpetrators of violence and witnesses at the same time.

The centrality of witness can often explain the dynamic of a Grand-Guignol play as it helps to locate the focal point of horror within a given scene and explain the motivation and the function of roles played by the various characters onstage. In our Laboratory investigation of *Les Diaboliques*, for instance, the 'death throes' of Delassalle may seem all-important but in fact the sequence requires a perfect balance between the three participating characters, their individual motivation and their body language. Similarly, with plays from the repertoire, meticulous care should be taken with witnesses and bystanders in a moment of horror, as their performance (whether turning away in disgust or watching every moment) can have a profound effect in enhancing a set piece. Such a dynamic comes back to the 'collaboration' Maxa referred to as we, the audience, are witnesses ourselves and in this way we are implicated more forcefully within the action. In many cases horror lies more firmly in the build-up to the climax, rather than in the delivery and mediation of a specific moment of horror itself. As much as this emphasizes the issue of pace, it also brings the *writing* into sharp relief.

## A Theatre of Writing

In 1931, a journalist argued:

> The Grand-Guignol actor does not simply live his part. He is a chronometer. The Grand-Guignol author is the perfect workings of a fine precision instrument: a well-crafted timing device. Second by

*Figure 6.* The high stylization of violence: Raymond murders Lionel in de Lorde and Binet's *L'Homme mystérieux* (sketch by D.O. Widhopff in *Monde Illustré*, number 2799, 1910, 31) (British Library)

second the mechanism turns, regularly, consistently, until the bomb finally explodes.

(Quoted in Pierron 1995, XV)

The idea of the 'chronometer' is an interesting way to think of the Grand-Guignol performer, as it clearly emphasizes the importance of *temporal* manipulation in the form. It is also significant that the journalist locates the Grand-Guignol writer as the all-important factor behind this process and indicates the extent to which the Grand-Guignol actor must give full consideration to a play's dramaturgy.

Vigor Mortis, a contemporary Grand-Guignol theatre company from Brazil, has developed original stage plays on serial killers such as Hindley and Brady, Jeffrey Dahmer and Charles Manson. The director Paulo Biscaia Filho explains:

> We believe that true stories are more effective than the old Grand-Guignol plays which are too melodramatic and would not work for a 1990s audience, except for laughs. However, their structure, especially the André de Lorde plays, are very interesting and we still use them for a basis. We use them in an almost mathematical way, for its control of the audience attention is outstanding.
>
> (E-mail to the authors, 8 February 1999)

Biscaia Filho implies that, although the content and detail may have to change in order to retain a contemporary relevance and impact, the manipulation of pace and suspense developed in the Grand-Guignol has a timeless effectiveness. Although we would take issue with the claim that the old Grand-Guignol plays do not work (in our experience many of them remain surprisingly effective to this day), Biscaia Filho's argument would certainly go some way towards justifying our own claims for the innovation and influence of this 'lost' theatrical form, and its continued relevance and potential as a mode of theatrical practice *and* as a generic form of writing.

Although Fluger and Williams's claim—that a moment of violence is a scene in its own right with 'a beginning, middle and end; but one which the playwright can only rough in'—is useful because it highlights the primacy of the practical rehearsal process (especially in relation to set pieces that are potentially dangerous or distressing), we should not underestimate the usefulness and careful construction inherent in the Grand-Guignol script. This was never a theatre of improvisation. For that reason, in our own experiments in devising contemporary Grand-Guignol plays, the purpose of an improvisational approach is to arrive at a script that is strictly adhered to in performance.

Almost every Grand-Guignol script demonstrates a meticulous exposition through which suspense is built up with an inexorable pace. This careful development of the script was often acknowledged by critics at the time: Edmond Sée, for instance, describes one of de Lorde's plays as an 'improbable drama' but goes on to praise its 'impeccable dramatic progression' (*Oeuvre*, 24 July 1921, 153). Examples of this include the creation of a context of excruciating tension that entraps all the stage characters (as in *La Dernière Torture* and *Gardiens de phare*), some utilize cat and mouse games (*Le Baiser dans la nuit*), while others use red herrings and surprise tactics (*Le Jardin des supplices*). A significant textual device to be found in many Grand-Guignol plays is the signposting of what is about to happen. In his essay 'Une dramaturgie de la parole?' (1998), Michel Corvin questions the assumption—so effectively built into its mythology—that the Grand-Guignol is a form that relies on the physical manifestation of violence for its effectiveness and success. Corvin's argument is that this mythology hides a more complex truth, a reality that assigns a more prominent role to the writing and the careful exposition of plot through dialogue in the creation of horror drama. In other words, the Grand-Guignol 'was not a theatre of the *seen*, but the *unseen* horror, a theatre of restraint, rather than the blood-fest it has been presumed to have been' (Hand and Wilson 2000, 270).

It is true that many Grand-Guignol horrors do not take place in view of the audience, but may be reported, as in Bornin's account of Boxer atrocities in *La Dernière Torture*. In *Le Baiser dans la nuit*, the initial attack on Henri happened before the play begins and in *Au téléphone* all the violence occurs several miles away at the other end of a telephone. In Corvin's own words, 'this is not a theatre of physical actions, but of spoken actions' (Corvin 1998, 150) and, although Corvin's statement might need qualifying, in the sense that the importance of physical action still cannot be denied, it is an idea worthy of exploration.

What is most admirable about Corvin's work is that he gives credit to a team of highly skilled genre dramatists to whom credit is long overdue. The fact that their contribution has for so long been overlooked is merely indicative of their success and skill as writers, for they have effectively, through clever writing, created the impression of an action-based theatre. It is a convincing argument that is centred on the careful management of information and the manipulation of the audience's expectations. Dramatic irony and the use of clearly recognizable narrative structures are the key weapons in the writer's armoury, allowing the audience to come gradually to a realization of what is about to happen.

In his discussion of *Un crime dans une maison de fous* by de Lorde and Binet, Corvin explains that 'everything is spoken about in Act One, before being very quickly shown in Act Two' (Corvin 1998, 151) and it is a structure that is repeated throughout the Grand-Guignol repertoire. Let us take, for example, *Le Baiser dans la nuit*. Level goes to great lengths to furnish his audience with all the information needed to anticipate the outcome before Jeanne enters and the real drama is played out. By the time that Henri is left alone awaiting Jeanne's arrival, the audience should be left in no doubt as to the inevitable conclusion of the piece. Likewise, in *L'Euthanasie*, the miserable condition of the cancer-patient Paul is constantly reiterated to the point that it is clear that one of the main characters will have to put him out of his misery. Even the title (as with many other plays) reflects the playwright's decision to foreground the central theme or action. This was also Grand-Guignol, of course, so the audience would know what to expect.

Corvin is right that this represents a very careful crafting of the script by the writer, but it also suggests that an understanding of the nature of audience is crucial to the writing process. It could be argued that the audience is a subconscious partner in the creation of a Grand-Guignol script. In Grand-Guignol horror the issue is not *what* will happen, or even *who* it will happen to, but rather *when* and *how* it will happen. This allows for a gradual increase in tension, which is only released when it finally *does* happen. As Corvin says, 'the emotional tension does not derive from seeing an odious act, but from the long drawn-out nature of the dialogue' (Corvin 1998, 154). In this sense it is not the aim of the Grand-Guignol performer to make the audience jump out of their skins, but to ratchet up the tension by playing with the audience's sense of anticipation, to the point that the climactic moment of the piece provides an almost welcome release. This is not to say that anticipation is never undermined, but the example of *Le Jardin des supplices*, where the tables are turned on the audience's expectations by making Clara, rather than Marchal, the victim at the very last moment, is the exception rather than the rule.

The careful signposting of events before they occur is closely linked to the device of narrating events as they happen onstage. Corvin convincingly argues that this plays a vital role in the execution of physical actions, which are necessarily often obscured from the view of the audience. For example, *Le Baiser de sang* opens with the gruesome scene of an operating theatre in the course of a trepanning. The stage directions, which include an actual drilling into the skull of the patient and the peeling back of the skin on the skull, potentially present some serious challenges for the designers of stage trickery and the actors charged with realistically conveying this. What is interesting is that every action is preceded by an announcement of what is going to happen. The audience knows to expect a trepanning before the drill is even switched on, so that when the actual act is obscured from the view of the audience by one of Leduc's assistants, the audience know what they are meant to be seeing, even if they cannot actually see it.

By the same token, in the Grand-Guignol Laboratory's production of the devised piece *Orgasm*, it did not matter that the final castration scene was largely hidden from the audience by the vengeful doctor straddling her victim. The audience saw the doctor take a scalpel and raise it up and out from her body, then down to her obscured victim. After this, the tension in her arm and the tug of her wrist as the blade cut into what was, in fact, a blood-filled condom met the expectations of the audience's imagination in this moment of horror. In de Lorde's words: 'Murder, suicide and torment seen on stage are less frightening than the anticipation of that torture, suicide, or murder' (quoted in Deák 1974, 36).

It is the economy of staged violence that defines the Grand-Guignol. There are many instances of horror occurring offstage, and when horrific acts are performed onstage, they are more often than not still recounted to the audience, whilst being obscured by furniture or actors' bodies. Consequently when these things are performed in full view, the resources of the theatre's technical department are put at their disposal and the audience is all the more appalled by it.

# 4

# Technical Aspects of Grand-Guignol Practice

There is no doubt that the Grand-Guignol relied substantially on technical support, especially at those moments of performed violence and blood-letting. Paul Ratineau developed an enviable reputation and secondary career for himself as a designer of stage tricks and technical effects, earning recognition as 'the third bandit of horror' (Rivière and Wittkop 1979, 84) in the creative team that shaped and defined the characteristics of the form. John M. Callahan—in contrast to Corvin's persuasive argument that technical effects remain subservient and supplementary to the dialogue—argues that Ratineau's repertoire of special effects was central to the inducement of fear in the audience, claiming that 'terror [was] incited through the tricks of stage violence' (Callahan 1991, 165).

The high profile often given to the technical aspects of the Grand-Guignol (Gordon, for example, devotes a useful chapter to the whole issue of stage trickery; and Deák gives an interesting account of how some of the specific effects of the Grand-Guignol were executed, 39–42) is no doubt partly reflective of the role these aspects played in the mythology created by Max Maurey as part of his marketing strategy. In this sense, the development of technical effects was driven by a desire for realism and sensation, very much in the tradition of nineteenth-century spectacular theatre. The Théâtre du Grand-Guignol, however, had very limited resources at its disposal and stage effects were largely kept in check by economic considerations. Special effects were rarely, if ever, gratuitous, and resources were invested in a small number of impressive effects rather than a large number of spectacular ones and were always used to enhance the dramatic development of a play. Although, through its relationship with the *fait divers*, the Grand-Guignol was not averse to sensationalism, the technical effects at the rue Chaptal were sensational because of the way that they were embedded into the play, rather than because they stood out from it. This was the particular skill of Ratineau, not just an ability to design ingenious effects and technical devices, but to do so in the service of the drama. As with so much else in the Grand-Guignol, with the technical aspects of the form we see a theatre of restraint rather than a theatre of excess.

## Independent Effects

Effects which were independent of the actor relied more on the ingenuity of the design than any specialist performance skills of the actor and ranged from the cheap and simple to the complex and cumbersome. At one end of the scale we might include standard props such as daggers with retractable blades and manually operated pumps containing stage blood in the handle, or knives with curved blades that would fit around the arm or leg. As simple as these effects may appear, the key to their use is in the preparation and their ability to operate smoothly. If an actor were to peer down at the blade of the knife to ensure it retracted, or conspicuously squeezed the handle of a dagger to eject blood, the effect would be lost. Even with simple props, things can go wrong and injuries were not entirely uncommon at the Grand-Guignol. According to Gordon, 'One actress almost hanged herself in a leather contraption; another was badly burnt during an incineration scene' (Gordon 1997, 33), although he attributes this to a lack of stage discipline creeping into the theatre during the 1950s.

Most usefully Gordon also gives an account of the ribbon of flesh torture from *Le Jardin des supplices*, which it is worth quoting in full:

> Before Ti-Bah's second entrance, prepare the following back stage: On Ti-Bah's back, at the level of her shoulder blades, affix a thin strip of adhesive plaster colored red on the bottom and flesh-color on top.
>
> When Han says: "I said it," Li-Chang grabs Ti-Bah, forces her to her knees and, facing the audience, tears off her shirt.
>
> As soon as Han gives the knife to Ti-Mao, Li-Chang, with one knee to the ground next to Ti-Bah, holds her wrists with one hand and with the other grabs her by the hair and pulls her head down.
>
> Ti-Mao uses this moment to simulate making two slits in her back. In reality, he bloodies her back with fake blood contained in a small tube or vial, which he then hides.
>
> As soon as Ti-Mao has finished this preparation, Li-Chang pushes down on the back of Ti-Bah's neck, forcing her forehead to the ground, thereby exposing her back to the audience.
>
> At the same time, Ti-Mao seizes the top end of the plaster and tears it very slowly down her back so that everyone has time to see the bloody scrap peel off Ti-Bah's shoulders.
>
> (Gordon 1997, 47)

Whilst this description is uncredited, making it difficult to determine its authenticity, it does give a useful insight into how the effect might be accomplished, and it is interesting in a number of respects. Firstly, it is worth noting the care and detail with which the preparation is made, even ensuring that the reverse side of the plaster is coloured red. Secondly, the whole sequence is made up of a complex series of moves, each of which requires a smooth execution. Even with such a simple effect, extensive choreography and rehearsal would be vital to its success. Thirdly, much of the action is obscured from the audience by Ti-Bah. The audience will only see her bloodied back, the plaster being torn off (everything else is achieved by mere suggestion) and, most significantly, her exposed breasts. Partial nudity was not uncommon on the stage of the Grand-Guignol (at least in Paris, in contrast to the heavily censored London stage), as contemporary photographs show (see for example plates on pages 4, 6, 7 in Pierron 1995, between 794 and 795), but this serves to shift the attention towards the erotic and away from the onstage preparations of the actors. Finally, we are told that the plaster is removed *very slowly*. Whilst this certainly has a pragmatic aspect to it, in that a rapid removal of the plaster might cause considerable pain to the actress playing the part of Ti-Bah, it is also consistent with what we know about the measured pace of staged violence at the Grand-Guignol.

Gordon alludes to the simplicity of most of the stage tricks at the Grand-Guignol (Gordon 1997, 44) and seems to suggest that it was as much the audience's willingness to suspend disbelief as the authenticity of the effects that determined their success. There would seem to be a good deal of truth in this, although the statement needs to be qualified. Special effects which were simple to the point of being unconvincing only served to disappoint the audience, as reflected in Pierre Breyssac's review of E.M. Laumann's play *La Marque de la bête* (based on a Rudyard Kipling short story):

> As it happens, the overwhelming feeling is that the leper is a man like you and me, and the red-hot iron is an electric light at the end of a tube. The smoke which rises from the supposedly burning flesh does not create the illusion of reality. The realistic details are insufficient to give us the illusion of reality.
>
> (*La Marseillaise*, June 1945)

Breyssac lays the blame for this at the door of the cinema which, he feels, is able to present realistic illusion far more effectively, although it is not really clear whether or not this is the case or whether this particular production was the victim of poor performance. Nevertheless, the unsophisticated nature of some of the tricks, if transparent, can work against their effectiveness.

It would also be misleading to suggest that all special effects at the Grand-Guignol were characterized by their simplicity of design. Some effects were of great complexity and required the specialist manufacture of not insignificant stage machinery. Callahan describes how the victim's arm is amputated in the Grand-Guignol footage in *Ecco*:

> This trick was accomplished by the woman pushing her arm down hard on a slat of the table made to roll over when pushed, the reverse side having been prepared with a fake arm dressed to match the actress's arm at the shoulder. At the moment the slat rolls over, the actor crosses in front of her to keep the audience from seeing the manoeuvre. He then proceeds to dissect the fake arm, with much blood coming from the handle of the cutting instrument, being squeezed out through the blade.
>
> (Callahan 1991, 172–73)

In fact, on closer inspection it would seem that the woman in the *Ecco* footage is initially subjected to the effect of a trick knife on her real arm before she is *completely* replaced with a mannequin that can be manipulated from below the table to give a semblance of some natural movement. The editing of the extract makes it unclear when the transfer takes place (no doubt the whole top of the table flips over, an effect common in magician shows, with the mannequin attached to the underside of the revolving tabletop). The implication here is that after the arm is slowly severed from the body (which is where the extract ends), Landru may proceed to remove the head, if not completely dismember the corpse in a set piece of Grand-Guignol 'ritual'. It is a testament to the success of the Grand-Guignol effects that the full-colour and mid-shot *Ecco* footage can continue to trick viewers, even on repeated viewing.

Needless to say, tricks of such sophistication and complexity may have helped earn the theatre its reputation, but these were probably the exception rather than the rule. Working from the texts and the available photographs, Gordon concludes that the range of props and special effects was characterized by simplicity of design and operation in order to facilitate their effective operation on stage by performers who were skilled as actors, but not—contrary to Callahan's claims that to 'act at the Grand-Guignol was to be a magician' (Callahan 1991, 165)—as illusionists.

## Performer-Dependent Effects

Many of the stage effects were utterly dependent upon the specialist skills of the performer for their successful execution, and, given the intimate nature of the auditorium at the rue Chaptal, this must have made considerable demands upon the actors. Certainly the actors at the Grand-

Guignol would have had to possess some basic skill in sleight-of-hand and illusion,[1] but nothing that could not have been developed through training and experience. For the magician, sleight-of-hand actually relies upon the illusion being performed in full view of the audience. Indeed an illusionist will go to great lengths to give the impression of transparency. This was not the case at the Théâtre du Grand-Guignol. These actors relied far more openly and unapologetically upon concealment and distraction, using the shadows of the stage, the stage furniture and the bodies of their fellow actors to momentarily obscure their preparations from the audience, as can be seen in both the examples from *Le Jardin des supplices* and the short clip from *Ecco*. The necessary ensemble nature of Grand-Guignol performance meant that rarely was an actor working on their own to create an illusion, but had the support and co-operation of all their colleagues. In this way the company could change the stage focus to one actor to enable another to make the necessary preparations whilst the audience's attention was elsewhere.

An example of this can be found in Level's *Le Baiser dans la nuit*. When the Grand-Guignol Laboratory staged its adaptation of the play, the greatest technical challenge was how to effect on stage Jeanne's disfigurement after Henri's revenge vitriol attack on her. Because it is the climax of the play, it is necessary to ensure that the action all occurs downstage in full view of the audience. Interestingly, both the Samouraï film version of the play (1997) and our own production used the same blocking principle as the original production (as illustrated by P. Delaroche in the first publication of the play in *Monde Illustré*, number 2917, 1913, 16) (fig. 7) with Henri holding Jeanne from behind so that both their faces are visible to the audience for full dramatic impact at this crucial moment in the play. The fact that both actors are command-ing the full attention of the audience gives neither performer an easy opportunity to conceal anything about their person. The solution we found was to transfer the focus of attention from Jeanne to Henri immediately after he has poured the acid onto her face. The 'acid' was in fact stage blood, used in case anyone caught a momentary glimpse before Jeanne covered her face with her hands and writhed in agony on the floor. Henri, meanwhile, moved centre stage, increasingly manic in his moment of revenge and became the focus of attention. This offered Jeanne the opportunity to reach under the drape which covered the *chaise longue* to a dish containing a mixture of raspberry jam, stage blood and

---

[1] Rarely a problem for the actors at the British Grand-Guignol, where the ever-watchful eye of the Lord Chamberlain, the official censor, ensured that any horror was confined to the realm of the imagination and that realistic horrors were never actually staged before an audience.

*Figure 7.* In full view of the audience: Henri maims Jeanne with vitriol in Level's *Le Baiser dans la nuit* (sketch by P. Delaroche in *Monde Illustré*, number 2917, 1913, 16) (British Library)

vaseline, which she was able to smear over her face before finally revealing herself to the audience at the play's climactic moment. Although crude, it was, in the context of the writing and the performance, an effective solution. But it is not the only solution. In Instant Classic Theatre Company's production of *The Final Kiss* (London Festival of Unusual Theatre 2001), the director explains that an equivalent mixture of make-up 'was concealed in a plastic carton in (the actor's) dress, so located that she could fish it out while being held . . .' (Letter to the authors, 23 March 2001).

What is significant in both productions of the play is the manipulation of the point of view of the audience. In the Instant Classics production, 'magician's techniques of concealment and misdirection' were utilized, just as the Grand-Guignol Laboratory used Henri's movement away from Jeanne and the intensification of his acting to momentarily distract the audience. It is in such moments that one comes to appreciate the proscenium nature of the Grand-Guignol stage, and its crucial role in the creation of stage illusion. Many of the stage effects we have already referred to would be impossible in, say, theatre-in-the-round. Likewise, effects such as the disembowelling trick revealed in Pierron (Pierron 1995, 1400) or the eye-gouging effect (where the attacker seems to press a sharp object into the eye while in fact s/he squeezes a concealed bulb of cochineal down the cheek of the victim who, a moment later, scoops up a clump of vaseline and red dye from the underside of a table and slaps it onto the cheek and slowly drags it down the face with his/her fingers) explained by André Chanu (in *Clive Barker's A-Z of Horror*, BBC TV, 1995), are only going to be effective when seen 'head-on' through the fourth wall.

The greatest part of the Grand-Guignol mythology in respect of special effects is the Grand-Guignol's use of blood, by which it set great store. According to Gordon the 'single most celebrated secret involved patented blood recipes' (Gordon 1997, 44) which 'came in nine shades' ('Outdone by Reality', *Time*, 30 November 1962, quoted in Callahan, 1991, 170) and 'also coagulated after a few minutes to form scabs' (Gordon, 1997, 44). Mado Maurin (in *Clive Barker's A-Z of Horror*, BBC TV, 1995) claims they 'threw [stage blood] all over the place' and Maxa herself indicates the near-omnipresence of blood on the Grand-Guignol stage in her comments on her role in de Lorde and Binet's *Un crime dans une maison de fous*:

> You had to wash your hair every evening, twice when there was a matinee. The large shirts that I had to wear for the role also had to be washed. The wings were like a laundry. On top of that, I also had to take a bath because I was red from head to toe.
>
> (in Pierron 1995, 1387)

One cannot discount a certain degree of hyperbole in these accounts, nor in Maxa's amusing anecdote of the occasion when the gelatine-based blood came out in an unsatisfactory shade, causing the entire batch to be discarded. Instead the cast used the mixture as the filling for flans. She concludes the story with the words: 'Only at the Grand-Guignol could you eat like that!' (in Pierron 1995, 1386). In each case it adds to the Grand-Guignol mythology that this was a theatre where 'the ubiquitous glistening-red stage blood (. . .) splattered and flowed in pailfuls' (Gordon 1997, 30). It was a mythology that clearly affected the new generation of theatre-makers who briefly re-opened the theatre in the rue Chaptal in 1974. The twelve-year break appears to have seriously affected the continuity of the Grand-Guignol tradition, as a critic writing in *Newsweek* describes the performance:

> Severed heads thud on a blood soaked floor. A glistening scalpel slices open the throat of a screaming victim. Knives tear into writhing bodies. A butcher reels out a woman's intestines, two novice nuns are raped and one subsequently impaled on a blood drenched meat hook . . .
>
> ('As the Stomach Turns', *Newsweek*,
> 18 February 1974, 22, quoted in Emeljanow 1991, 151)

And so the review goes on. The kind of gore-fest which is described here is seriously out of line with what documentation and practice leads us to believe was the reality at the Théâtre du Grand-Guignol. The use of stage blood was a key feature of Grand-Guignol performance, but its effective use is dependent on care and restraint: a matter of quality rather than quantity, or—in that surprising motto of Grand-Guignol performance—'less is more'.

There is a photograph from the Grand-Guignol (see Gordon 1997, ix and Emeljanow 1991, 152) showing a formally dressed middle-aged man slitting the throat of a younger, but also formally dressed woman. There is no indication of the play to which this photograph belongs, but it is notable for the restrained use of blood. In fact there is far less blood than would be present if this were a real-life throat-slitting. The stage blood has been theatrically smeared in a wide and visible band across the throat by the blade of the knife whilst two thin trickles of blood run down towards the woman's breast, over her shoulder and down her arm. Most significant is the positioning of the female actor, as her arm is deliberately outstretched in a fashion that allows the blood to trickle *erotically* down her arm. This effect and the layering of eroticism into the meaning of the scene is totally dependent on the limited use of blood. If the stage blood really had flowed, rather than trickled, the effect would be lost. Other photographs tell the same story: the amount of blood used is enough to give the desired effect without being so much as to obscure the actors' gestures or expressions.

In *Orgasm* (Grand-Guignol Laboratory 1999), a scene was included that portrayed a woman receiving an internal examination from a female doctor, who was her vindictive rival in love. It was for many the most chilling moment of the play when the doctor removed her hand to reveal a single bright red spot of blood upon the white surgical glove. By contrast the closing scene of the play involved the castration of the male protagonist, which was performed, in the early performances, with a good deal of blood and even a pair of sheep's testicles! Consequently—and most unfortunately—the effect crossed the line into comedy. By the time the show reached the Edinburgh Fringe, however, the effect was fine-tuned so that the doctor slit open a condom filled with a smaller amount of stage blood (concealed in the victim's *white* boxer shorts), so that the audience witnessed a small, but spreading, pool of red on the victim's underwear. With this decision, the desired effect of horror was at least more likely to be successfully achieved. The Grand-Guignol may be synonymous with excess, but with regard to its blood effects it was comparatively restrained—and all the more effective in consequence.

The central plank, however, of performer-dependent special effects at the Grand-Guignol was not, as might be supposed, sleight-of-hand, but rather the acting skills of the company. Whilst the sleight-of-hand trick relies, to some extent, on a swiftness of movement, the Grand-Guignol has less use for this than an eye-gouging, disembowelment, stabbing or throat slitting which is performed slowly, with care and precision, enhanced by the gestures and the facial expressions of the actors. Production photographs show victims who have contorted their bodies and faces into living images of agony, whilst the murderers show rigid bodies, clenched teeth and taut facial muscles just at the moment the knife enters the flesh.

## Offstage Technical Aspects: The Use of Make-Up, Lighting and Sound at the Grand-Guignol

The preparation in advance of wounds that would be hidden beneath clothing or bandages played an important role within the Grand-Guignol. In this respect the level of sophistication could be much greater than make-up applied quickly and surreptitiously in the middle of a performance, such as in *The Final Kiss*. Henri's ravaged face can be concealed beneath the bandages until the appropriate moment, whereas Jeanne's must be applied on-stage. Inevitably, Jeanne's make-up, whilst remaining effective, is likely to be much cruder, and production photographs (see Pierron 1995, plates on 4, between 794 and 795) bear this out. After seeing the 1938 production, Montboron commented that 'M. Dartiall's make-up is enough to make one faint with terror' (*La Transition*, 16 January 1938). It is a comment which also indicates the importance of make-up as perceived by the Grand-Guignol audience.

Make-up was used, beyond merely the presentation of realistic wounds, disfigurements and deformities, in a stylized manner to enhance certain facial features of the actor in accordance with the character they were playing. For example, the cover to the published edition of René Berton's *L'Euthanasie* (1923) shows the actor Paulais in a pose from the production (reproduced in Hand and Wilson 2000, 269). In this extra-ordinary photograph Paulais can be seen contorting his mouth, flaring his nostrils and moving his eyeballs beneath his lower eyelids in a melodramatic representation of a man driven to lunacy through the suffering of cancer. What is also noticeable from the photograph is the black and white maculated hair and the heavy greasepaint on the eyebrows, around the eyes and on the cheeks to give the face a drawn and sunken appearance.

In the clip of Grand-Guignol performance in *Ecco* the murderer also appears in heavy make-up. The beard is shaped to reflect a melodramatic stylization of the villain and the cheekbones are also accentuated. Most noticeably, the murderer's forehead appears to have been substantially enlarged, made all the more obvious by the baldness of the actor's head. It is unclear whether this prosthetic is concealing some special effect (we are reminded here of the end of *Le Laboratoire des hallucinations*, where de Mora cracks open Gorlitz's skull) or whether it is an attempt to enlarge the skull so as to suggest the distorted mind of the psychopath, but the effect is certainly to enhance the actor's sinister appearance. This aspect is further supported if we consider the appearance of his victim, a young woman, dressed mainly in white, with long flowing locks of red hair: the very image of a melodramatic heroine. It is another fascinating and contradictory aspect of the Grand-Guignol genre that make-up served to enhance both its realistic and stylized aspects.

The principles of lighting and sound design at the rue Chaptal are again generally accredited to Paul Ratineau and were inevitably deter-mined by the intimate nature of the auditorium. The importance of lighting within the theatre's production values is made clear by Maxa when she states that 'a certain kind of lighting is indispensable' (in Pierron 1995, 1392). The principal feature of Grand-Guignol lighting design appears to have been the use of shadows achieved through 'some green or red in a corner giving an all-pervading sense of mystery' (ibid.).

This use of shadows served two specific functions, the first of which is simultaneously to illuminate and obscure the actions and execution of effects on stage, demonstrating an advanced and sophisticated application of lighting. The second function of lighting in the Grand-Guignol and, according to Maxa, its primary purpose, is contained in her statement that 'the most important thing, first of all, is to create an atmosphere' (ibid.). We have already seen how the creation of an appropriate atmosphere, designed to enhance the emotional experience of the spectator, is a crucial part of the pre-show game played with the audience. The purpose of the lighting is to extend that atmosphere onto the stage and into the programme itself. In doing so it clouds the distinction between stage and auditorium, further drawing the audience into the action and involving them within it. When the curtain rises it merely represents a continuation and an intensification of what already exists both inside and outside the auditorium. This is most obvious in the original design for the 1911 premiere of Level and Rey's *Sous la lumière rouge*, when the red set was bathed in the red light of a darkroom lamp which, in the words of Louis Schneider reviewing in *Comoedia*, 'throws a sinister light upon the stage' (9 May 1911, quoted in Pierron 1995, 440). Charles Atamian's sketch of the darkroom scene (fig. 8) taken from the production in the first publication of the play (*Monde Illustré* number 2831, 1911, 9) successfully conveys the sinister atmosphere created by the careful mediation of light. The predominance of the colour red simultaneously symbolizes blood and the opulence of the middle-class surroundings, yet this can only work because it is a *bloodless* play[2] and because the red light is 'real'—in other words, accountable—as it directly appertains to Philippe's beloved technology.

It is worth noting that even complete darkness has a role to play. One of the most effective moments in *L'Horrible Expérience* is when the stage is plunged into darkness just as Dr Charrier and his assistant are attempting to resurrect Charrier's daughter:

[Charrier] lets the head of the corpse fall onto the table with a bang. At that moment a strong gust of wind blows outside; one of the shutters which has come undone crashes against the window, stage right, causing the pane to rattle violently and the window to suddenly open; a gust of wind blows into the room with a mournful

---

[2] The temptation always to bathe the stage in a sinister red hue is to be resisted as a matter of urgency in respect of the use of stage blood, as under red light it has the look of chocolate sauce.

*Figure 8.* A sinister atmosphere created by the careful mediation of light: Philippe and Didier in Level and Rey's *Sous la lumière rouge* (sketch by Charles Atamian in *Monde Illustré,* number 2831, 1911, 9) (British Library)

whistle. The lantern goes out. The stage is in darkness. A long pause.
The monotonous, sinister hum of electricity can be heard. The stage
is only lit by the electricity which is running through the equipment.
Jean and Charrier emit an involuntary cry of terror.

(Pierron 1995, 399)

Thus de Lorde and Binet establish an evocative moment of suspense
with the extinguishing of the lamp, a moment of darkness and then,
very slowly, the illumination of the stage by the light of the electric
current. Here we have a use of specific light similar to the use of red in
*Sous la lumière rouge* that is eerie and yet, once again, *accountable* as it
belongs to the scientific equipment. Moreover, it is a light source that is
emanating from an object *onstage* and this will certainly enhance the
effectiveness and 'realism' of this suspenseful moment. However, this
scene from *L'Horrible Expérience* is not simply about lighting, it is also
about the performers' ability to enhance the technical adjustment of the
environment (note the involuntary scream the two men emit). But it is
also an excellent demonstration of the use of sound in Grand-Guignol,
with the noise of the storm outside suddenly smashing the window
open and filling the laboratory with its lugubrious whistling, followed
by the ensuing silence, eventually broken by the hum of the electrical
current.

Sound effects as a whole were treated with great seriousness at the
Grand-Guignol. It is remarkable how many of the plays include significant use of offstage sound, whether it is the sounds of the storm
outside the house in *Au téléphone* or in the example we have just seen,
the distant explosions in *La Dernière Torture*, the ship-bells and
Chinese oarsmen in *Le Jardin des supplices* or the noise of the seagulls
pecking against the glass dome of the lighthouse in *Gardiens de phare*.
These are examples where strictly offstage sounds help to establish the
context, environment and mood of the plays, and substantial time and
resources were invested in perfecting such sound effects. Maxa recalls
spending up to two days perfecting an offstage scream (Pierron 1995,
1386).

What is borne out by Maxa's testimony is that the technical practices
at the Grand-Guignol were developed on the job. Ratineau developed his
specialist skill whilst working as a member of the acting company: it was
not necessarily knowledge that he brought with him. Gordon explains
that Ratineau 'discovered the further away the sound source was from
the audience, the more effective (or chilling) it was' (Gordon, 1997, 44).
This was a theatre that was not working so much to a fixed set of rules
as making those rules and generic conventions up as it went along. It is
clear from anecdotal evidence, as much as anything else, that the creative

use of sound was a crucial part of the Grand-Guignol experience,[3] and effects such as Ratineau's seagulls became classics in their own right (Pierron 1995, 118).

We turn finally to the role (or evident lack) of music within Grand-Guignol performance. Music, used in order to convey meaning (non-diegetic music), was a common device in nineteenth-century melodrama and has a near-omnipresence in cinema. Nowhere is this more evident than in the horror film, where a soundtrack is used to communicate atmosphere and to signpost certain actions and events. It may be surprising, therefore, that there is no evidence that music was ever used in the Grand-Guignol in this way. Any use of music in the Grand-Guignol is strictly diegetic, such as the chapel bell and nuns singing in *Un crime dans une maison de fous*. The non-diegetic music used during the brief clip of Grand-Guignol performance in *Ecco* was added by the filmmakers. Even in the British Grand-Guignol, where programme notes do reveal the presence of a small orchestra, this was only used to provide music (in the way of light classical pieces) *between* plays and not during them. There is nothing to suggest that the rue Chaptal ever hosted such an orchestra. After all, Maurice Magney originally designed the theatre as a forum for turn-of-the-century naturalism which would have little use for live music. In an auditorium of such limited size an orchestra pit may well have been a luxury that Magney felt he could not afford, as it would have significantly reduced the number of seats available for paying customers, in addition to the cost of employing musicians. This would no doubt have been welcomed as a blessing by Méténier and his successors, as an orchestra pit situated between stage and audience would have had serious implications for the intimacy of performance on which the Grand-Guignol genre depended and thrived. It should also be

---

[3] The use of sound was also one technical aspect which the British Grand-Guignol was able to import from Paris without fear of the censor's intervention and it seems that they took on these tasks with equal seriousness and commitment to that of their French counterparts. This, however, was not always without its problems as is shown by the story that, during the 1921 production of Maurice Level's *The Kill* (adapted by W.H. Harris), the offstage imitations of howling wolfhounds by the actors were so realistic that the R.S.P.C.A. was called in to investigate amidst concerns about animal cruelty:

> The R.S.P.C.A. inspector saw the show and demanded to be allowed back stage at the next performance. 'Nothing could make the dogs howl in this way,' he declared, 'except the most vicious cruelty'. I was there that night and I well remember his discomfiture. When the moment came he was shown Lewis dressed only in his underclothes (he was also making up for the next play) and the stage manager standing in the wings baying like the hounds of hell into lamp glasses!
> (Casson 1972, 71–72)

remembered that the Grand-Guignol was a genre that relied heavily upon well-crafted dialogue and it would have been important not to lose the actors' voices beneath the sound of orchestra music. Whether the emphasis on dialogue was developed in response to the lack of music, or vice versa, it is impossible to say, but it is clear that the continuing absence of music at the Grand-Guignol contributed to the development of the genre and gave it a significant distinction from melodrama.

Considerable time and effort were invested in the technical dimensions of theatre production at the Théâtre du Grand-Guignol and some of these devices acquired a certain notoriety in their own right. Nevertheless, Ratineau was not a showman in this respect. The technical devices and special effects were always employed sparingly and for the enhancement of the play and, ultimately, the complete theatrical experience. There was a genuine creative partnership between author, director, actor and technician, each working for the betterment of the project. The prime function of the technical designer was not simply to shock or disgust the audience but to feed and nourish that central factor in the creation of effective Grand-Guignol drama, namely the imagination. Let us give Maxa the final word: 'Imagination always transcends reality and it is the imagination, along with a shiver of the soul, that constitutes the poetics of fear' (in Pierron 1995, 1393).

# 5

# Issues of Audience and Reception at the Grand-Guignol

'It's queer people on the streets of Montmartre at this time of night'
(*Mad Love*, Karl Freund 1935)

Most commentators agree that one of the most remarkable features of the Grand-Guignol audience was its eclectic nature, the ability of the theatre to attract support from across the whole spectrum of society. In spite of Homrighous's suggestion that this ability to transcend class boundaries is what defines Grand-Guignol as truly popular theatre (Homrighous 1963, 177), this claim to universality is potentially problematic when trying to construct an argument for placing Grand-Guignol within a popular theatre tradition. John McGrath (1981) and others more convincingly argue that popular theatres more often address *specific* (and working-class) audiences, rather than attempting to reach out to the complete spectrum of society. Besides, Homrighous's statements are loaded with an inference of the artistic inferiority of the popular form.

In fact, to suggest that the Grand-Guignol was able to please all of the people all of the time is a simplification of a far more complex situation. It would be more accurate to say that the Grand-Guignol retained a core popular audience, whilst at certain times in its history also drawing considerable support from different sections of society, a model entirely consistent with McGrath's own. The picture was complicated from its very early days. When Méténier opened the Grand-Guignol in 1897, it was an avant-garde experiment supported by the radical artistic community, but it also had a significant local clientele in this traditionally working-class—and red-light—district. Under Max Maurey, the theatre began to tip the balance from naturalism towards melodrama and subsequently draw in a more popular audience, a development for which Homrighous unfairly and rather patronizingly levels the accusation that the 'grandguignolesque is not art, but it is artfully contrived' (Homrighous 1963, 67–68). It was also a time when, according to Gordon, the Grand-Guignol became fashionable with the Parisian upper class and visiting minor European royalty (Gordon 1997, 22, 26–27), as well as becoming one of 'the best known tourist attractions in Paris by 1910' (23). This love affair with tourism is one that continued up until 1962, when the audience consisted mainly of tourists and die-hard regulars (33). The years of Occupation brought a more unwelcome kind of tourist to Paris in the shape of the German Army. Although the authorities attempted to suppress it as *entartete Kunst* or 'degenerate art' (30), the Grand-Guignol not only survived but continued to be popular. Hermann Goering was amongst its regular patrons (Gordon 1997, 30, and Callahan 1991, 169). Even after the Liberation in 1944, the theatre proved itself equally popular with the Allies (Callahan 1991, 170), aptly symbolized by the high-profile visit of the appropriately nicknamed General 'Blood and Guts' Patton to the theatre (see Pierron 1995, XXXIII).

Throughout its life, the Grand-Guignol audience always contained a significant element for whom the genre had become, albeit temporarily, fashionable. However, this ability to appeal across social boundaries is not quite the same as a claim to universality. Callahan captures the essence of any universality that might be inherent in the Grand-Guignol genre:

> For its patrons, the Grand-Guignol offered a chance to be scared in complete safety. Audiences enjoy being frightened, as the movie box office has continued to prove. Most people are vicarious lovers of violence and danger, and the majority of people find the theatrical depiction of violence to be cathartic. People went to the Grand-Guignol to be scared, to be able to hug their girl friend or boy friend, to laugh, to release their own sadism and/or masochism. It was a good night out. People have enjoyed, and always will enjoy, being stimulated and shocked.
>
> (Callahan 1991, 166–67)

At the same time as recognizing that the 'universal' appeal of Grand-Guignol lies primarily in its content (i.e. horror and comedy), Callahan rightly identifies a number of elements common to a range of popular theatres, and John McGrath would no doubt agree that an essential ingredient of popular forms is the 'good night out'. What is particularly interesting in Callahan's observation, however, is the way that he uses the example of the cinema audience to prove his point about the attraction of stage violence.

This may be serendipity, of course, but what is remarkable about the Grand-Guignol audience captured on film in *Ecco*, in the photographs in the documentary *Clive Barker's A-Z of Horror* (BBC TV, 1995) or in the still photograph produced by Gordon (Gordon 1997, 116–17) is that it has the exact look of a popular cinema audience, rather than a theatre audience. There is a significant degree of informality: not a dinner suit, evening gown or any formal dress in sight. Instead the audience is dressed casually and contains a very clear gender mix and is representative of the whole adult age range. In the Gordon photograph, dated around 1954, there are both couples and single-sex groupings with the back row of seats clearly occupied by the younger members of the audience. The posture of the audience is also striking: this is no usual passive theatre audience, but rather all spectators are either leaning forward, craning their necks or resting their chins on their hands, not in boredom, but in active engagement with the onstage proceedings. Similarly, in *Mad Love*'s Théâtre des Horreurs, the audience—complete with in-house 'nurse'—is presented as being intensely engaged with the onstage action. In all these examples we are very clearly witnessing an audience fully participating in the intensity of the experience: whether individually perceiving it as an erotic show, performance ritual or theatrical spectacle, they are all participating in a 'good night out'.

## The Guignoleurs and the Idea of the Playful Audience

One of the more remarkable aspects of the Grand-Guignol was the emergence of the *guignoleurs*,[1] a group of regular audience members at the rue Chaptal. According to Gordon, they shouted '"Assassin!" at the various "villains" and . . . liked to repeat the number of times that the house physician was called to treat temporarily sickened spectators' (Gordon 1997, 27). The *guignoleurs* clearly identified themselves with the theatre and both understood and participated in the development of its conventions. This is redolent of the popular audiences who attended the Montmartre melodramas in the nineteenth century but it is also reminiscent of the contemporary cinema audience that can, on occasions like a late-night horror show, be similarly active, and similarly enjoy sharing a laugh and a delighted *Schadenfreude* 'at the expense of the Grand-Guignol virgins' (Hand and Wilson 2000, 271). However, we would not wish to patronize the *guignoleurs* and their pleasures and motivations, since a familiarity with generic conventions can often liberate—and sophisticate—the process of interpretation. Tony Williams, discussing the contemporary horror film, argues:

---

[1] Gordon (1997) uses the term *'guignolers'* to describe the regular Grand-Guignol audience members. We have adopted the term *'guignoleurs'* as a linguistically more logical form upon the advice of Claude Schumacher.

> [Viewers] may choose to read 'against the grain,' bypassing
> spectacular violent mechanisms within slasher films to privilege
> neglected thematic motifs within the text and discern what exactly
> suffers repression. Viewers have the potential of reading beyond
> deceptive formal devices.
>
> (Williams 1996, 19)

The attendance of a regular audience also has an interesting implication in the process of reception and 'horrality'.[2] Plays would be on for a
few weeks at a time, and some of the classics of the repertoire would
return to the stage, and so we find a regular clientele who are familiar
with the works, no longer surprised by the narrative but enjoying the
process, technique and delivery of the works, and also being able to
interpret complex and obscured meanings. Moreover the plays in the
Grand-Guignol exploit the spectators' expectations with horrality in
mind. Brophy defines the playful functions of horrality in the following
terms:

> 'Horrality' involves the construction, employment and manipul-
> ation of horror—in all its various guises—as a textual mode. The
> effect of its fiction is not unlike a death-defying carnival ride: the
> subject is a willing target that both constructs the terror and is
> terrorised by its construction. 'Horrality' is too blunt to bother
> with psychology—traditionally the voice of articulation behind
> horror—because what is of prime importance is the textual effect,
> the game that one plays *with* the text, a game that is impervious to
> any knowledge of its workings. The contemporary Horror film
> *knows* that you've seen it before; it *knows* that you know what is
> about to happen; and it knows that you know it knows you know.
> And none of it means a thing, as the cheapest trick in the book will
> still tense your muscles, quicken your heart and jangle your nerves.
> It is the *present*—the precise point of speech, of utterance, of plot,
> of event—that is ever of any value. Its effect disappears with the
> gulping breath, the gasping shriek, swallowed up by the fascistic
> continuum of the fiction. A nervous giggle of amoral delight as you
> prepare yourself in a totally self-deluding way for the next shock.
>
> (Brophy 2000, 279)

---

[2] Horrality is a term coined by Philip Brophy, being a compound of horror,
textuality, morality and hilarity (see Brophy 2000, 277). It was intended to be
applied to what Brophy argues was, post-1975, 'a small "golden period" of
the contemporary horror film' (Brophy 2000, 276), but it can also be
profitably applied to the Grand-Guignol.

Likewise, the Grand-Guignol is a kind of carnival ride belonging to the tradition of popular entertainment, a Big Puppet Show or a Puppet Show for Grown-Ups as a literal translation of the theatre's name suggests. Its location emphasizes its 'adult' appeal as something along the lines of a sex-show or cabaret. Although there is rich material for psychoanalytical interpretation in the Grand-Guignol repertoire, during the experience of watching a play such concerns are probably shelved for the sake of the 'present': the carefully manufactured thrill of the passing moment. The Grand-Guignol may have arisen at the same time as psychoanalysis but perhaps its primary function is as a sensationalist spectacle, thriving on adrenaline and delighting in the visceral effect it has in manipulating willing targets who participate in the construction of terror and are likewise terrorized by its construction. David Cronenberg emphasizes a similar point of view in relation to attempts at political interpretation when he writes that 'the appeal of horror is beyond politics' and argues that, although it can be *eventually* interpreted politically, its appeal is 'right into the viscera, before it gets to the brain' (Cronenberg 1997, 60). Brophy argues that horrality engages

> . . . the reader in a dialogue of textual manipulation that has no time for critical ordinances of social realism, cultural enlightenment or emotional humanism. The gratification of the contemporary Horror film is based upon tension, fear, anxiety, sadism and masochism—a disposition that is overall both tasteless and morbid. The pleasure of the text is, in fact, getting the shit scared out of you—and loving it; an exchange mediated by adrenaline.
>
> (Brophy 2000, 279)

There is a great deal of game-playing in the Grand-Guignol, especially with the *guignoleurs* who know and understand its conventions, but even with the spectators who willingly suspend their disbelief and yet, underneath it all, know that they are watching artifice (even if they may need to pinch themselves when they start to forget).

The great directors and writers of the Grand-Guignol demonstrated a willingness to play with the audience (just as the audience displayed an equal willingness to be played with). Méténier was fully aware of the importance of audience as he performed his pre-show antics, and Maurey, the arch-publicist, was keen to encourage all popular aspects of the form, and the incorporation of the audience as willing players in the entire event was part of this strategy, perhaps best exemplified by his installation of the house-doctor.[3] While masquerading as a comfort, the result of such measures was probably entirely disconcerting. The significance of such stunts is that they break down the border between art and life: Grand-Guignol, the 'slice of death' theatre, was naturalistic or ultra-realist in its performance aesthetic, and the audience witnessed, like Peeping Toms, extremes of behaviour through the fourth wall. By employing a doctor, Maurey told the Grand-Guignol audience that there was the potential of *real* danger. The implied danger would manifest itself in spectators being 'overcome' by what they will witness. This functions as an ingenious strategy in the suspension of disbelief as it strives to prove that, although the theatrical spectacle may only be art, even art can seriously damage your health. Simply by noticing—let alone, as it seems sometimes happened, being examined by—the house doctor on entry, the spectators were left wondering whether what they were about to witness would make them lose their self-control or their dinners.

The playfulness of the event is something that the Grand-Guignol Laboratory has embraced fully in its public output. Of course, it is difficult to compare these experiments with the authentic Grand-Guignol as we did not have the benefit of an audience of regular *guignoleurs*, familiar with the generic conventions or the repertoire. Nevertheless, these performances incorporated a pre-show ritual of one sort or another that invited the audience to play the Grand-Guignol game. When the Laboratory was, for example, performing at the University of Exeter in May 1999, the audience was led round the side of the building to accordion music, before being subjected to a 'medical examination' by two actors playing the roles of doctor and nurse, before being admitted to the theatre. This was not an attempt at historical authenticity, but rather a recognition of the performer-audience conventions of the genre.

## Eroticism and the Grand-Guignol

No discussion of audience and reception at the Grand-Guignol would be complete without a consideration of the undeniably erotic—even pornographic—dimension to the form, a dimension that links it to the

---

[3] His gimmick of employing a resident doctor would be later emulated by Hollywood, most famously by 1950s American horror movie director William Castle who, amongst many other ingenious publicity stunts, employed actors to play doctors, nurses and life insurance brokers assessing spectators on entry. Even Alfred Hitchcock (or at least the marketing executives at Paramount) hired uniformed Pinkerton guards to enforce the director's policy that no latecomers should be admitted to the first screenings of *Psycho* (1960) and early British screenings of *The Exorcist* (1973) included genuine St John Ambulance assistants in attendance.

cabarets, burlesques and other onstage entertainments available in Pigalle. The Grand-Guignol also came into being during the confidently open-minded era of *la belle époque*, and Homrighous even links the cradle of the Grand-Guignol, naturalism, to the erotic, arguing that one aspect of the 'revolution of naturalism was that it became a rationalization for the proliferation of pornography' (Homrighous 1963, 5). Whatever the reason for its erotic genesis—geographical, historical or cultural—not only does the Grand-Guignol present us with erotic titles like Régis Gignoux's *Le Kâma sutra, ou Il ne faut pas jouer avec le feu* (1922), Jack Jouvin's *Sexualité* (1932), or Eddy Ghilain and Fernand Millaud's *L'École du strip-tease* (1956), but eroticism in the shape of adultery and sadomasochism runs deep through the Grand-Guignol repertoire and, in addition to the titillating slap-and-tickle frolics of the comedies, the horror plays also succeeded in sexually arousing some spectators. The process of witnessing a Grand-Guignol play can thus transform a spectator into a voyeur, depending on one's predilection. In a humorous cartoon of 1922 (see Pierron 1995, XV), two women are seen discussing the Grand-Guignol, with one claiming that her sex-life has improved since her husband began attending the theatre. The joke is that since seeing the horrors at the rue Chaptal, her husband is unable to sleep at night. 'And I'm the one who benefits . . .' she adds. Furthermore, there is evidence to suggest that the sexual arousal of some spectators *during* a show was not an unusual occurrence at the Grand-Guignol. Bernard Charlan (an actor at the Grand-Guignol) claimed that he was once obliged, mid-performance, to harangue a courting couple in one of the boxes with the words, 'You enjoy yourselves in there!' (quoted in Jones 1997, 112). This anecdote suggests that couples would frequent the theatre for the purpose of what used to be euphemistically called 'heavy petting', in the same way that they might seek anonymity in the darkness of the back row of a cinema. It is a notion that is confirmed by Pierron in a recent interview:

> Until the Nazi occupation in World War Two, theatres provided trysting places. There were stairs at the back of the theatre that led ticket holders to private boxes. The boxes were designed with lattice work so that audience members could see the play, but not be seen. The Grand-Guignol was the last theatre in Paris to offer this kind of seating.[4]

(26 October 2000)

---

[4] This interview took place on 26 October 2000 at the EXIT Theatre, San Francisco when Pierron shared the stage with Mel Gordon in post-show discussion as part of the SCHOCKTOBERFEST!!, hosted by Thrillpeddlers, a contemporary Grand-Guignol company based in San Francisco.

The key difference is that at the Grand-Guignol, the onstage entertainment added to the arousal. Pierron informs us that 'cleaning ladies would find traces of sexual pleasure from the audience' (quoted in Jones 1997, 112) and in her own study of the form she comments: 'it was well-known that during the notorious Monday matinees, that women would prepare for adultery by snuggling, half-dead with fear, into the arms of the man in the next seat' (Pierron 1995, XV). Certainly, some of the more robust critics of the Grand-Guignol during its heyday—such as Émile Mas—highlight the dangers of a form which, as they saw it, functions like a kind of addictive drug on its spectator and can, worst of all, instigate a 'physical excitement':

> I consider this kind of theatre to be very dangerous . . . [I] do not really see any difference between the absinthe addict, for example, and the fervent enthusiast of these plays which offer nothing but physical excitement! If alcohol corrodes the body, certain displays unhinge the mind and I do not see what distinction can be made between these 'products'.
>
> (Émile Mas in *Le Petit Bleu*, 28 April 1921, 77)

In the same article, Mas, who had just seen the highly acclaimed revival of *Le Laboratoire des hallucinations* featuring Paulais as de Mora, goes on to plead with de Lorde to turn his eyes to 'that which is beautiful and healthy . . . and renounce despair . . . '. While Mas can only praise de Lorde's skill as a playwright (he also celebrates the quality of the acting), he is deeply troubled by the themes and images of the plays and their potential effect on an audience. The physical effects he refers to might include one of the theatre's celebrated faintings, but we may assume that he is principally referring to sexual stimulation.

Unlike Mas, Colette regrets that in the Grand-Guignol 'there are many more ways to die than there are to make love' (in Pierron 1995, 1380) and she goes on to lament the fact that the erotic dimension of the genre did not evolve as quickly, or as imaginatively, as its portrayal of violence. Perhaps, in the light of this, we could argue that the Grand-Guignol was not so much inventively erotic as mundanely pornographic. While it could be asserted that many Grand-Guignol plays function along similar lines to the thriller, there is also a similarity between the structure of pornographic literature and performance and many a Grand-Guignol play. The plays are short and the narrative is often very simple with an uncomplicated and unambiguous exposition heading towards a clearly signposted ending. Suspense and tension are developed with tantalizing and excruciating care and the plays frequently climax in an intense display of violence. David Cottis of Instant Classics likens this to 'the "money shot" . . . in pornography' (Letter to the authors, 23 March 2001). While the violence in more substantial Grand-Guignol plays such as *Le Jardin des supplices* is as formulaically orchestrated as sex scenes in an erotic movie, there is a distinct parallel to be drawn between the shorter Grand-Guignol plays and the numerous pornographic one-reelers privately produced in Pigalle by such figures as the shady-named amateur film-maker 'Monsieur X' (who flourished in the 1930s).[5] These short films, like Grand-Guignol plays, include mundane settings such as the contemporary home or workplace, but also display the exotic with works of fetishist, orientalist or historical fantasy with performers in costume. It is often said that pornographic narratives are generally designed for the sexual response of the male spectator. This is undoubtedly accurate, although it is worth noting that the Pigalle one-reelers avoid obvious gender demarcation and are significantly bisexual in their imagery, including scenes of gay and lesbian sex as well as heterosexual intercourse. It is rather like violence in the Grand-Guignol, inasmuch as there does not seem to be an obvious process of gender-specification in terms of perpetrators and participants (or, in terms of horror discourse, monsters and victims): at the end of the day, the Grand-Guignol is probably universally misanthropic rather than specifically misogynistic.

All in all, we would argue that the presence of the erotic in the Grand-Guignol should not be underestimated. It is in all the plays as a subtext if not blatantly foregrounded, and this serves as a clear exploitation of the sadomasochistic potential in the plays, which recurrently explore guilt, sexual violation and sexual punishment. If, in the golden age of the Grand-Guignol, these themes were elaborately developed or located in a sophisticated subtext, in the last days such themes were less subtle: Pierron includes a photograph from Eddy Ghilain's 1961 play *Les Blousons sanglants* (Pierron 1995, plates on 4, between 794 and 795) in which a woman's nipple is cut off with scissors. The depiction of extreme sexual violence, whilst rare within the Grand-Guignol, points to its moral complexity.[6] Our investigation of the erotic in the Grand-Guignol suggests that there is a key dialectic in the form between the corporeal senses and the moralizing intellect. This dialectic (only one of many dialectical structures inherent in the form) is often teased in the Grand-Guignol and is perhaps one reason why it can be such a problematic and disquieting form. Gordon writes that 'There is

---

[5] For examples of the genre see *Vintage Erotica, anno 1930* (DVD, Cult Epics, 2000), a collection of short French erotic films from the 1920s and 1930s.
[6] For a discussion of morality within the Grand-Guignol, see Hand and Wilson 2000, 272.

something embarrassing about the Grand Guignol . . . [It] still touches upon our secret longings and fears' (Gordon 1997, 2), and we would argue that the dialectic Gordon highlights between longing and fear is parallel to the one we have located between the senses and the intellect (which can certainly be just as 'embarrassing'). Similarly there is the dialectic of humour and horror, although contemporary theoretical investigation would argue that these are not so far apart as they seem.

## The Reception of Violence

Anecdotal evidence suggests that the Grand-Guignol audience behaved towards scenes of obscured violence in the same way that they would have had the acts been performed in full view. The creative core of the Grand-Guignol is such that the effective execution of horror, through a heady blend of anticipation and suggestion, allows the audience to see, or at least believe it has seen, what it clearly has not. It is a key concept in horror performance and is regularly employed as a cinematic technique, as in Quentin Tarantino's *Reservoir Dogs* (1991), where many of the audience believed that they had seen the severing of an ear, when in fact all the film shows is a movement of the arm and the resulting wound. Of course, cinema has always been able to use its key technique of montage to its advantage as a horror effect—we need only consider the opening moments of Luis Buñuel's *Un Chien Andalou* (1928) or the shower scene in *Psycho* (1960)—but the technical capabilities of modern-day cinema allow film-makers to achieve other horror effects in increasingly sophisticated and effective ways. It is all the more impressive that this could be achieved within the context of an intimate theatre at the beginning of the twentieth century. If audiences genuinely believed, whilst watching *Le Baiser de sang* in 1929, that they had really seen the drill enter the skull, as seems likely if we are to credit André Antoine's account of multiple faintings (see Pierron 1995, 1113), it says much about the nature of communication between performer and audience in relation to the willing suspension of disbelief, an issue we would tend to associate with controversial episodes in more recent drama such as Edward Bond's *Saved* (1965) or Howard Brenton's *Romans in Britain* (1980).

Pierron's anecdote relating to the performance of Eddy Ghilain's *Les Coupeurs de têtes* (1960) at the rue Chaptal would suggest that such creative imagining on the part of the audience was commonplace:

> For example, there was a play which featured a naked woman tied to a post being shot with arrows. As an actor 'shot' the arrows, arrows would pop out of the post. Audience members swore that

they could hear the arrows whizzing through the air towards the woman—but it was just their imagination.

(Interview at the EXIT Theatre,<br>San Francisco, 26 October 2000)

A story, told about a performance of Richard Berkeley's *Eight o'Clock* at the British Grand-Guignol in 1920, indicates that even at London's tamer imitation of the genre, such things were also possible. The play deals with

> the last half-hour of a man's life before he was hanged at eight in the morning. Russell [Thorndike] was the condemned man and Lewis [Casson] the prison chaplain. Their dialogue not unnaturally made frequent references to the time, gradually increasing the tension as the minutes ticked by. One night after the show a retired prison governor came round to say that although he had enjoyed the play there was one bad mistake that he had to point out to them. There would never have been a clock on the wall of a condemned cell, and in any case how on earth did they manage to make the dialogue keep so accurately in time with it. Lewis at once took him on to the stage where the cell was still standing. There was no clock on the wall. The governor had been so aware of the time by the playing of the scene that he had actually 'seen' a clock on the wall.

(Casson 1972, 72)

This has significant implications for the nature of the role of the audience in the creation of Grand-Guignol drama. If one of the achievements of the actors is to enable the audience to 'see' what it has not seen, then the audience is irrefutably implicated in the creative process and an equal partner in the audience-performer dynamic. Once again the fourth wall is penetrated to allow the audience to take their part as meaning-makers in the dramatic process, so that form and meaning are negotiated and created in the space between actor and performer. It is arguable, of course, that the meaning of all performance, indeed all art, is formed within the dialogue between creator and receiver, but when it is done so openly, it is usually an indication of a popular theatre form. Such democratization of meaning-making is a significant consideration in assessing the Grand-Guignol and, in particular, its relationship with its audience. This democracy needs to be qualified, however. Maxa talks about the performer's need to exercise focus and control in the performance (Pierron 1995, 1393) and Gordon comments that 'the smallest manual slip or false note in the acting could thoroughly ruin a twenty-minute scenario' (Gordon 1997, 25–26). This focus and control is not restricted to voice and movement. It also applies to the actor's relationship with the audience, because the actor must always remain in control of that dynamic. The audience is allowed to interpret and make meaning, but only because it has seen or heard what the performer allows it to see and hear, so that the meaning that is made is the meaning that the actor wishes to make. In this sense, consent is a crucial factor. The audience submits itself to the play and the actors, so that any negotiation of meaning occurs only within the parameters set out by the actors.[7] This contract between them is dependent on the very trust and loyalty of the audience that the Grand-Guignol undoubtedly enjoyed. To return once more to the clip from *Ecco*, at that moment when the actor acknowledges the presence of the audience, we perceive the embodiment of that contract. There are elements of collaboration, voyeurism and democratization, but we are never in any doubt as to who is in control. There is definitely something of the Svengali in that moment.

A study of the Grand-Guignol demands that we continually return to issues of audience and reception. It is a form that presents a provocative mixture of the horrific and the erotic, the satirical and the realist, the reactionary and the radical, the frightening and the funny, the thrilling and the theoretically determined. No one aspect is clear-cut. All these central issues are issues of *response*, relating to the individual psychology and experience of the spectator and the dynamic of the audience. What one spectator watches as artful construction, another sees as an escapist 'ride'. One person's repugnant nightmare is another's outrageous comedy, while the same thing is yet another person's erotic fantasy.

---

[7] Furthermore, Deák (1974, 43) claims that the Grand-Guignol employed a 'plant' in the audience 'to encourage and secure the desired reactions'. Although this appears to be an unsubstantiated claim, it would not be surprising if this had been the case, as it would merely be a later example of the nineteenth-century French theatrical convention of the *claque*.

Part Two

# Ten Plays of the Grand-Guignol

THE GRAND-GUIGNOL LABORATORY

The work of the Grand-Guignol Laboratory at the University of Glamorgan is ongoing and the authors are very keen to know if anyone in theatre companies, drama groups, educational environments etc. makes use of the material in this book for practical workshop investigation. The authors would be delighted if anyone undertaking such work would contact them via the publishers to let them know about the experience of using this book as a way to undertake experiments and research into Grand-Guignol.

# A Note on the Translations

The particular problems associated with the translation of dramatic texts have been the subject of much debate amongst scholars within the discipline of translation studies. It is not our intention to revisit those debates here in any great detail, but they are largely concerned with the tensions that exist for the translator between the literary and performative imperatives of a particular text. According to Susan Bassnett-McGuire, 'all kinds of factors other than the linguistic are involved in the case of (translating) theatre texts' because 'a theatre text exists in a dialectical relationship with the performance of that text' (1985, 87). It has been our intention during the translation of these Grand-Guignol plays to remain as honest as possible to the original French without compromising the performative potential of the plays within the Grand-Guignol tradition. With the exception of *L'Euthanasie*, the original scripts used (and to which the reader may wish to refer) are those published in Pierron's *Le Grand-Guignol* (1995), an anthology based on previously published scripts and the collections in the Bibliothèque de l'Arsenal. The text used for *L'Euthanasie* is that published by Librairie Théâtrale in 1925.[1]

During the process of translation our overriding priority has always been to produce scripts that are *playable*. We have attempted to translate *accurately* from French to English, but, in doing so, to embrace the *spirit* and the *performability* of the form in the first instance. To this end, any differences between the translation and the original can be summarized thus:

- In all scripts we have dispensed with the French convention of marking each entrance and exit of a character by a new scene. This seems rather odd to the English reader and unnecessarily breaks up the flow of dramatic action. The scripts are instead simply divided into acts according to a change in setting, as in the original French.

---

[1] Readers should refer to these two volumes for complete cast lists of the original productions. Additionally, Pierron includes a 'Calendrier des Spectacles' (1401—24), which lists the performance dates of all the plays presented at the Grand-Guignol.

- We have also at times taken the liberty of making more concise the often lengthy and detailed descriptions of stage scenery which regularly precede each act.
- Because of its length and the size of its cast list, *The Torture Garden* has been purged of non-speaking walk-on characters to enable the script to be used with smaller groups of actors.
- French idiom, slang and expletives have not been literally translated, but replaced with English equivalents or approximations. This is particularly the case with *Tics* which relies heavily upon colloquialisms and innuendo for its humour.
- Very occasionally lines of little significance have been cut in order to maintain the pace of the original French script which might otherwise have suffered in the process of translation. This is most evident in *Jack*, the quick-paced *The Ultimate Torture* and the longest piece in this collection, *The Torture Garden*.

*The Final Kiss* is the one play which stands out from all others in this collection in that it is best described not as a translation, but an *adaptation*. Our version was developed as part of a programme of three Grand-Guignol plays, and pragmatic considerations led to our concentrating on what is the second act of Level's play. This has resulted in a much shorter piece and the elimination of a number of minor characters. The essential information revealed in Level's Act 1 has been concentrated into the opening scene of our version which focuses much more upon the final encounter between the former lovers. In spite of it being an adaptation of the original, we have included it here as it still closely conforms to the generic conventions of the Grand-Guignol and is the script which has been most subjected to practical experimentation.

Our intention with these translations has been not only to give the English-speaking reader a true and accurate feel for the Grand-Guignol, but to provide some raw material for practical work and we would advise users of these scripts to make any minor modifications that they see fit. The translations in this volume have not been written so that they can remain on the page, but rather so that they can be liberated in the studio.

# Jack

## (Lui!, 1897)

*by*

### OSCAR MÉTÉNIER

## Preface

Oscar Méténier's *Lui!* (1897), one of the first Grand-Guignol plays, was included in the year of the theatre's inauguration. The play was first performed on 11 November 1897 and was revived at the Grand-Guignol as late as 1940.

The fact that it is an early play is evident in the naturalistic essence of the piece. The play is set within a brothel and the characters in the play are predominantly working class: such slice-of-life surroundings and proletarians are the stock-in-trade of naturalism. It is a short play (very much a 'studio' piece), as were the majority of naturalistic plays in that era. Interestingly enough, the concept and tradition of a medley of short plays became one of the most significant trademarks of the Grand-Guignol.

The author can be seen to be exploiting aspects of contemporary French (or even Parisian) culture. The prostitute at the beginning is reading *Le Petit Parisien*, a pulp magazine full of sensational stories. This magazine and others like *Le Petit Journal* were an extremely popular form of literature, full of *faits divers*. It is interesting that Méténier makes such ingenious use of this form. This news genre exploited the readership's lurid appetite for taboo and sensation, which probably bordered on *Schadenfreude*. The fact that Violette and Madame Briquet dwell on the horrific demise of Madame Dubois is Méténier's ploy in setting them up as targets of the killer. This, in turn, manipulates the audience into feeling simultaneously titillated and at risk themselves. The 'real', or at least 'possible', horrors of the Grand-Guignol consistently manipulate the audience's anxiety about their own vulnerability. The cathartic experience of watching something terrible happen to someone else is always tempered by the fact that 'next time it could happen to *you*'.

The build-up of the play is such that, in the Grand-Guignol Laboratory, some participants expressed disappointment that Violette escapes the clutches of Luc ('Jack') Martinet! It may have seemed inevitable that Violette would meet her demise at the hands at the killer, and that is precisely what one would expect in the 'Theatre of Horror'. We should remember, of course, that Méténier's play is an early work before the Grand-Guignol established its winning formula and sensational identity. Nevertheless, the fact that the killer is apprehended may prove a surprise, and in that way it still makes a significant contribution to the repertoire: the question of predictability is an interesting one in Grand-Guignol drama. Sometimes the audience can anticipate what will happen in a play, so that the pertinent issue is not so much *what will happen* as *when it will happen*. In other instances, the surprise or shock moment is all-significant. The last minute rescue of Violette is a case in point.

It is clear that Jack is the killer; he matches the description in all respects and the booty he produces seems to be that of the murdered woman in the village. Nevertheless, the end of the play is interesting: the playwright does not give us a typical melodramatic ending where the villain of the piece acknowledges that it has been a 'fair cop'. Méténier's preference is to leave the play open-ended, and we are left to speculate whether Jack will ever confess to the crime. Moreover, this finale does also allow the possibility that, by some grotesque chance, Jack is innocent and the real killer is still on the loose.

In the original French play, the killer on the loose is actually called Luc. We have decided to call him Jack rather than Luc in an allusion to the 1880s Whitechapel murderer, Jack the Ripper. This play may be set in Paris, but is located in roughly the same temporal context as the notorious serial killer of London, and clearly exploits the same situation and the same fears inherent in the audience. The Parisian setting of the play evidently feeds off the metrophobia of the audience: the killer has left the village to lose himself in the anonymity of the crowd and the brutality of the metropolis.

Around the time Méténier's play was produced, Frank Wedekind (1864–1918) was writing the second of his Lulu plays, *Pandora's Box*. Wedekind wrote the play over a period of nine years (1892—1901) and it was not performed for many years because of the controversial nature of the piece. Wedekind, as ever, was uncompromising in his assault on bourgeois hypocrisy, and in his forthright depiction of sexuality and violence. In the Stephen Spender translation of the Lulu plays (1972), Wedekind's achievement is described as 'a fascinating mixture of Morality Plays and Grand Guignol' (back-cover summary). The scandalous Lulu, Wedekind's complex *femme fatale*, ends up as a prostitute in a London attic, not dissimilar to Violette's Parisian bedroom. Unlike Violette, however, Lulu is not rescued by the police in the nick of time, but dies at the hands of Jack the Ripper.

*Jack* is an interesting example of naturalist drama developed before the Grand-Guignol genre had come into being. However, with its milieu, theme and extraordinarily effective pace and suspense it is easy to see how influential the play would be on what would become the Grand-Guignol genre.

# JACK

*(Lui! 1897)*

*by*

OSCAR MÉTÉNIER

---

Madame Briquet
Violette
Voice of newspaper seller on the street
Jack
Police Inspector
Three police officers

---

*(A room in a brothel. Stage right, a bed and the door to the bathroom. Stage left, a door and a window overlooking the street. The window is open, but the blind is partly drawn, so that although it is daytime the room is lamp-lit. Violette sits knitting on the windowsill. There is a knock at the door and Madame Briquet sticks her head in.)*

| | |
|---|---|
| MME BRIQUET | *(cautious)*: Can I come in . . .? You're not with anyone . . .? |
| VIOLETTE: | Nah—no one at all. Not even a cat! It's so quiet today—even the street's deserted. |
| MME BRIQUET: | Violette . . . have you seen the picture of Madame Dubois in the *Petit Parisien*? |
| VIOLETTE: | Madame Dubois? Who's she when she's at home? |
| MME BRIQUET: | That poor old dear in Vincennes—they found her murdered . . . in her own home. Have a look at the picture. |
| VIOLETTE: | Oh God! Her head's nearly off her body—some bastard did a good job on her. |
| MME BRIQUET | *(sitting)*: Things like that really get to me . . . I haven't been able to eat a thing all day after seeing *that*. |
| VIOLETTE: | Oh don't worry . . . I mean we wouldn't get anyone here who'd do something like that . . . would we? |
| MME BRIQUET: | I spoke to Inspector Nez-Cassé this morning. You see, I run a decent house here and the police say we're safe because we have a visitors book and everyone has to register . . . |
| VIOLETTE: | But . . .? |
| MME BRIQUET: | Don't worry, love. |

VIOLETTE:     Imagine being in a room with a killer like that . . . I'd die of fear, I know I would.

MME BRIQUET:  Oh Violette, *don't worry*—he wouldn't be after someone like you—or me—we haven't got a penny, and it's the money he's after. Now that Mme Dubois was pretty well off.

VIOLETTE:     I just hope they get him—put him away.

MME BRIQUET:  It's just a matter of time, thank God . . . Inspector Nez-Cassé said so this morning . . . They know who the killer is, and they're pretty much hot on his heels.

VIOLETTE:     They know who he is?

MME BRIQUET:  Yes—he's a butcher.

VIOLETTE      (*looks at the paper again*): I suppose it could only be a butcher to do something like that to a woman.

MME BRIQUET:  They've got his name in the paper. (*Takes it and struggles to read through her glasses*) 'The . . . police . . . would like to . . . question . . . a man . . .'

VIOLETTE      (*grabbing paper back*): Give it here—I can read better than you. 'The police would like to question a man called Jack Martinet, butcher's assistant in the town of Vincennes, in connection with the ghastly murder of Mme Dubois. Martinet has not been seen since the day of the murder, but the police are confident that they will apprehend Martinet within a "matter of hours".'

MME BRIQUET:  Thank heavens! But it's a race against the clock . . . A man like that, he could chop someone up into tiny pieces . . . There's some poor old lady scraping together her savings and suddenly—(*gestures slice of the throat*) you're gutted like an animal! To do that, you'd have to be the *devil*!

VIOLETTE:     I know—and hanging's too good for someone like that. They're not human—they're savage animals! (*Looks at paper*) There's a description of him. He's got long red hair and a moustache . . . Ah, he's got a scar on his left arm . . . That's all it says! (*Throws paper away*) I'm going to have nightmares about this—and I'm going to see him everywhere . . .

MME BRIQUET:  You don't think he'd come here do you—to the middle of Paris . . . two steps from the police station . . . and to a street that the coppers watch as carefully as this one!?

VIOLETTE:     It's horrid being watched by the coppers all the time . . . but sometimes you can't help feeling grateful . . .

VOICE ON THE
STREET:       Extra! Extra! *Evening News!*

MME BRIQUET:  Quick—get a paper, maybe they've caught him!

VIOLETTE:     I don't think I've got any cash—have you?

MME BRIQUET:  No . . .

VIOLETTE:     Hold on—I've got some. Hey! Paper over here please! (*She reaches out of the window and takes a paper. Reads quickly.*) I can't see anything—they obviously haven't caught him yet . . .

|  | Hold on, here's something . . . 'The Vincennes Murder' . . . Let's see . . . 'Mme Dubois had a cash box with, it is reckoned, about twenty francs in it. She was not known to part with her money easily but she loved jewellery . . . She always carried jewel-encrusted rings with her . . . and very expensive earrings . . . All these objects are missing . . .' |
|---|---|
| MME BRIQUET: | Shh—someone's coming! |
| VIOLETTE: | Yes? At last—some business! |
| MME BRIQUET: | I'll leave you to it! (*Exits hurriedly. Violette glances in the mirror, tidies herself and then opens the door.*) |
| VIOLETTE: | Do come in, sir. (*Jack Martinet enters. He is clean-shaven and his hair is cropped. He looks around then sits down heavily. Violette closes the window.*) |
| JACK: | Close the door! |
| VIOLETTE | (*aside*): Another drunkard. |
| JACK: | Is this your room? |
| VIOLETTE: | Yes, my bedroom . . . Let me take your hat. (*She does so. Jack points at the bathroom.*) |
| JACK: | What's in there? |
| VIOLETTE: | That's the bathroom . . . |
| JACK: | And what's through there? |
| VIOLETTE: | That's where you came in . . . Look, love, just calm down. No one can hear a thing next door if that's what you're worried about. |
| JACK: | Yes, it's nice here. |
| VIOLETTE: | Well it's definitely better in here than out there. It's so hot today . . . So, love, are you going to give me something? |
| JACK | (*distant*): What? |
| VIOLETTE: | Something . . . to drink? |
| JACK: | Yes, yes—a drink! |
| VIOLETTE: | How about some champagne . . . that'd be nice . . . and not at all expensive really when you think about it . . . |
| JACK: | Yes—champagne. |
| VIOLETTE: | So are you going to give me some? |
| JACK: | What? |
| VIOLETTE: | Champagne. It's worth paying the Madame for a good one . . . Mmm . . . A nice drop of champagne . . . We can get a bit tipsy together—how about that? |
| JACK: | (*hands some money over*): Here. |
| VIOLETTE | (*aside as she goes to the door*): He doesn't look like a rich man but he's certainly loaded! (*At the door*) Mme Briquet! A bottle of champagne and three glasses please! |
| JACK | (*serious*): Who's Mme Briquet!? |
| VIOLETTE: | She's the Madame . . . Seeing that you're such a nice guy, you're going to have a really good time . . . (*She exits and returns with a bottle and three glasses. She struggles with the bottle.*) |
| JACK: | Give me that . . . you're making me feel nervous . . . (*He takes the bottle and pops the cork effortlessly.*) |

VIOLETTE:    You're strong.

JACK:    Why three glasses?

VIOLETTE:    I meant to tell you. Mme Briquet likes a glass or two, and she's nice to me so . . . Do you want to see her?

JACK:    No—I want to be alone with you. I don't want anybody else around.

VIOLETTE:    Fine, fine—don't worry . . . I'll just take her a glass, okay?

JACK:    Get on with it.

VIOLETTE    (*aside as she exits*): Impatient sod. (*Offstage*) Here you are, Madame. Lovely, eh? (*Violette re-enters.*)

JACK:    What did you say?

VIOLETTE:    Nothing—Mme Briquet sends her thanks . . .

JACK:    Now lock the door.

VIOLETTE:    But we don't normally do that, sweetheart.

JACK:    *Lock it.* Now that I've paid, I don't want to be disturbed.

VIOLETTE:    No one will disturb us!

JACK:    God Almighty! Will you do what I tell you!

VIOLETTE    (*aside as she goes to the door*): What's his problem? (*She locks the door and puts the key on the mantelpiece.*) There. You can calm down now.

JACK:    Me? I'm always calm.

VIOLETTE:    You're a bit on edge.

JACK:    I'm not on edge—I'm just thirsty. (*Drains his glass dry*) Fill it up.

VIOLETTE    (*aside*): A pisshead. I thought so.

JACK:    Great isn't it—the more I drink, the more thirsty I get! (*Roars with laughter.*)

VIOLETTE    (*sits on his knees*): Look, sweetheart, I'm going to give you a really good time . . . but the only thing is . . . you know . . .

JACK:    Don't worry—I won't be ungrateful . . .

VIOLETTE:    You *know* you're going to have a good time . . .

JACK:    I don't doubt it. And I'm going to give you a little something, something really special . . .

VIOLETTE:    Give it to me now.

JACK:    But, I'm not going.

VIOLETTE:    Give it to me now, darling. It's better that way, then we needn't give it any more thought . . . (*Aside*) Always get the money up front.

JACK:    You don't seem to trust me. (*Stands up*) Have some dosh then. (*He pulls out some gold coins from his pocket and shakes them in his hands.*)

VIOLETTE:    Blimey! They look like gold sovereigns!

JACK:    Yeah—'blimey'—they are! (*Sits*) They're all mine, all this money . . . I earned it you see, yes, I earned this lot.

VIOLETTE:    And if you're generous to a little woman like me, fortune will really smile on . . .

JACK:    Fortune will smile on me, will it? Here you are then—have a sovereign. (*She takes one and then goes over to the bed and pulls the covers open, while Jack continues to count his money.*) Yes, I earned this lot . . . I earned this lot alright . . . (*Laughs loudly.*)

VIOLETTE: What is it?

JACK: Nothing—I just thought of something and it made me laugh . . .

VIOLETTE: What? Go on—I like a laugh!

JACK: Nothing to do with you—God, I'm thirsty. Aren't you?

VIOLETTE: I'm always thirsty.

JACK: Come on then—drink up! (*He fills up the glasses.*) You're a bit of alright, aren't you?

VIOLETTE: You've noticed have you? (*He puts his hands around her hips.*) You know, you look so worn out.

JACK: Worn out? Me?

VIOLETTE: Yeah, you live life at breakneck speed, don't you . . . I bet you haven't had a good night's sleep for days . . . (*She takes the glass from his hands just before he drops it.*)

JACK: Yeah, you're right. I haven't slept for a week.

VIOLETTE: And you thought I couldn't tell? You know what you're going to do? You're going to lie down and have a kip. A good long sleep. Then, tomorrow morning when you're refreshed we're going to . . .

JACK: Yeah, a sleep . . . a good kip . . .

VIOLETTE: But not on the chair—come on, get into bed, wake up . . .

JACK: I am awake . . .

VIOLETTE: You're dozing off. Come on, get undressed. I'll help you. (*She helps him to his feet and starts to undress him while he rubs his eyes.*)

JACK: Wait a minute . . .

VIOLETTE: Come on, you're so tired . . .

JACK: Let me empty my pockets first . . . (*Violette shrugs rather dejectedly and sits at the foot of the bed. She watches Jack empty his pockets.*) Here's some bank notes . . . and here's some pearls . . . and, look at this, look at my diamond ring . . . (*Holds the diamond up to the light*) Look at it gleaming . . . it's beautiful, isn't it . . . you'd look like a princess if you put that on your finger . . .

VIOLETTE: That's a woman's ring.

JACK: Listen—it's *mine*. You've never seen anything quite so beautiful have you . . . (*Pulls out some earrings*) And look at these . . . wouldn't you love a pair of these? These aren't paste you know, these are the real thing . . .

VIOLETTE: They certainly are beautiful.

JACK: Haha . . . you'd like some too wouldn't you . . . You'd settle for a pair of these! Tell you what . . . if I ever get another pair like it you can have them . . . but until then these are *mine*.

VIOLETTE (*subtly concerned*): Where did you get all these?

JACK:   I bought them . . . probably. (*He puts the earrings down and pulls out a revolver which he handles nonchalantly.*) Not a bad little shooter this. But it's not what I'm after—*this* is what I'm after . . . (*He pulls out a huge butcher's knife. He touches the tip of the blade and then runs his finger along the back of the knife. He studies it for a while, smiling.*) This is my best friend . . . never lets me down . . . (*Violette looks terrified so Jack tosses it onto the table with ironic casualness.*) You see how much I trust you? I'm leaving all my stuff on the table here and I know that you won't try to nick it.

VIOLETTE:   If you are . . . worried . . . why don't you . . . lock it in the desk drawer . . .

JACK   (*takes the knife and stabs it into the table*): No . . . no . . . *as I said*, I don't think you'll try and nick anything from *me*.

VIOLETTE:   Honestly, it'd be better to lock it all up . . . in the desk . . . That's what we'd normally do . . .

JACK:   How many times . . . No! (*Takes the knife again*) The first person who touches anything . . . anything of mine . . . I will slit his gizzard . . . *Like that!* (*Violette jolts back in terror and Jack laughs and licks his lips in delight.*) Slitting a throat . . . it's like peaches and cream!

VIOLETTE:   Please put the knife down . . . you're scaring me . . . (*Jack stops laughing in a flash.*)

JACK:   You're so annoying . . . you're no fun at all . . . (*Stabs the knife into the table again*) I'm only having a bit of a laugh . . . (*Gathering all his things on the table.*)

VIOLETTE   (*aside*): He needs to sleep it off!

JACK:   You're no fun at all . . . I wouldn't hurt you, you silly tart . . . I wasn't going to cut you up . . . (*He goes over to the bed, dragging Violette with him and forces her to sit down next to him.*) I cut the throats of lambs . . . of lambs, you silly woman! I'm a *butcher* . . . (*At this word Violette stiffens in terror and then extricates herself from Jack who gradually topples over onto the bed murmuring to himself.*) Lambs . . . lambs' throats . . . not your throat . . .

VIOLETTE   (*stands frozen, staring at Jack and the knife, her voice very deep*): My God! The butcher . . . It's him!
(*A long silence. Suddenly inarticulate voices are heard in the street and then certain phrases are clear: 'Open the door! Let me in! Let me in or I'll smack you in the face!' Jack wakes up and grabs his knife and stares at the door while Violette moves in terror to the far corner.*)

JACK:   What's going on? I'll slice up anyone who comes near me! For Christ's sake!

VOICE OFFSTAGE:   Leave him alone—he's just had a bit too much to drink that's all! He's *drunk*!

JACK:        It was just some pisshead . . . Blimey—frightened the life out of
             me . . . Just a pisshead, that's all . . . (*Looks around*) Hey, where
             are you? Oh, you're there—what are you doing in the corner?
             Are you scared? Don't worry it was just some pisshead . . . a
             pisshead, that's all . . . Come on—come over here . . . (*Violette
             approaches slowly.*) You still scared? Is it because I was
             shouting? I was just dozing off and I heard all that noise! I hate
             sudden noise . . .! I'm quite sensitive . . . and it was just some
             old wino out in the street . . . Come over here . . . He gave me a
             headache—silly old bastard . . .! I should cut his throat for him
             . . . that'd sort him out . . . old git . . . (*Dozing off*) Slice . . . slice
             . . . his throat . . . like . . . peaches and cream . . . (*Asleep*)

VIOLETTE     (*walks over to the bed and looks at Jack, her eyes wide*): He's
             asleep . . . (*looks at the knife*) I'm so scared . . . I think he must
             be . . . Slicing throats . . . a butcher . . . the paper said he was a
             butcher . . . the diamond ring . . . the earrings . . . and red hair
             . . . he's got red hair! (*Silence. She tries to examine his arm
             without waking him.*) A scar . . . he's got a scar . . . on his left
             arm . . . It's him! He's the killer! (*She staggers back and
             screams, Jack rouses.*) Oh God—he's waking up . . . I'm so
             scared—so scared! (*She staggers across the room, tripping over
             the furniture while Jack continues to slowly wake up. She gets
             to the door but it is locked and looks around for the key in
             panic. She finally locates it and unlocks the door and slips out.*)

JACK:        Peaches and cream—slicing throats . . . (*The door opens and
             Mme Briquet comes in.*)

MME BRIQUET: Come in—you must come back in . . .

VIOLETTE:    I can't! I can't!

MME BRIQUET: He's asleep . . . there's nothing to fear . . . he's asleep . . . We
             must get the police . . . we'll send Addy . . . but come back in
             . . . it'll only be five minutes . . . but you must stay here until
             then . . . (*Mme Briquet exits and Jack wakes up when she
             closes the door.*)

VIOLETTE     (*aside*): He's waking up! Oh God!

JACK:        What? What's up? What you doing by the door?

VIOLETTE     (*aside*): I want to go!

JACK:        Is someone outside the door . . .

VIOLETTE     (*aside*): Oh God, he'll hear them!

JACK:        Is someone there?

VIOLETTE     (*aside*): I'm done for now! (*to Jack*) No . . . Mme Briquet
             wondered if I wanted a bit of supper, but I'm not hungry . . .
             I'll stay here with you . . . I'll stay here . . .

JACK:        Come here—come and lie down with me . . . Have I got to
             come and get you? Come and lie down . . .

VIOLETTE     (*approaching the bed*): Yes, yes, I will . . . go back to sleep . . .
             go on . . .

JACK         (*dozing off*): Come and lie down . . .

VIOLETTE: (*sitting on the bed*): Yes . . . sleep . . . I'll lie down in a moment . . . go to sleep . . . (*she holds him*) Go to sleep, darling, go to sleep . . .
JACK: (*growing weaker*): I'm knackered . . . so knackered . . .
VIOLETTE: I know you are . . . so sleep, sleep . . .
JACK: You're . . . so . . . beautiful . . .
VIOLETTE: Yes . . . And I love you . . . love you . . . Sleep, darling, sleep . . .
JACK: Slitting throats . . .
VIOLETTE: Sleep . . .
JACK: Peaches and cream . . .
VIOLETTE: Sleep, sleep . . . (*Jack is asleep. Violette extricates herself very slowly. She hears a noise outside.*) Here they are!
(*The door opens without a sound and Violette hides behind a chair. A police inspector enters followed by three officers. They carry truncheons. They approach the bed silently.*)
INSPECTOR: It's him alright . . . Take that gun and the knife . . . (*An officer does so while another gets ready to grab Jack.*) Wait a moment! (*He taps Jack on the leg.*) Jack! Hey, Jack!
JACK (*leaps up and reaches for his loot*): Hey! Get off! *I'll kill you!* (*The officers grab him and pin him down on the bed.*)
INSPECTOR: Kill us, eh? Handcuff him. (*The officers do so while Jack struggles.*)
JACK: I'll kill you—I'll slit your throat! You'll see! I'll get you!
INSPECTOR: Let's see . . . diamond ring . . . earrings . . . it's him . . . we've got our man. Take him away . . .
JACK: Bastards! Bastards!
INSPECTOR: Where's the lady who . . .
MME BRIQUET: Violette, sir . . .
INSPECTOR: I want to thank you, my dear . . . you have done a great service to society . . .
VIOLETTE (*anxious*): Here's the money he gave me . . .
INSPECTOR: I must take it, but I promise you, you will be rewarded. (*Exits.*)
MME BRIQUET: Just think—we caught the killer! We caught the killer in our own house!
VIOLETTE (*hysterical*): I'm scared—so scared!

THE END

# The Ultimate Torture

## (La Dernière Torture, 1904)

*by*

### André de Lorde and Eugène Morel

## Preface

André de Lorde and Eugène Morel's one-act play *La Dernière Torture* premiered at the Grand-Guignol on 2 December 1904. The production enjoyed a controversial, but highly successful, run and was revived for the August 1920 season. Pierron informs us that, in the latter production, the celebrated designer Ménessier created an impressive and elaborate set that came as a shock to a Grand-Guignol audience used to 'modestes intérieurs' (Pierron 1995, 102).

The play is set during the closing days of the Boxer Rebellion of 1900 in the French consulate in Beijing. The fact that the play ostensibly recreates true—and recent—events makes it an instance of documentary drama. The play can be seen as providing a fascinating insight into the propaganda and anxieties of *belle époque* France in its international context.

In global terms, the international politics of the opening years of the twentieth century are characterized by the arms race and the tensions within Europe which would ultimately lead to the Great War of 1914–18. However, the context for this lies in the scramble for Africa and the rise of the colonial powers in the final decades of the nineteenth century, which held particular importance for France.

Mayeur and Rebérioux (1987, 99–100) maintain that French colonial policy was based upon three justifications. The first was that a colonial empire was a necessary development for a post-industrial nation, providing new opportunities for the export trade in manufactured goods. Second, there was the belief that modern European nations had a moral duty to civilize and educate the heathen native populations in the colonies. It was these racist assumptions that led to the large amounts of missionary work undertaken in the colonies during the nineteenth century. On these two accounts France did not differ greatly from her European neighbours.

However, whereas Great Britain used her Empire to reassert her position as a Great Power, and Germany used hers to claim her right on that same stage in spite of being a fledgling unified state, France also sought, through colonial expansion, to re-establish her status on the international stage following the humiliation and defeat at the hands of Bismarck in the Franco-Prussian War. As Mayeur and Rebérioux say, there was a 'haunting worry about national decline ( . . .) the obsession with "status" which was at the heart of French nationalism of both the left and the right after the defeat of 1871' and that colonialism 'was of a piece with patriotism and the wish to regenerate France' (Mayeur and Rebérioux 1987, 100).

Nevertheless, the colonial road often provided a rough ride for France, perhaps best exemplified by the Fashoda Incident of 1898, whereby a stand-off with Great Britain over territorial claims in Eastern Africa led to a humiliating French climb-down. Although France was later compensated with territory in the Sahara, it was an event that further fuelled French uncertainty about its international stature. At the same time Germany had become allied with Austria-Hungary in the Dual Alliance of 1879, which was joined by Italy in 1882 in the Triple Alliance (Hayes 1992, 108), so forming a potentially anti-French power block along its eastern frontier stretching from the Baltic to the southern Mediterranean.

French ambivalence towards the benefits or otherwise of the repositioning of the European powers in the age of colonialism is at the heart of *The Ultimate Torture* and its reconstruction of the Boxer Rebellion. The Rebellion itself came about as a direct result of a western colonial policy that displayed an arrogant superiority over non-European culture. The Great Powers had long coveted the economic resources of China and had carved it up into areas where individually they enjoyed exclusive trading rights. France too had interests in the region and had been involved in a war with China over Tonkin in the 1880s, the aftershocks of which continued until the end of the century (Mayeur and Rebérioux 1987, 96–97).

In 1900 the Fists of Righteous Harmony, a secret society which practised martial arts (hence the nickname 'Boxers'), encouraged by the Empress-Dowager Tsu Hsi, went on the rampage throughout the country, attacking missionary outposts and slaughtering foreigners. By the summer the Boxers had entered Beijing and laid siege to the compound in which the foreign diplomats and their families had taken refuge. The siege continued for two months until, just as the compound was about to fall to the Boxers, the International Relief Force arrived to relieve the city. The events of the Boxer Rebellion struck at the very heart of European assumptions about racial superiority and represented the greatest fears of the European colonizers. The barbarity with which the Boxers dispatched the Western Christians fuelled European xenophobia and the eleventh hour dramatic lifting of the siege was the stuff of heroic legends.

De Lorde and Morel were writing a drama about events still fresh in the minds of the Parisian audience, representing perhaps the worst imaginable fate of any individual in colonial France of the time. It is a piece which reflects the ambiguities of France during *la belle époque*—a country which on the one hand enjoyed the confidence that came with a sizeable colonial empire, whilst on the other hand harbouring a paranoia about losing that very status.

Although ostensibly being an example of documentary drama, the play is very much of its time in asserting the hegemony of Western Imperial values: it fulfils the stereotypical scenario of European masters holding out against the 'restless natives'. The 'savages' are never *seen* but are *heard* (albeit with Chinese gongs replacing the rhythmic jungle drums of a more familiar African cliché). The play functions on a structure of binary oppositions, most centrally identifiable as a dialectic between the individual characters of the besieged French and the anonymous, seemingly invisible 'dirty yellow faces' of the Boxers. Much of the narrative thrust relies on the savagery of the 'uncivilized' Boxers and anticipation of what might happen to the 'civilized' Europeans inside the consulate once they are finally overrun. The siege is ghastly enough as it is driving everyone insane and has directly caused the death of a baby: but the Boxers' invasion will be a fate worse than death. This overt racism runs throughout the action. The pivotal moment occurs when the marine Bornin returns from outside the consulate to reveal the bloody stumps where his hands have been severed, an act that blatantly illustrates the Boxers' brutality. Furthermore, if the death of a baby was not crime enough, the mutilated marine—drifting in and out of consciousness—relates the calculated and sadistic horrors that the Boxers exacted on that ultimate signifier of Christian virtue and innocence: a nun.

The horror structure of the play exploits violent action. We have *descriptions of violence* (most importantly, Bornin's account of the nun's death); graphic images of the *result of violence* (Bornin himself); and *onstage violent action* (Kerdrec's grotesquely ironic attack on Clément and, above all, the murder of Denise). However, it is not de Lorde and Morel's exploitation of violence that is the ultimate torture of the title. The structural climax to this particular Grand-Guignol play is D'Hémelin's shooting of his daughter. This may seem to be the ultimate, tortuous horror. It is an act nevertheless rendered necessary by the situation and, moreover, in the circumstances, the justifiable action of a loving father and civilized Frenchman: it is an act of *honour* not *horror*. This onstage murder is a moment for pity for both D'Hémelin *and* his daughter. The horror is reserved for the bitter irony of the moment that D'Hémelin realizes that the cacophony everyone has taken to be that of the Boxers' final onslaught is in fact that of the international force relieving the consulate. The penultimate torture is the terrible realization that he has murdered his daughter needlessly. This action took place at the moment D'Hémelin believed was the annihilation of civilization but was, in fact, the reassertion of European supremacy. This realization drives D'Hémelin insane and it is insanity rather than violence *per se* that is the ultimate torture and the enduring horror. As in many classics of Grand-Guignol the play concludes with onstage insanity. Homrighous argues that the play is an example of the 'negative or reversed application of the Scribean technique' (1963, 50) because the final irony of the play suggests that the ending is not a logical conclusion of the events, but is based on misunderstanding: if the play had followed the Eugène Scribe model it would have ended with the arrival of the Boxers, not the Allies.

Although the Eurocentrism and racism of the play are predominant, there is an argument in seeing its irony as subversive. A contemporaneous work of fiction such as Joseph Conrad's *Heart of Darkness* (1900) could be seen as a more sustained critique of European Imperialism: set in the Belgian Congo, the novel is arguably a devastating exposé of the unacceptable face of colonial expansion. The climax of the novel is the lunatic Kurtz's apocalyptic realization of 'The horror! The horror!' This is more than an expression of the guilty white man's burden, it is a moment of nihilism revealing the irredeemably 'dark heart' of European oppression. *The Ultimate Torture* in its way is similarly ironic as it also presents the disintegration of a stalwart 'hero of the Empire'. The meaning and impact of both works hinges on the insanity and horror of Kurtz and D'Hémelin. Moreover, both works reflect the *Zeitgeist* of their context: early modernism where nineteenth-century certainties are replaced by a profoundly twentieth-century doubt.

Leaving aside the politics of the play and its significance as a complex work of imperialistic propaganda, the modern dimension of the play is inherent in its establishment of the siege metaphor. This has, of course, been a staple situation in the war genre since Homer. The psychological breaking point caused by the war situation is a recurrent theme in cinema: it is memorably explored in Robert Aldrich's *Attack!* (1956) and is a key motif in the Vietnam War genre of American film. Aside from the war genre, de Lorde and Morel's situation has become a paradigm in the modern thriller and horror genres. We need only think of the claustrophobic siege in a horror novel like Richard Matheson's *I Am Legend* (1954). Several 'suspense' film-makers have exploited a situation parallel to *The Ultimate Torture* in films like Alfred Hitchcock's *The Birds* (1963), George A. Romero's *Night of the Living Dead* (1968), Sam Peckinpah's *Straw Dogs* (1971), Saul Bass's *Phase IV* (1973) and John

Carpenter's *Assault on Precinct 13* (1976). Romero's masterpiece is a particularly apt comparison as, unlike the others, it concludes with an ironic ending that is as shocking and as audacious as the finale of the 1904 play. Romero's choice of an 'unhappy ending' has been traditionally perceived as a revolutionary moment in contemporary horror. De Lorde and Morel's decision to single out the bourgeois figure of D'Hémelin for onstage deterioration into insanity makes for a tempting comparison with Luis Buñuel's surrealistic *El Angel Exterminador* (Mexico, 1962). In this ruthless satire we watch the demise of 'civilized' values as the dignified bourgeois dinner guests drive themselves insane when they turn their meal into an absurd and pointless self-imposed siege. Buñuel's film is a masterpiece of comedy and, appropriately enough, Serge Douay highlights *The Ultimate Torture* as a key play of the repertoire as it was, as he saw it, the first—and influential—example in the repertoire where 'comedy mixes with horror' ('Le Grand Guignol a Cinquante Ans' in *Javroche,* 10 October 1945).

In 1948, the journal *Bataille* asked 'Will Jean-Paul Sartre replace André de Lorde?' (10 November 1948), perceiving a 'Theatre of Horror' in Sartre's drama, albeit less explicitly gruesome. Certainly a work like *Huis Clos* (1944), with its dramatic investigation of aspects of existentialism, is a play set in a grand-guignolesque realm of godlessness and claustrophobic terror not far from *The Ultimate Torture*. When Estelle attempts to stab Inez and fails (because she is already dead) Sartre uses absurdity to defuse a scene of bloody stage violence that the Grand-Guignol would have adored. Nevertheless, the 'moral' of the play, 'Hell . . . is other people', was something that not only had been demonstrated nightly for decades at the Grand-Guignol, but was at the heart of the genre's meaning.

# THE ULTIMATE TORTURE

*(La Dernière Torture, 1904)*

*by*

ANDRÉ DE LORDE AND EUGÈNE MOREL

---

D'Hémelin, a consul
Gravier, a treasurer
Bernard, an interpreter
Morin, a corporal in the marines
Loreau, a marine
Kerdrec, a marine
Bornin, a marine
Clément, a volunteer soldier
Denise, the daughter of D'Hémelin
Woman

---

*(The fortifications of the French Consulate, China, July 1900, during the Boxer Rebellion.)*

| | |
|---|---|
| GRAVIER: | Look at the flames! |
| BERNARD: | The whole city's on fire. |
| GRAVIER: | The cannons . . . like last night! |
| BERNARD: | They're pounding away over there . . . |
| GRAVIER: | By the pagodas. |
| | *(Silence. Suddenly Bernard points at the horizon where jets of flames can be seen.)* |
| BERNARD: | God almighty! |
| GRAVIER: | What is it!? |
| BERNARD: | They've set the customs house on fire! |
| GRAVIER: | Yes . . . they're advancing nearer and nearer . . . |
| | *(Silence)* |
| BERNARD: | We're done for. |
| GRAVIER: | Don't say that! If the soldiers can push the Boxers back we might still have a chance. We'll gain some time and the Allies will be able to disembark. |
| BERNARD: | We've been waiting thirty-two days! |
| GRAVIER: | Perhaps they're here already! Perhaps it's them doing the blasting, right now! We've got no idea what's happening! |

THE ULTIMATE TORTURE 99

BERNARD: We're going to die.

GRAVIER: But if the soldiers . . .

BERNARD: What soldiers!?

GRAVIER: The Imperial Chinese Army! The Boxers are *rebels*!

BERNARD: They're all fighting together—the Boxers *and* the 'Imperial Chinese Army'!

GRAVIER: We've . . . we've got to cling to something . . .

BERNARD: Cling to something! We should run away! Yes—*run*! Down to the canal, like the others. We shouldn't stay locked in here, 'under the protection of the French flag'. Yes, it protects us well, doesn't it! Perhaps there's still time to escape . . .

GRAVIER: Escape? Now! You honestly think we can get out of here?

BERNARD: Bornin managed to get away. So did Carel! And others!

GRAVIER: Where are they right at this moment?

BERNARD: Safe, perhaps . . . If they got to the river they could get to Tien-Tsin, and there they would find the French: lots of them! Alive! With weapons!

GRAVIER: They'd come back and rescue us.

BERNARD: Yes, perhaps they're coming. I'm counting on them. What I wouldn't give to hear the sound . . . the sound of French bugles! The sound of the army *advancing*! (*He sings an advance and pounds his rifle butt on the ground.*)

GRAVIER: Shut up! (*Points at the sleeping men*) Don't wake them. They deserve to sleep.
(*The consulate door opens and we catch a glimpse of a room. D'Hémelin appears on the step with a lantern. He closes the door, descends the steps slowly, and steps over the sleeping men.*)

D'HÉMELIN: Guard?

GRAVIER: Present.

D'HÉMELIN: Oh, it's you, George. Any news?

GRAVIER: Nothing. (*Points at the city*) They're blasting over there.

D'HÉMELIN: Yes, I know . . . Who's there? Is that you, Bernard?

BERNARD (*comes closer*): Yes, sir.

D'HÉMELIN: No news?

BERNARD: At about midnight I thought I heard something down there, in the undergrowth . . . I went near it to check . . .

D'HÉMELIN: Well?

BERNARD: I saw nothing . . . The grass was so high . . . Maybe that's the point, someone could hide there, listening . . . waiting . . .

GRAVIER: We won't be attacked at night—the Boxers are frightened of evil spirits!

D'HÉMELIN: I know. All the same, the silence makes me anxious. What are they scheming?
(*Suddenly desperate cries of grief are heard from inside the consulate.*)

BERNARD: Oh my God, that noise . . . it's the women . . .

GRAVIER: All night you can hear them sobbing.

D'HÉMELIN:    They are going insane—and so are we! What are we going to do?

(*The cries grow much louder.*)

GRAVIER:    Shall I go in and see them?

D'HÉMELIN:    What good will that do? (*The cries stop. Silence.*) They're calm now . . . quiet.

(*Bernard moves away.*)

GRAVIER:    What about Mlle Denise?

D'HÉMELIN    (*with anguish*): My daughter, my daughter!

GRAVIER:    Is she any worse?

D'HÉMELIN:    I watched over her all night. She had a fever and was delirious . . . She put her hands round my neck and said: 'They want to take me . . . save me . . . save me!' She's so tired and weak . . . I've never seen her so frail.

GRAVIER:    The deprivation . . . the hunger . . . She's starving!

D'HÉMELIN:    I wish we were back in France . . . I want to go home! You know I even asked to return . . . Since the death of my wife, my daughter's wasted away; I knew that if we didn't return at once, she'd be lost . . . this country'll take her like it took her mother. She actually seemed better when we made the decision to return to France. Back there in that climate, under that gentle sky I would've made my daughter healthy again— I would've cured her! But as things are . . . it's another . . . death . . .

GRAVIER:    Sir!

D'HÉMELIN:    It's true . . . I can't do anything . . . I'm in command . . . I *must take* command . . . if only I could give some hope to everyone . . . Oh, my friend . . .

GRAVIER:    Hope, sir, hope—it's your duty to . . .

D'HÉMELIN:    My duty? Yes. That's easy. But I have another duty as well.

GRAVIER:    What do you mean?

D'HÉMELIN:    Another . . . duty . . . a horrific duty . . . I'm scared to think of it . . . But when the time comes . . . The time when there's nothing else we can . . . George—if everything is absolutely hopeless . . .

GRAVIER:    Yes?

D'HÉMELIN:    Nothing . . . I'll tell you later . . .

BERNARD:    Sir! Sir!

D'HÉMELIN:    What is it?

BERNARD    (*pointing at the horizon which grows more and more red*): Look to the east! It's the Austrian Embassy . . . It's burning! An inferno!

D'HÉMELIN:    So that's what they've decided to do.

GRAVIER    (*desperate*): Burning down all the Embassies!

D'HÉMELIN:    It'll be our turn soon.

(*Silence. A cannon fires in the distance.*)

BERNARD    (*energetically*): So what are we waiting for, sir!? Let's at least try to escape!

D'HÉMELIN: Run away? If it was even possible, do you think I could do that . . . and what about my daughter? Anyway, we're encircled with fire now . . . Escape! The Boxers are everywhere. The whole country is behind them . . . Not a single village—not a single house—would see us as anything but enemies . . . (*In speaking he knocks into a sleeping man.*)

MORIN: Eh! What! What is it!?

D'HÉMELIN: Nothing, my friend. I'm sorry—it was me . . .

MORIN: Ah, sir . . . It's you . . . I was terrified . . . I thought it was . . .

D'HÉMELIN: It was nothing . . . Sleep! Go back to sleep.

MORIN: Yes, sleep . . . that'd be good . . . sleep . . . I was having a wonderful dream. What was it now? Oh yes—I dreamt I was back in the country and it was harvest time . . . Yes, harvest time! It was wonderful . . . (*He falls asleep.*)

BERNARD: Harvest time in the country. Will any of us ever see it again?

D'HÉMELIN: Let them hope so . . . Let them believe that they will go home until the very last moment . . .

(*The door opens and Denise comes down the steps.*)

DENISE: Father—come quickly.

D'HÉMELIN: What's happened? (*Cries of grief are heard.*)

DENISE: Quickly . . . it's horrible . . . the poor woman . . .

D'HÉMELIN: What is it?

DENISE: Oh, father . . . one of the women . . . her baby's just . . . died. She's gone insane. Listen to her . . . His body's already cold; and she's trying to breast-feed him . . . We've tried to get the body away from her . . . but we can't. (*The cries turn into nervous laughter, then singing.*) Listen, now she's singing . . . She's insane! (*A woman appears at the doorway.*)

WOMAN: Miss—we can't hold her! She trying to escape! (*Goes back inside.*)

D'HÉMELIN: Keep her there! Keep her there! (*To Denise*) Go back in with her, my darling.

DENISE: Yes, father. But . . . (*She sees the horizon.*) The sky's red . . . It's like fire!

D'HÉMELIN (*gently pushing her back inside*): No, my darling, it's nothing. Now go back inside.

DENISE: But what's burning?

D'HÉMELIN: It's just the sun coming up.

DENISE: The sun . . . No . . . look . . . over there!

GRAVIER (*coming over to her*): It's just the dawn . . . The dawn of our hope! The soldiers are coming—to rescue us!

DENISE: Really! Is it true! Father—is it true!?

D'HÉMELIN (*with difficulty*): Yes . . . yes . . . we're going to be saved. It's only a matter of hours now . . . Now go back inside and tell everyone to be brave . . . (*She exits.*) Bernard! You must get the baby's corpse and bury it . . . quickly . . . it doesn't matter where . . . in a ditch!

BERNARD: Is there some cloth I could use?

D'HÉMELIN: Any cloth we have is for the wounded, not for the dead; the child doesn't need a shroud!

BERNARD: What about the mother, sir. If I've got to take the body by force, I don't think she'll be . . .

D'HÉMELIN: Wait a moment—I'll come with you. Gravier, keep watch. (*D'Hémelin and Bernard go into the house. The cries get louder and then stop. Gravier listens to them and then surveys the horizon. Cannon fire in the distance. The dawn begins to come up. Loreau wakes up and presses his ear to the ground.*)

LOREAU: Someone's digging—I can hear them! Under the ground! I'm not dreaming—under the ground . . . It's like the sound of a mine—it's a tunnel . . . beneath us! They must be planting explosives! We're going to be blown up! Clément! Clément! Wake up!

CLÉMENT: Eh, what!? Is that you Loreau?

LOREAU: Wake up! *Listen!*

CLÉMENT: What is it?

LOREAU: I think I heard something . . . (*Sober*) But you didn't, did you?

CLÉMENT: Bah! You're just feverish.

LOREAU: No, listen, *listen.*

CLÉMENT: I can hear the cannons.

LOREAU: No, here, beneath the ground.

CLÉMENT: No!

LOREAU: Well, I heard it—I heard it! They're digging beneath us. We must give the alarm . . . (*Silence*) I don't hear them anymore . . . I'm going crazy—crazy . . . Why am I so scared? I wasn't when I fought them face to face . . . But at night, when we're alone . . . when it's so quiet . . .

CLÉMENT: You're just hungry, that's all.

LOREAU: Yeah, maybe . . . that would explain it. Hallucinations . . .

CLÉMENT: (*hands his bottle to Loreau*): Here—have a swig of this. That'll calm you down . . . let's finish it off.

LOREAU: Thanks. To your health—cheers!

CLÉMENT: (*finishes the bottle*): The last one! Another thing the Chinese won't get their hands on. They'll never get my bottle—or me! (*He throws the bottle far away and it shatters. Kerdrec wakes up in panic at the sound and picks up his bayonet.*)

KERDREC: To arms! (*He leaps to his feet and lunges at Clément, jabbing him on the shoulder. Gravier enters.*)

LOREAU: Oh my God!

MORIN: You're insane—what are you doing!?

GRAVIER: What the hell's happening!?

KERDREC: (*seeing Clément*): It's you . . . what have I done?

LOREAU: Are you hurt?

CLÉMENT: No. It's nothing. More scared than injured.

| | |
|---|---|
| D'HÉMELIN | (*entering*): What's happening? |
| KERDREC: | I don't know. I panicked . . . I thought it was them, all around me . . . I could hear them screaming . . . (*Tearfully*) You . . . it was you! I've hurt you . . . |
| CLÉMENT: | Oh, enough now—it's nothing. |
| D'HÉMELIN: | You're injured? |
| CLÉMENT: | Just a little cut, that's all. It's my own fault—I shouldn't have smashed that bottle. |
| KERDREC: | I could've killed you . . . I'm a swine—a complete swine! |
| GRAVIER: | Calm down. |
| LOREAU: | It's not your fault! |
| D'HÉMELIN: | It's cabin fever. We've been besieged for thirty-two days. Come on—chin up—it's nothing. Morin, go and look over there. (*Morin goes off right.*) |
| KERDREC: | Everywhere . . . all around me . . . their little yellow faces, grimacing . . . screaming! What a nightmare. |
| D'HÉMELIN: | I think we're all having those. |
| KERDREC: | Perhaps they're killing themselves off—fighting each other . . . |
| CLÉMENT: | And then what? Sooner or later, they're going to be here, you fool. And perhaps it'll be *me* who will have to kill *you*. Or would you prefer *them* to get hold of you alive? |
| KERDREC: | To be butchered? No thank you! |
| CLÉMENT: | Well, that's settled. Perhaps we will kill each other this evening—kill each other because it'll be the kindest thing to do! |
| D'HÉMELIN: | Will you two keep quiet—the women can hear you! |
| CLÉMENT: | Yes, the women. |
| LOREAU: | It's turned us all into cowards having *women* here. |
| KERDREC: | Yes—if they weren't we— |
| CLÉMENT: | If it'd just been men here we could've broken out . . . |
| KERDREC: | We could've got to Tien-Tsin. |
| LOREAU: | Like Bornin did—and Carel . . . |
| CLÉMENT: | Like Robert and the rest. |
| KERDREC: | They're saved—every one of them! |
| LOREAU | (*furious*): I've had enough! Thirty-two days stuck in here, starving away . . . When I hear their war cries . . . I just want to lay into them, kill them. |
| ALL | (*variously*): Me too—by God yes—to the end—kill 'em! |
| D'HÉMELIN: | We all feel the same way—every one of us. Me too—I'd love to get out there and fight them, man to man. I was at Gravelotte—a glorious battle. But for us today it's much, much harder. We need another kind of courage. It's not only a case of protecting the French flag like it is in every conflict. There are the weak and the frail, women and children to protect. It's our duty—it is a *sacred* duty . . . |
| CLÉMENT: | I've got a wife—and kids—it's *my* duty to care for *them*—and I want to see them again! |
| KERDREC: | Well come on—let's go! |

D'HÉMELIN:    Leave here? Don't be ridiculous! You'd be slaughtered after two steps. And even if you escaped the Boxers . . . The whole country's in ruins, everyone is hostile . . . An enemy at every turn . . . Food rotting away . . . the rivers choked with corpses. Where would you go? What would you eat? What would you drink?

KERDREC:    I don't know . . . I could at least try . . . But here I'm going—

CLÉMENT:    I'd get out there and *kill*!

KERDREC:    No one's coming to rescue us.

LOREAU:    None of us believe that any more.

CLÉMENT:    Not even you, sir.

D'HÉMELIN:    I believe . . . I believe that the seven of us have held this place for over a month . . . There are hundreds of them out there and they see this building—they think it's well defended, impregnable. All their fury is set against us—against seven men! But we're here—united, disciplined—and they've no idea how many we are. What power is greater than courage? If you leave here you become just men—seven men against thousands, against a raging horde!

CLÉMENT:    But what about Carel, Bornin . . .

D'HÉMELIN:    They tried to escape . . .

LOREAU:    They're miles away now . . .

CLÉMENT:    They're saved!

D'HÉMELIN:    They are dead. Yesterday, by the canal . . . didn't you see it? The Boxers paraded by with a basket. And inside it . . . was a severed head.
(*A horrified silence*)

CLÉMENT:    So, if we can't leave here, what should we do?

KERDREC:    If no one alive can help us, what's the best thing for us to do?

LOREAU:    When there's no ammunition left, no rice, no water . . . what will we do then? Tell us!

D'HÉMELIN:    We will fight . . . fight to the end! I promise you that I will *not* surrender.
(*Bernard enters.*)

BERNARD:    Sir, she's gone crazy—we've locked her up.

D'HÉMELIN:    And the body?

BERNARD:    It's done.

D'HÉMELIN:    You've done it?

BERNARD:    Yes.
(*Silence*)

KERDREC:    She had no milk left—the kid died of starvation.

LOREAU:    I've got a child that age.

CLÉMENT:    They'll pay for that!

KERDREC:    Yes! Before we die—let's kill them! Kill them! Now!

LOREAU:    They're still so far away—I would like to see their dirty yellow faces.
(*A muffled cry*)

| | |
|---|---|
| D'HÉMELIN: | Silence! Listen . . . |
| LOREAU: | Who is it? |
| GRAVIER: | Someone's wounded . . . Morin's on guard! |
| CLÉMENT: | He's been attacked! |
| D'HÉMELIN: | He's trying to give the alarm! |
| MORIN'S VOICE: | Help! |
| D'HÉMELIN | (*takes Bernard's rifle*): Go and see . . . (*Indicates Kerdrec.*) |
| MORIN'S VOICE: | Help! |
| GRAVIER: | Watch out—get down everyone. (*They grab their weapons and crouch down.*) |
| MORIN: | Don't shoot, don't shoot! |
| D'HÉMELIN: | What is it? |
| MORIN: | A man . . . crawling . . . in the grass . . . I saw him . . . |
| GRAVIER: | A Boxer . . . |
| D'HÉMELIN: | A spy? |
| BERNARD: | A sapper? |
| CLÉMENT: | Let's kill the— |
| MORIN: | No—a European . . . wounded, covered in blood! Crawling . . . It's . . . I think it's him . . . |
| D'HÉMELIN: | Who? |
| MORIN: | Bornin! I think it's him. |
| ALL | (*variously*): Him . . . Bornin . . . Impossible! |
| MORIN: | Crawling . . . so weak . . . like a ghost. |
| KERDREC: | Bornin? |
| CLÉMENT: | Listen . . . |
| D'HÉMELIN: | Get him to safety . . . (*Everyone moves.*) No, just you, Kerdrec. The rest of you, over there. |
| VOICE OF BORNIN: | Help, help . . . |
| | (*Kerdrec drags Bornin in and D'Hémelin rushes over to assist. Bornin falls heavily to the ground.*) |
| ALL | (*variously*): It is Bornin . . . Is it you . . .? Where have you been? (*Bornin moves and we see that his hands have been severed.*) |
| BORNIN: | Help . . . |
| ALL | (*variously*): Oh my God . . .! Jesus! (*Silence*) |
| CLÉMENT: | What about everyone else? |
| BORNIN: | Aagh . . . |
| CLÉMENT: | Robert? |
| BORNIN: | Dead . . . |
| KERDREC: | Carel? |
| BORNIN: | Dead . . . |
| LOREAU: | Jean-Louis? |
| BORNIN: | Dead—all dead . . . massacred . . . tortured . . . And me . . . I saw Carel die: they tore out his fingernails and ripped out his eyes . . . I heard his screams . . . Then it was my turn . . . they put me on the same floor, all covered with blood . . . and my hands—they cut them off . . . And then . . . I heard a noise—cannon fire—and I |

was alone . . . pools of blood . . . I called out for Carel, I looked for his body . . . there was nothing left . . . blown to pieces . . .

D'HÉMELIN:    Bornin, be brave.

MORIN:    You're safe now.

BORNIN:    Aagh . . .

D'HÉMELIN:    Be brave!

BORNIN:    My hands, my hands.

CLÉMENT:    We'll take care of you now.

BORNIN:    They took a nun, took her and tied her up, choked her . . . tore out her fingernails and toenails . . . and then . . . with red-hot tongs they ripped out her tongue, tore off her breasts . . . (*Passes out.*)

D'HÉMELIN:    Bornin!

BORNIN (*last effort*):    They are there . . .

D'HÉMELIN:    Where?

BORNIN:    Along the canal . . . thousands of them, thousands . . . hidden in the grass . . . everywhere . . . there's no hope . . . you can't escape . . . you're done for . . . So . . .

D'HÉMELIN:    Yes?

BORNIN:    Think of Carel . . . look at me . . . Don't let them get you alive . . . Don't let them get you alive . . . Don't let them get you alive . . . (*Collapses.*)

MORIN:    Oh my God!

D'HÉMELIN:    Bornin . . . Bornin . . .

CLÉMENT:    He's gone . . .

GRAVIER:    There's no pulse.

D'HÉMELIN:    Dead!

GRAVIER:    Dead.

D'HÉMELIN:    Those who believe in God, pray for his soul. (*Long silence in which only Kerdrec makes the sign of the cross.*) Clément, Kerdrec. (*They take up the body and carry it away.*)

GRAVIER:    It's the end.

D'HÉMELIN:    And now we know what's in store for us. Well, I have an order I must give you . . . horrific though it is.

GRAVIER:    Sir?

D'HÉMELIN:    Yes—for you, and you alone. I can't do it. My hands are shaking at the thought . . . It is so horrific . . . but I can't stand the thought of them taking her . . . So you . . .

GRAVIER (*stares over to the door where Denise is hiding*):    Me?

D'HÉMELIN:    You alone . . .

GRAVIER (*terrified*):    Not me—not me!

D'HÉMELIN:    You! I beg you, I beg you . . .

GRAVIER:    I can't do it! Just think . . . here . . . in the same place . . . She was here and we spoke of our hope . . . and I promised her . . . I promised that I'd talk to you . . . because . . . I love her . . .

D'HÉMELIN:    You love her! (*Bitter laughter, then sobers*) There's nothing for it then. It'll have to be me . . . her father . . . (*Resolutely*) I

don't want them to get her alive . . . no, not alive . . . not alive!
*(An explosion followed by cries and gunfire.)*

GRAVIER:  Get down! Get ready to fire . . .
*(All the men go to the barricades and fire. More explosions and then the cries of the Boxers and the sound of gongs and bells.)*

BERNARD:  Get down, sir! They'll hit you!

D'HÉMELIN:  They're not very good shots!
*(A cannon ball strikes the barricade.)*

MORIN:  Not bad!

LOREAU:  Their aim is getting better.
*(The noise gets louder.)*

BERNARD:  They're by the canal!

CLÉMENT:  They're by the walls!

GRAVIER:  Fire at the grass! Shoot! Shoot!

LOREAU  *(abandoning his post)*: We're overrun!

D'HÉMELIN:  They're everywhere!

GRAVIER:  The swarming mob . . .
*(Cannon fire)*

ALL  *(variously)*: Here! Here! Face the right! There they are! There they are!
*(A cannon blasts very close.)*

GRAVIER:  It's over—we can't hold out!

D'HÉMELIN:  Get down—into the cellars—don't stay here!

LOREAU:  In the name of God, let's fight!

KERDREC,
MORIN, AND
BERNARD:  *Charge*!

KERDREC:  We don't stand a chance, but let's *kill*!

LOREAU:  They want our skin!

ALL:  Charge! *(They advance. Only Gravier and D'Hémelin remain.)*

GRAVIER:  Don't stay here, sir . . .

D'HÉMELIN:  Leave me.

GRAVIER:  You'll die out here . . .

D'HÉMELIN:  What is left but death? *(He pushes Gravier away.)* Denise . . . Denise . . .
*(Cannon blast. The consulate door is being pounded, the women scream. Denise runs out and into her father's arms.)*

DENISE:  Father . . . help us . . .

D'HÉMELIN:  Are you hurt?

DENISE:  I'm scared—so scared!

D'HÉMELIN:  Denise!

DENISE:  Father—save me—the Boxers . . . Save me!

D'HÉMELIN:  Yes, I will save you.

DENISE:  It's them! *(The sound of gunfire and cries of the wounded.)* The screaming! Father! Save me! It's them!

D'HÉMELIN:     Don't be scared . . . Don't be scared . . . Denise, my darling . . .
               (*Slowly he takes his revolver and puts it to Denise's head and shoots her. Suddenly all the gunfire stops.*)

VOICES OF
KERDREC,
MORIN,
BERNARD,
CLÉMENT:       It's the allies! We're saved—*saved*!

GRAVIER        (*bleeding*): Sir, sir—it's the allies! The allies! We're saved!
               (*D'Hémelin still holds Denise's body tightly in his arms.*)

D'HÉMELIN      (*laughing insanely*): Saved! We're saved!
               (*He drops her body to the ground and the sound of the victorious European troops can be heard as the curtain slowly descends.*)

THE END

# The Lighthouse Keepers

*(Gardiens de phare, 1905)*

*by*

PAUL AUTIER AND PAUL CLOQUEMIN

## Preface

*Gardiens de phare* premiered at the Théâtre du Grand-Guignol in May 1905 with Henri Gouget in the role of Yvon, the son, and it soon established itself as a classic of the repertoire, being reprised on a number of occasions until 1933 under Jack Jouvin, including a 1918 production with Paulais.[1] Jean Grémillon even made a film version in 1929. Its success makes it even more remarkable that this was Autier and Cloquemin's only contribution to the Grand-Guignol.

In 1925 Choisy programmed it on the same evening as de Lorde and Binet's *Un crime dans une maison de fous* with its gruesomely violent set pieces (this was clearly a juxtaposition in *la douche écossaise* that was deemed to be successful, as Jouvin did the same in 1933). *The Lighthouse Keepers*, in contrast, is a play that does not require visual special effects: all its emphasis is on accomplished and intense acting to achieve a mood of claustrophobic terror and a double climax of horror (Yvon succumbing to rabies and being strangled by his father).

The horror within *The Lighthouse Keepers* operates on a number of different levels and in each case it is exacerbated by the effective symbol of the lighthouse, which represents claustrophobia, isolation and a haven surrounded by a danger (the elements), which may penetrate the defences at any moment. Unsurprisingly, the lighthouse was used as a setting in a number of Grand-Guignol plays (Pierron 1995, 118), most notably Marcelle Maurette's *La Tour d'amour* (1938) and Alfred Machard's[2] sex horror, *L'Orgie dans le phare* (1956).

---

[1] In her brief introduction to the play (1995, 118–19), Pierron lists 1913 and 1918 as reprise production dates, although in her 'Calendrier des Spectacles' (Pierron 1995, 1403–24) these are listed under 1915, 1925 and twice in 1933. Gordon dates the premiere of the play as 1918 (Gordon 1997, 58).

[2] Leopold Marchard in Gordon (69 and 110).

The play is about contamination, a popular theme in a number of Grand-Guignol plays, and in this case rabies. This is the horror of Yvon's realization that he has contracted the disease and is going to die. As Pierron points out, 'rabies had lost none of its immediacy', (1995, 119) even though Pasteur had discovered a vaccine twenty years earlier. As in many other plays from the genre which deal with medical issues, *The Lighthouse Keepers* successfully combines the fiction of the drama with the facts of the disease, such as Yvon's fever and his hydrophobia (again made worse by the fact that he is stranded in the lighthouse surrounded by sea).

It would be a mistake to assume that the horror focuses most strongly on Yvon's visible deterioration. Yvon, it seems, already suspects that he may have been contaminated after the dog that bit him died of rabies. As far as Yvon is concerned there is more horror in imagining the progression of the disease. However, the main horror is reserved not for the victim, but for the witness. For Bréhan the horror is multi-layered.

There is the horror of watching his son die and the horror of killing his son. Like D'Hémelin in *The Ultimate Torture*, he is faced with the agonizing choice of becoming the murderer of his own child or leaving him/her to face an even worse fate and, like D'Hémelin, he chooses to kill. It is a theme that is also present in *Euthanasia* where Saint-Géry is faced with a moral dilemma and also concludes that a mercy killing is justifiable. For Bréhan the greater horror is what lies ahead, and that is not simply having to live with his memories and his conscience. The father and son are on their first night of a month-long tour of duty at the lighthouse and by the end of the play, Bréhan must face that month alone, in the presence of the rotting corpse of his son. The horror remains strictly offstage and located around the victim.

Interestingly Autier and Cloquemin cleverly lead us to expect a different horror, namely that the play will end with a shipwreck due to Bréhan's failure to light the lamp in time to avert tragedy. Bréhan's prime motivating force is his sense of duty. It is this which causes the argument between the two men early in the play, it is out of a sense of duty to his son that he commits filicide, and it is his final despairing cry as the curtain falls. However, this turns out to be only a red herring. As Yvon lies dead in his arms, Bréhan hears an approaching ship and, in horror at his dereliction of duty, rushes to light the lamp, just in time. However, his success merely serves to emphasize the other horror that awaits him. Having fulfilled his public duty he must now spend the next month alone in his own private hell.

In analysing horror films using Kristevan theory, Barbara Creed discusses the construction of the maternal figure as abject (see Creed 2000, 66–67). She cites films like *Psycho* (1960) and *Carrie* (1976) as examples where the father is absent and the maternal figure is monstrous. To this we might add films like *Evil Dead II* (1987) where a demon emerges from the cellar in the form of the lullaby-singing mother of one of the characters. The Grand-Guignol, however, does not obviously exploit the monstrous-maternal. In terms of familial relationships, in *The Ultimate Torture* we witness a father forced to kill his daughter, and in *The Lighthouse Keepers* a father kills his own son: these are examples of the monstrous-paternal in worlds where it is the *mother* who is significantly absent.

*The Lighthouse Keepers* is one of the shorter plays in the Grand-Guignol repertoire, but this merely intensifies the action. The suspense is further increased by a series of sound effects, originally devised by Ratineau, and including the sound of the seagulls hammering their beaks against the windows. It was, according to Pierron (1995, 118), an effect that became legendary in the history of the genre, but also seems to anticipate Hitchcock's use of the same in *The Birds* (1963). The use of sound effects in the Grand-Guignol is often seen by critics as secondary to the use of visual special effects, and yet it would appear that much use was made of offstage sound (as well as onstage sound, from the cracking sound of bones to Maxa's inimitable, piercing scream) and Ratineau employed as much energy in creating these as he did the more complex sleight-of-hand visuals. As Maxa says, 'crying and wailing coming from quite a distance was particularly effective' (in Pierron 1995, 1392). At the same time sound effects were always balanced with silence, just as visual effects were balanced with stillness and anticipation.

# THE LIGHTHOUSE KEEPERS

*(Gardiens de phare, 1905)*

*by*

PAUL AUTIER AND PAUL CLOQUEMIN

---

Bréhan
Yvon, his son

---

*(The action takes place on the top floor of the Maudit Lighthouse, on an isolated rock, two leagues from land. A simple room, circular or with cut-off corners, a door to the right. On the left, a bunk; in the centre, a table and two wooden stools.)*

*(As the curtain rises, Bréhan is busy wiring up an electric switch on the left-hand wall.)*

BRÉHAN: Five o'clock. Soon it'll be too dark to see anything. I'll be finished in a minute, thank goodness . . . the mechanism seems to be in good condition. All the same, they're wonderful things these electric lamps! In the old days it used to take ages . . . now a turn of the wheel . . . *(Bréhan gives it a turn and the footlights get brighter.)* Great! All the filaments are alight! There . . . *(Bréhan turns it in the opposite direction and the footlights get dimmer.)* We're all ready for lighting-up time.

YVON *(appearing from the right)*: Phew!

BRÉHAN: Are you all finished down there?

YVON *(a coil of rope over his shoulder)*: Yes, I've refilled the tank and come all the way back up . . . two hundred steps to the top . . . I'm done for! *(He throws the coil of rope to the left of the bunk.)*

BRÉHAN: You're lucky they didn't build this lighthouse even higher.

YVON: Being stuck fifty metres up in the air is quite enough for me, thank you!

BRÉHAN: What weather! Just listen to that wind!

YVON: For sure! *(Pause)* It's going to be a long night. *(Sitting on the bunk and stretching out)* I'm bored! I'm so bored!

BRÉHAN: Already?! *(Taking the coil of rope which Yvon left by the bunk, he walks in front of him and goes to the door on the right.)* And it's not even seven hours since we started our shift. Never mind, a month will soon pass, eh, my boy? Life here isn't as much fun as it is in the village, eh? You'll miss those parties at your cousin Santec's place, I expect. So many people went to those! Yes, indeed! And here we are all alone! (*Bréhan sits down on the stool to the right of the table.*)

YVON: Alone . . . just the two of us all alone . . . separated from all of Christendom by more than six miles of sea.

BRÉHAN: Hey, listen to that . . . what a storm! Can you hear that noise?

YVON: Yes. (*Pause*) I've never felt quite so isolated as I do today.

BRÉHAN (*smiling as he pours himself a drink*): The fact is that there's not another living soul for miles. The Maudit Lighthouse, the bleakest in all of Brittany—that's how it was described to me when I got this job twenty years ago. Bleak—that's for sure. The nearest those administrators have come to this place is when they've been out for a spot of fishing! (*A prolonged rumble of thunder*) Ah! They probably have a right old laugh about it, while they're putting their feet up in front of the fire. Ah well, here comes the thunder, the sound of the big bass drum! (*He puts the goblet to his lips. Pause.*)

YVON (*sitting on the bunk*): Father, if one of us were to die, what would become of the other?

BRÉHAN (*stopping drinking, goblet in his hand*): What are you talking about? Dying without the last rites? God wouldn't allow such a thing to happen. Dying without seeing your mother again? While she's waiting for us across the water? Without embracing her . . . (*He places the goblet on the table.*) What's the matter with you? In the three years since you took over here from your brother, Pierre, God rest his soul, I've never seen you like this . . . (*Reassuringly*) You're not going to die and neither am I. (*He takes the goblet, empties it in one gulp and places it on the table. Pause.*)

YVON: Poor Pierre. If only he had stayed.

BRÉHAN: If he had stayed, he wouldn't have ended up as shark food. Poor boy!

YVON: Mother will never get over it. The day before we left I caught her reading that letter again from the captain of the ship Pierre was sailing on to the South Seas.

BRÉHAN: Ah, that letter, I know it off by heart. (*Reciting*) 'During a south-south-easterly storm, I ordered a change of course. Your son was the first to climb the rigging. Half-way up he lost his footing and disappeared into the swell. God took him.'

YVON: My fate might have been the same. I used to have a life of freedom, a life without boundaries, a life of danger, instead of being a prisoner like a rat in a trap.

BRÉHAN (*getting up*): A life of danger, that may be fine, but working here is a hundred times better. (*He takes a step towards Yvon.*)

YVON: Still, it's tough being shut up.

BRÉHAN:    Pah! Every thirty days, when we go home for a month, we can
be proud of ourselves. Thanks to our lighthouse, a good many
return to port who otherwise . . . (*He goes to examine the
lantern on the left-hand wall.*)

YVON    (*standing by the bunk*): This pride you talk of, father. I used to
feel it. You remember how happy I was on my first tour of
duty, when I was given the job of working with you after I left
the navy. Well, since we got back, I haven't felt the same. I
don't know . . .

BRÉHAN:    Don't worry, it'll pass.

YVON:    Yes, it'll pass . . . tomorrow. (*Pause, during which he moves to
the right.*) A nor'westerly. It's going to be one hell of a night!

BRÉHAN    (*kneeling in front of the lantern and opening it*): Listen to those
seagulls outside! What a racket! That means stormy weather . . .
(*Pause. Yvon goes to the door on the left.*) Calm down, Yvon!
(*Taking the lantern downstage to the wall on the left*) Will you
stop wandering about?

YVON:    No! This is all too much . . . I need to keep moving!

BRÉHAN:    (*approaching Yvon*): Oh, I wonder whether it might be another
kind of sickness you're suffering from. The kind that ends in
wedding bells.

YVON    (*standing at a right angle to the bunk*): You've guessed right,
father. Marie is going to be my wife . . . we got engaged the
other day.

BRÉHAN:    Of course! That's what your problem is. Don't think about it
anymore. (*He turns towards the lantern downstage right by the
wall.*) Mind you, you certainly kept that one quiet. (*He kneels
down in front of the lantern, back to the audience.*) I'd never
have guessed otherwise. She's got taste, though . . . our Yvon . . .
and a lighthouse keeper as well . . . she'll never have cause to
be jealous, anyway.

YVON    (*standing in front of the bunk*): Stop teasing me, father . . . we
love each other very much.

BRÉHAN    (*standing up and going over to Yvon*): I'm not teasing you. I'm
looking forward to you giving me a strapping young grandson
who can look after this lighthouse when my old bones are
resting with my ancestors in the village graveyard.

YVON    (*sitting down on the bunk*): That's all a long way off yet!

BRÉHAN:    Yes, there's plenty of time for that. I'm in no hurry to book my
ticket to the afterlife. (*He goes centre stage and looks up.*)
What's got into those birds out there? The way they're pecking
at it with their beaks, they'll end up breaking the glass. (*He
picks up his sou'wester and puts it on.*) And it wouldn't be the
first time either! (*He makes his way towards the door.*)
Nevertheless, in this weather, you can't just leave them to it!
Thankfully they don't like humans, so if I just open the door . . .
Shoo! Go on, get out of it! (*Exit Bréhan.*)

YVON:    What on earth's the matter with me? I'm cold . . . I'm so cold . . . and at the same time, here (*He taps his chest.*) I'm burning, simply burning. I've never felt anything like this before. The old man's going to worry . . . I feel so restless. (*He gets up and moves stage right.*)

BRÉHAN    (*entering*): Brrr! What weather! I'm absolutely drenched! The great storm four years ago was the last time it was as bad as this. (*He takes off his sou'wester and his oilskins.*) At least our lighthouse is built on solid foundations. Nothing's going to blow it down, that's for sure! Just think of those poor boats out there. You just try struggling against a wind like that. (*He picks up a lantern from the floor upstage left and carries it over to the table.*) But our light will shine tonight and they'll see their way safely home, eh, Yvon? (*He sets about polishing the lamp.*)

YVON    (*to the far right of the stage*): Yes. (*Pause*) Father, what are you doing?

BRÉHAN:    What does it look like? I'm polishing. A good seaman must always be prepared.

YVON:    Just leave it be. Leave the lantern alone.

BRÉHAN    (*surprised*): But why?

YVON    (*brusquely approaching Bréhan to take the lantern*): For the last time, will you just leave it?!

BRÉHAN:    What's got into you?

YVON    (*without taking his eyes off the lantern, with his back to the audience, moving left*): The glare from the brass is hurting me. It's like red-hot needles being driven into my brain.

BRÉHAN:    Don't be ridiculous! Have you gone mad?

YVON:    I don't know . . . I don't know anymore . . . I'm scared.

BRÉHAN:    Scared?

YVON    (*standing stage left*): Yes, scared . . . This is all beginning to get to me . . . being alone here for months . . . for years . . . (*turning*) oh, I envy those sailors in the ships out there, heading for port, towards civilization . . . whereas us . . . (*He moves to the footlights on the right.*)

BRÉHAN:    Don't get yourself worked up like this! You'll tire yourself out and then you'll be falling asleep on duty tonight.

YVON    (*collapsing onto the stool*): So much the better! Sleep! If only I could sleep!

BRÉHAN    (*standing to the right of Yvon*): Shut up, Yvon, don't talk like that . . . falling asleep on duty! You're putting your very soul in danger! (*Seriously*) If a ship were to founder on the rocks through negligence whilst we were on duty, we would have the deaths of every single person on our hands. Right, let's get the oil. Let's get cracking!

YVON:    I'm just going to get some fresh air. Maybe that'll make me feel better. (*He gets up and goes towards the door.*)

BRÉHAN:    Watch out and be careful, the wind's strong out there! (*Exit Yvon.*)

BRÉHAN    (*moving centre stage*): Poor boy! Hopefully it won't get any worse, or we'll be in a right mess here. In weather like this no boat would be able to get near the lighthouse and the local doctor with his boneshaker and his old grey mare certainly couldn't get out to Maudit tonight. Just think, if you fell ill, you could die out here for want of a doctor. (*A cry is heard.*) Ah! What was that? I thought I heard a cry . . . no . . . (*Cupping his ear with his hand*) I can't hear it anymore. Nothing. You're going senile, you old fool. (*He approaches the table. Another cry is heard.*) No, no, I didn't imagine it. (*He returns to centre stage.*) But there's only Yvon and me here . . . My God, what on earth can have happened? (*Enter Yvon. Bréhan moves centre stage.*) Yvon, what did you cry out for?

YVON    (*stopping*): Did I cry out? Yes, maybe I did. I seem to be doing things in spite of myself today.

BRÉHAN:    Come here, you're soaked to the skin.

YVON    (*moving downstage*): There's something wrong, isn't there?

BRÉHAN:    Has that awful storm made you feel worse?

YVON    (*moving centre stage*): Yes, I'm burning up. Here, feel. And I'm thirsty . . . so thirsty.

BRÉHAN:    Don't drink anything! It'll just make your fever worse.

YVON:    But just give me some water . . . a little water.

BRÉHAN:    No.

YVON:    Give me some water. I want some.

BRÉHAN    (*picking up the jug of water from the floor and carrying it over to the table*): Don't be angry.

YVON    (*standing in front of the bunk*): I'm sorry. But you don't know what it's like. You can't know. I'm not myself anymore. I don't know what's happening to me . . . it's as if something has taken control of me . . . I want a drink! Oh, I want a drink!

BRÉHAN    (*pouring some water into a goblet and passing it to Yvon*): Ah well, drink then . . . but just sip it. (*He puts back the jug.*)

YVON    (*taking the goblet and immediately putting it down again*): Ah! What's wrong with me now? This is something else . . . I'm thirsty, I want to drink, but I can't.

BRÉHAN    (*returning to the table*): You see, it's the fever!

YVON:    But I want to drink . . . I'm thirsty, I want to drink as if my life depended on it, for God's sake! (*He goes to pick up the goblet.*)

BRÉHAN    (*stopping him*): Leave it. You can have a drink a bit later.

YVON:    Yes . . . a bit later. Keep it away from me . . . far away from me. (*He sits down on the bunk, his head in his hands. Pause.*)

BRÉHAN    (*filling his pipe*): Are you feeling any better?

YVON:    Please, don't fuss about me. Oh, this rain . . . this rain!

BRÉHAN:    I think God's left the tap running. (*He strikes a light.*)

YVON:    Don't joke . . . you're always joking. And put that light out, it's hurting my eyes.

BRÉHAN:  Good God, what's got into you? (*He puts his lighter on the table.*) There. Are you happy now?

YVON:    Yes, that's better. What a day! Will there be no end to it?

BRÉHAN:  It's no longer than any other.

YVON     (*raising himself up, about to take his jumper off*): I'm too hot . . . I'm suffocating!

BRÉHAN:  Look at you, you're shivering. Wrap yourself up.

YVON:    No, I'm too hot.

BRÉHAN   (*stopping him from getting undressed*): Wrap yourself up, I tell you! I'm your father and you'll do as I say! (*He makes him sit down again on the bunk.*) What on earth's the matter with you? (*Turning his back on the audience and looking at Yvon, who doesn't take his eyes off him.*) Why are you looking at me like that? I've never seen you like this before . . . there must be something wrong with you. (*He approaches Yvon.*)

YVON:    Listen, father. There's something I want to tell you. It's . . .

BRÉHAN:  What is it?

YVON:    I'm worried . . .

BRÉHAN:  Worried? Why?

YVON:    The other day . . . when I was round at cousin Santec's house . . . I got bitten.

BRÉHAN:  Bitten?

YVON:    By the dog.

BRÉHAN:  Which dog?

YVON:    Toby.

BRÉHAN:  The one they had to have put down?

YVON:    They had him put down?

BRÉHAN:  Yes, didn't you know?

YVON     (*getting up*): But, he was . . . he went mad then! (*Sitting down again*) Then that's why I've been feeling odd for the past two days. This terrible sickness has been simmering away. And then now . . . it's boiled over. It's invading my whole body. It's overrunning me . . .

BRÉHAN   (*taking hold of him by the shoulders*): You're wrong.

YVON:    Look, when Guérec the butcher died of rabies, he had the same symptoms—fever, pains in the eyes, followed by thirst. And he couldn't drink. There you are, you see. It's all over. I have rabies, don't I, father? I'm going to die of rabies.

BRÉHAN:  No, no . . .

YVON:    I'll be rabid, rabid like a wild animal . . . never . . . never . . .

BRÉHAN:  Yvon!

YVON:    Father! Father! Save me! Don't let me die!

BRÉHAN:  No! No! I will save you!

YVON:    I don't want to die! I want to live! I want to live!

BRÉHAN:    Yes, yes . . . you will live, my son . . . you will live . . . there, it's all right. (*He sits him down on the bunk and sits next to him. Pause.*)

YVON:    Tell me, father, have there ever been any lighthouse keepers who have died all alone, helpless and isolated.

BRÉHAN:    Yes.

YVON:    And the other one . . . his companion, what did he do with the body, day after day until someone came to relieve them? It's horrible . . . I don't want that to happen.

BRÉHAN:    Don't even think about it, Yvon.

YVON:    But that's what it'll be like for you . . . with my body . . . no, no, that would be awful for you. I'm going to end it all now. (*He gets up and lunges for the door.*)

BRÉHAN    (*getting up and holding him back by the shoulders*): No . . . please . . . don't do this to your old man.

YVON:    Let me go!

BRÉHAN:    Think of me!

YVON:    You're the one who should think of me. Won't you let me finish it? (*He brutally pushes his father away.*)

BRÉHAN:    No! Yvon!

YVON    (*leaning against the wall, left*): Oh! Water . . . more water . . . everywhere there's water . . . I'm scared . . . I'm scared!

BRÉHAN    (*returning to Yvon and leading him to the bunk*): Yvon, my son, come here. Next to me . . . I'll look after you, I'll make you better.

YVON:    There's nothing that can be done. Not by you. Not by anyone.

BRÉHAN    (*making him sit down on the bunk*): I'll swim ashore. I'll bring back help . . . a doctor . . .

YVON:    You're mad . . . swimming all that way in weather like this!

BRÉHAN:    Yes, I'll go . . .

YVON:    No . . .no . . . don't leave me . . . I don't want you to leave me. (*He makes him sit down next to him.*)

BRÉHAN:    You're right.

YVON:    It's the best part of a month before anyone will come.

BRÉHAN:    I'll send a signal. Somebody will come.

YVON:    In winter the storms go on and on and this place is so godforsaken . . . nobody could get up to the lighthouse.

BRÉHAN:    God will protect us.

YVON:    God!

BRÉHAN:    Don't blaspheme, Yvon! God is just, he remembers everything. I have risked my life enough times for my fellow creatures over the last ten years on the lifeboat . . . he owes me your life.

YVON:    Yes . . . perhaps. (*Pause*) Oh, it hurts.

BRÉHAN:    There's nothing . . . there's nothing I can do for him. My boy . . . my son. (*He gets up.*) Ah! You're right. It's this lighthouse that's to blame for everything . . . Otherwise help would come, you'd be looked after.

YVON      (*groaning*): Oh, I feel awful . . . I feel so ill . . .

BRÉHAN    (*returning to Yvon*): Yes, my son, I know how you suffer . . . if
          your mother were here, she would speak to you, she would
          speak to you as only mothers know how . . . the way they
          speak to their children when they are ill. I don't know how to,
          you understand. (*He sits down on the stool.*)

YVON      (*rolling over on the bunk*): Mother!

BRÉHAN:   My God! And so helpless!

YVON:     Oh, mother . . . mother . . .

BRÉHAN:   My son . . . my poor son . . . (*He weeps silently. Pause.*)

YVON      (*getting up*): I don't want to die like a rabid animal . . . a
          terrifying death . . . no, no.

BRÉHAN    (*also getting up*): Yvon!

YVON:     But I can't do it. I don't have the strength to . . .

BRÉHAN:   Stop it!

YVON:     You'll have to put me out of my misery. Put me out of my
          misery like a dog . . . that's what I am, an animal.

BRÉHAN:   What is it you want me to do, my son?

YVON:     You gave me life, take it back again. There's nothing else you
          can do for me.

BRÉHAN:   Kill you?! Kill you, my own son?!

YVON:     Father, you have to! Please, I beg of you. Have you no pity for
          me?

BRÉHAN:   But I'll make you better . . .

YVON:     Nobody can make me better . . . before long a wild animal will
          attack you and you will have to defend yourself . . . you have
          to live . . . for the sake of the lighthouse.

BRÉHAN:   Shut up, shut up and don't talk like that.

YVON:     I'm suffering, I'm suffering!

BRÉHAN:   My God! My God!

YVON:     Father! Father! Help me! It's getting worse! I can't bear it any
          longer .. I can't bear it . . .

BRÉHAN:   Yvon! My dear Yvon!

YVON      (*walking up to Bréhan*): Go away! Go away! Quickly, get away
          from me! I can feel myself wanting to bite you. Look out! I'm
          going to bite you! (*He lunges at Bréhan and grabs him round
          the neck.*)

BRÉHAN:   Ah, no!

YVON:     Ah! Ah!

BRÉHAN:   What are you doing? Let go! Will you let go?! In the name of
          God! I'll have to . . . (*Just as he is about to be bitten by Yvon,
          Bréhan strangles him. Yvon falls. Bréhan throws himself on the
          body.*) Yvon, my boy, my son, I've killed him. I've killed my
          son. (*He sobs. The wind grows stronger, the storm rages. He
          gets up.*) Yes, bastard sea! You bastard! Are you happy? Now
          you have my two boys. For twenty years at this lighthouse I
          have robbed you of your victims, but today you've taken your

revenge, you bastard. Oh, I hate you! I hate you! Yvon! Poor Yvon! (*He collapses in front of his son's corpse. Pause. The sound of a siren in the distance. He doesn't hear it. The siren again, this time closer. Bréhan pricks up his ears.*) Eh? What? A siren! A ship! (*Siren again and again, getting nearer.*) The lighthouse! I've forgotten to switch on the lamp. The ship will crash on the rocks! It'll be lost! They'll all be killed! I didn't switch on the lamp . . . they haven't come to rescue us. I want to stay with my son . . . my child. (*Sirens, increasingly strong.*) No, I can't . . . I have to help them find a safe passage through. (*He slowly goes to the electric switch and turns it. The footlights come on, the siren stops.*) It is my duty . . .! (*He returns to kneeling by Yvon.*)

THE END

# Chop-Chop! or The Guillotine

## (La Veuve, 1906)

*by*

EUGÈNE HÉROS AND LÉON ABRIC

## Preface

Eugène Héros and Léon Abric had already established reputations for themselves as comedy writers by the time *La Veuve* premiered in the impasse Chaptal in March 1906, having previously written *Le Pont d'Avignon* (1902) and *Paquerette* (1905) for the Théâtre du Grand-Guignol, as well as a number of songs, revues and operettas for the Parisian music-halls and cafes (Pierron 1995, 206).

As might be expected, it is a fast-paced farce that takes place in a single setting and revolves around the themes of infidelity, sexual deviance and being caught *in flagrante delicto*. Structurally, the play conforms to the expected conventions of farce, a view that is further strengthened by the stereotypical nature of the numerous additional characters. The Museum Curator, for example, is portrayed as a self-important jobsworth, a satire on the French minor civil bureaucrat, and the English visitors as pompous, empty-headed tourists. The guillotine, centre stage throughout, makes the play curiously macabre as much as it is a satirical sex romp.

If the comedy associated with the peripheral characters centres around the portrayal of type, then the opposite can be said of the three central characters. That is to say that the basis of any comedy around them lies in their behaving contrary to the audience's expectations of their stereotype. In this way, Palmyre, who on the surface would seem to be a respectable married Parisian housewife, turns out to be an independently minded, even dominant, woman with unconventional sexual proclivities. Lecardon, a former wrestler and the handsome lover, finds himself symbolically emasculated by the guillotine, whereas Letocard, the meek cuckold, transforms himself (much to Palmyre's admiration) into the mouse that roared. Millet, on the other hand, is the only character to maintain any sense of dignity, remaining—like the audience—the rather distanced and amused observer of ludicrous events.

The guillotine is arguably the central character in the play. The very title testifies to this (the French title literally means 'the widow', but is also a colloquial term for the guillotine), and it is important not to forget the significance of the guillotine as a cultural icon in France. It is a potent symbol of the Revolution and, by implication, the Republic and democracy itself. More than that, however, as the most efficient means of execution of its day, it stands as a symbol of French civilization and over the years acquired an air of romanticism, evident in the way that the guillotine is discussed in the opening scene of the play. The guillotine plays a key role in a number of Grand-Guignol plays, including *Au petit jour* (André de Lorde and Jean Bernac 1921), *Vers l'au-delà* (Charles Hellem and Pol d'Estoc 1922) and *L'Homme qui a tué la mort* (René Berton 1928)[1] and considering the national obsession with it, it would be extraordinary were this not the case. After all, executions were still sometimes held in public in France until 1937 and the death penalty was not finally abolished until 1981 (Pierron 1995, 875).

What is extraordinary about *Chop-Chop!* is that it is a comedy. The guillotine was taken very seriously in France and was the focus for ongoing public debate amongst theologians and members of the medical profession (Pierron 1995, 874); its presence on the stage was normally limited to dramas, rather than comedies. Interestingly, when Samouraï Films produced a version of the play on video (1997), the ending was changed, transforming the piece into a horror play with the decapitation of Lecardon. It is as if the Samouraï version feels *compelled* to use what is now an 'historical' machine as a climax to the macabre theme of the play, although the distinct anticlimax and humiliation of the manly Lecardon was obviously a careful decision on the part of Héros and Abric, especially in the context of an explicitly realist theatre of horror.

The seriousness with which the French public viewed the representation of the guillotine on stage can be measured by the scandal that erupted following the original staging of *Au petit jour* in 1921, the only time that the Grand-Guignol seems to have transgressed the boundaries of public decency. The play, which concerns the tormenting of a condemned man by the father of the woman he has murdered, ends with his beheading.[2] Camillo Antona-Traversi recounts the audience's reaction to the closing scene:

---

[1] Berton's play—in which a scientist conducts a Frankenstein-style experiment to resuscitate a guillotine victim—reflected the real-life experiments, in 1905, of a certain Dr Burieux who attempted to communicate with the severed head of a condemned man (Kerekes and Slater 1995, 162).

[2] For an explanation of how this illusion was achieved, see Pierron 1995, 1399.

At first there was dead silence throughout the auditorium; then some timid applause, obscured by whistling, could be heard. Then a spectator in the balcony began protesting that it was a scandal.

(Antona-Traversi 1933, 72)

What followed was uproar in the auditorium from outraged members of the audience and the ensuing debate ran in the Parisian press for several days. As a result Choisy, de Lorde and Bernac were summoned to the offices of the Chief of Police, where they gave an undertaking to rewrite the final scene, so that the curtain fell just as the condemned man was being led to his execution (Pierron 1995, 874).[3]

The offence had been caused, it seems, not because of the reference to, or even presence of a guillotine, but rather because to show a functioning guillotine was considered an act of sacrilege towards a national icon. One can almost imagine a similar sense of outrage over the unflattering portrayal of royalty on the British stage during the same period. With *L'Homme qui a tué la mort* there was no such problem.[4] Bearing this in mind, it is perhaps the case that *Chop-Chop!* is able to give such prominence to the guillotine precisely because it is a comedy and the functioning of the guillotine is permissible because the blade is only made of cardboard.

As regards *Chop-Chop!* the guillotine also takes on an unambiguous symbolism in terms of the charged eroticism that runs through the play. To be caught in such a compromising position is a great humiliation to Lecardon and his 'emasculation' results because of helplessness or impotence to extricate himself from the situation. The precarious position in which he finds himself suggests as much a threat of castration as decapitation. The guillotine may have a phallic (even, in terms of French culture, phallocentric) significance, but it is also 'la veuve': it is a power-

---

[3] This requirement to change the ending of a play to protect the audience from the full excesses of the Grand-Guignol, although rare in France, was a common strategy of the censors of the Lord Chamberlain's office in Britain in their dealings with Levy's Grand-Guignol at the Little Theatre.

[4] Rather interestingly, when Jose Levy obtained a licence for an English version of the play for his ill-fated revival in 1928, on condition that the severed head remained invisible to the audience, one argument that was put to the censors on its behalf was that since, according to the play, a severed head could communicate for a short while before death, then this suggested that hanging, the preferred method of execution in Britain, was superior (and, by implication, so were the British) since death was instantaneous. The play, therefore, was used as evidence that the French were less civilized than the British, quite the opposite meaning of the guillotine in France! (Memo from Mr Gordon to Lord Chamberlain, 8 May 1928).

ful, blatant—and, in this instance—amusing incarnation of the Freudian *vagina dentata* that permeates the Grand-Guignol whether in the form of the castration complex or the *femme fatale* that threatens male power (the unruly Palmyre and a guillotine is a dangerous combination!).

*Chop-Chop!* ultimately shows that the difference between Grand-Guignol horror and comedy does not necessarily lie within the subject matter itself. The themes of sex and revenge can be found in many of the classic horrors of the genre from Level's *The Final Kiss* (1912) to Ghilain and Larroque's *La Loterie de la mort* (1957). The distinction lies rather in the *consistency* with which the material is treated by both writer and actor alike.

# CHOP-CHOP! OR THE GUILLOTINE

*(La Veuve, 1906)*

*by*

EUGÈNE HÉROS AND LÉON ABRIC

---

Lecardon
Ernest Letocard
The Curator
The Interpreter
Millet
John Matthews
Palmyre Letocard
Kate Matthews
English Tourists

---

*(Paris in the early twentieth century.)*

*(Ernest, perched on a stepladder, is busy with a lamp adding the finishing touch to a new exhibit—a guillotine. The sound of hammering and the tightening of screws continues for some time.)*

CURATOR *(entering via staircase)*: Well, how are you getting on?

ERNEST: Pretty well. Just a few finishing touches, but most of it's done.

CURATOR: Fiddly work, eh?

ERNEST: By and large. You need a sensitive touch to prepare a machine like this.

CURATOR: And not a job for weaklings either.

ERNEST: Professionally speaking, I see myself as a locksmith, unlocking the secrets of an exhibit.

CURATOR: The guillotine, now there's a fine old lock—the lock of eternity!

ERNEST: You speak like a work of literature! A true poet!

CURATOR: There's not a single work of literature in the whole collection as clever as that thing.

ERNEST *(climbing down the stepladder)*: Exactly! Look at the neck brace. Say what you like about the guillotine, it's still a fine instrument, beautifully worked out . . .

CURATOR:    Looking at it like this, in the cold light of day, it does something to me, you know. This machine is a part of history . . . it's dealt with some famous people, some real characters!

ERNEST:    Yes, the guillotine has a way of making the murderers more respectable. It makes them grow in stature.

CURATOR:    By making them shorter!

ERNEST:    This one consigned Pranzini to posterity. And Carrara. And many others.

CURATOR:    Before the baying mob . . . there's nothing like a good old public execution.

ERNEST:    Oh yes, the fresh air, the guards, the state prosecutor, the priest with his crucifix . . . the military cordon . . .

CURATOR:    'Present Arms!' Then, silence . . . then the small click of the release catch that jolts the crowd like cannon fire!

ERNEST:    Ah, but imagine an execution in a dungeon like this? Would it be more picturesque? More theatrical? Absolutely not!

CURATOR:    And the poor guillotine would be too hemmed in between these four walls. At least in the public arena it has a certain style. It is the dispenser of justice!

ERNEST    (*gathering up his tools and putting them into his bag on the bench on the left*): In here it is nothing more than a machine.

CURATOR:    A nasty machine for cutting off heads. Don't you think that the condemned prefer the old system?

ERNEST    (*sitting on the bench*): Oh, undoubtedly!

CURATOR    (*sitting next to Ernest*): Just think about it! To be executed behind closed doors! Like getting a divorce! What they call in the theatre, a technical rehearsal!

ERNEST:    Just for the stage crew!

CURATOR:    That's terrible. I wouldn't wish such a death on my worst enemy. What about you?

ERNEST:    Me neither. Wait a minute, though. There is somebody I know, whom I would take great pleasure . . . (*He points to the guillotine.*)

CURATOR:    Who's that? Your mother-in-law?

ERNEST:    You're not even warm. (*He gets up.*)

CURATOR:    Your wife then?

ERNEST:    Not my wife either. But someone rather close to her.

CURATOR:    How close?

ERNEST:    Too close. Her lover.

CURATOR    (*standing up*): She's cheating on you?

ERNEST:    Probably.

CURATOR:    Then take your revenge!

ERNEST:    It's all I ever think about . . . but how?

CURATOR:    If you have proof, divorce her.

ERNEST:    I haven't got any hard evidence . . . and anyway I love my wife . . . she's a very beautiful woman.

CURATOR:    Well then, kill the fellow.

ERNEST:    Thank you, but there's the trial, and prison . . .

CURATOR:    You'd be acquitted.

ERNEST:    Possibly. But that's all conjecture. I'd rather just wait for the right opportunity. One will come along sooner or later.

CURATOR:    But seeing as you know who your wife's lover is, you could always pick a fight and give them a good thrashing.

ERNEST:    Who, my wife?

CURATOR:    Oh no, just her lover.

ERNEST:    No, no, it's just not practical.

CURATOR:    Why not?

ERNEST:    Why not? Well, for a start he's bigger than me. He used to be a wrestler, now retired with a private fortune. I daren't lay a finger on him—he'd send me flying with a flick of his wrist. And then where would I be?

CURATOR    (*moving to the right*): Well, whatever. I was only saying it to pass the time.

ERNEST    (*getting up and slinging his bag over his shoulder*): Thanks for listening.

CURATOR:    Is the exhibit ready?

ERNEST    (*approaching the guillotine*): Yes, it's working beautifully. Watch. If you press the lever on the right, the neck brace lifts up. If you press the lever on the left then (*draws finger across throat*) justice is done!

CURATOR    (*next to the guillotine*): Right for the neck brace, left for the blade. (*Draws finger across throat.*)

ERNEST    (*going to get the stepladder*): Perfect. You know as much as the finest executioner. Now, I must be off. I've still got things to do.

CURATOR:    Right. I'll stay here and wait for the signal.

ERNEST:    Good. Bye then! (*He leaves, carrying the stepladder, along the corridor to the left.*)

CURATOR    (*alone in front of the guillotine*): The lever on the left for the neck brace, the lever on the right for the blade. A simple little action and there we are—one less person! And to think it's now ours. It's just right. (*A whistle offstage*) Ah, this sounds like the moment of truth. (*He goes to the parlaphone and puts the horn to his ear. He listens and replies.*) Good, everything is ready. Has the electricity been fixed? Go on then, switch it on. (*Light*) Good, you can let them in now. (*Back by the machine, speaking to the guillotine*) Are you ready? The whole world's coming to see you! (*Pause. Sound of footsteps. Visitors, Matthews, Kate, the Interpreter, numerous English tourists come down the stairs. The original English as used by Héros and Abric is here underlined. Ultimately much of the humour centres on the misunderstandings of the English characters and it is important to make clear when the tourists and the Interpreter are speaking an 'English' that cannot be understood by the other characters. One possibility would be to have the tourists and the Interpreter speak their 'English' with outrageous French accents.*)

TOURISTS: It was beautiful! Very nice indeed . . .

INTERPRETER: This way, if you please, to the famous French guillotine.

CURATOR (*reciting*): Ladies and Gentlemen. Here we have the very guillotine used by M. Deibler Senior for twenty years. The Daumier Museum, of which I have the honour of being the curator, has been able to acquire it at great cost. This machine, which has recently been restored, cut short the lives of many famous murderers, amongst whom I could name Pranzini, Anastay, Carrara, Géomay and many others.

INTERPRETER: A great many notorious murderers whose names you know; Carrara, Géomay, Anastay and many others were beheaded by this guillotine.

CURATOR (*reciting*): I will now explain to you how this instrument works. The blade is raised and secured here in the neck brace, which closes automatically. Simply press the lever here on the right to release the blade. To release the neck brace, simply press the lever on the left. The whole business takes between five and seven seconds, just long enough for the condemned to repay his debt to society. (*To the Interpreter*) Have they understood?

INTERPRETER (*quietly, walking in front of the Curator and standing before the guillotine*): Not a single word! Just a moment. (*Melodramatically, with grand, sweeping gestures*) The murderer is put on this board, his head comes in that hole, then if you push the déclic here, the knife fells on the neck, and the head in a basket full of sand. Then, the executioner takes the murderer's head by the hair and says, 'Look out, you all, that's the head of the murderer!' and then he let it fall down in the basket again. (*During this explanation, he has taken his cap in the right hand and let it fall on the words 'the head in the basket'. He picks it up again on the words 'the murderer's head', and holds it out to the tourists as if he were holding the head of the executed man and lets it fall again at the end of the phrase.*) That's all for the guillotine. (*He puts his hat back on.*)

CURATOR: And now I would like to show you how, in the Colonies, the natives were persuaded to pay their taxes. That is to say, the impalement stake, the tooth extractor and the gunpowder cartridge. Let's start with the gunpowder cartridge . . . (*He turns to the exit on the right.*)

MATTHEWS (*to the Interpreter*): Is it all right for young ladies?

INTERPRETER (*to the Curator*): The gentleman is asking whether all this is going to be suitable for young ladies?

CURATOR (*to the Interpreter*): That depends on one's views on such matters. If I had a sister I would ask her to wait for me here.

You're thinking of the gunpowder cartridge, of course, and where it was inserted?

INTERPRETER   (*to Matthews*): It's quite impossible for young ladies, you better give her a newspaper and tell her to wait till we come back.

MATTHEWS   (*seating his daughter and giving her a copy of The Times, before leaving with the rest of the party*): Here you are, Kate. Sit down and read.

CURATOR:   The methods of persuasion are this way, Ladies and Gentlemen! (*He ushers the visitors through the small door on the right.*)

KATE   (*going to the right-hand door and trying to see*): Silly old fool! (*She returns to the left.*)

CURATOR   (*appearing in the doorway*): Did you call me?

KATE:   No. (*The Curator disappears. Kate sits down on the bench, back to the audience, reading* The Times, *motionless. Pause.*)

LECARDON   (*enters with Millet via the stairs on the left*): Ah! Look, here is the guillotine . . .

INTERPRETER   (*rushing up to give his explanation with melodramatic gestures*): That is a French guillotine. A great many notorious murderers whose names you know were beheaded by this very guillotine. The murderer is put on this board, his head comes in this hole, then if you push the déclic here the knife fell on the neck and the head in a basket full of sand. Then the executioner takes the murderer's head by the hair, like this, and says to everybody, 'Look out, you all, that is the head of a murderer', then he let it fall down in the basket. That's all for the guillotine.

LECARDON:   I'm sorry, but I didn't understand a word of that. I'm French.

INTERPRETER   (*angry*): For goodness sake, you might have said so earlier! (*He leaves. The Curator returns.*)

CURATOR   (*aside*): More people! I'll soon deal with them. (*He takes a clothes brush from under the guillotine and brushes his clothes during the following speech. He recites very quickly.*) Ladies and Gentlemen (*Stuttering over his words*) Here we have the very guillotine used by M. Deibler Senior for twenty years. Erm, erm . . . face upwards on the board and his neck is secured here in the neck brace. (*Less quickly*) Simply press the lever on the left. You see? (*He replaces the brush beneath the guillotine.*)

MILLET:   Perfectly. Right for the blade, left for the neck brace.

CURATOR   (*turning towards the right-hand door*): Good, now are you coming, because I have some other visitors through here . . .

LECARDON:   Don't worry about us. We're waiting for somebody.

CURATOR:   Right, I'll leave you then. If you want to catch up with us, it's straight ahead. But remember, don't touch anything!

LECARDON:   What do you take us for? We have been to the Louvre, you know! (*Curator leaves by the right-hand door.*)

MILLET:   So what's all this about? It's jolly nice here!

| | |
|---|---|
| LECARDON: | Yes, this rendezvous is another one of Palmyre's ideas. |
| MILLET: | Well, she's always game for a laugh, your girlfriend. |
| LECARDON: | What do you expect? She's a very well-read lady. So she's always on the look-out for new thrills. She wants to make love in the most unlikely of locations. Oh, I've had to do it in some pretty weird places, I can tell you. |
| MILLET: | Well, if I were you, I'd finish with her. |
| LECARDON: | I've often considered it. This is no way to carry on, after all. But I'm afraid she'll resort to a bottle of acid. And this idea of making love by the guillotine! Oh, when she saw the poster announcing this new attraction at the Daumier Museum, she didn't hang about. And here we are—our usual meeting time and on the same day as the grand opening. I'm just glad that you're here. Maybe we'll be able to spend the whole time talking. Whatever happens, don't leave me! |
| MILLET: | You can count on me, old boy. (*Noticing Kate, still motionless*) Look, a lady! |
| LECARDON: | Don't be daft, it's a joke. It's just a wax mannequin that's been sat on a bench. |
| MILLET | (*walking behind the bench*): Yes, but I bet you that her legs are made of wood. |
| LECARDON: | Let's have a look. (*He lifts Kate's skirt a little, which causes her to cry out with all her might.*) |
| KATE: | Help! (*She flees to the exit, crying, 'Help, help!' and then she turns around and shouts contemptuously.*) Pervert! (*She exits right.*) |
| LECARDON | (*to Millet*): She meant you, old boy. |
| PALMYRE | (*entering left*): I've kept you waiting, darling . . . |
| LECARDON: | Oh no, no. Allow me to introduce my friend Millet, a travelling salesman—surgical supplies. Madame Palmyre, Letocard, my girlfriend . . . |
| PALMYRE: | Charmed, I'm sure. |
| LECARDON: | I met him quite by accident here at the museum. |
| PALMYRE: | Have you come to see the latest attraction? |
| MILLET: | Certainly, Madame. |
| PALMYRE | (*crossing the stage, Lecardon follows*): Ah, here it is, the famous guillotine. |
| LECARDON: | Yes, here it is. |
| PALMYRE: | I'd imagined it to be somewhat larger. |
| MILLET: | I think it's quite large enough. |
| LECARDON: | How about going for a drink? |
| PALMYRE: | Oh no, it's far too much fun here. |
| LECARDON | (*hiding behind Millet*): She's planning something. Don't leave me. |
| MILLET: | Don't worry, old boy. |
| PALMYRE: | Ah! This dungeon! (*Facing the guillotine*) This dismal machine, with its menacing blade, gleaming . . . what a perfect spot for making love. |

| | |
|---|---|
| LECARDON | (*to Millet*): Here we go! |
| PALMYRE | (*to Millet*): Oh, M. Millet, the joy of exchanging caresses in strange and atmospheric corners! My friend, M. Lecardon, and I love that. |
| LECARDON: | Yes, she loves that. |
| MILLET: | There's no accounting for taste. |
| PALMYRE: | If you only knew of some of the delightful spots that have borne witness to our kisses. One day we had a cosy cup of tea in the catacombs! |
| LECARDON: | Yes, we were surrounded by piles of bones. |
| PALMYRE: | And another time, thanks to one of our friends who is a charge nurse at the hospital, we had a candlelit dinner for two on the dissection table in the operating theatre. |
| MILLET: | Charming! |
| LECARDON: | Isn't it just? |
| PALMYRE: | And then there was the time we had high tea in the furnace at the crematorium. |
| MILLET: | No? |
| LECARDON: | Yes! |
| PALMYRE: | Not to mention our little get-togethers at the morgue . . . |
| MILLET: | You *are* a right pair! |
| PALMYRE: | But none of those places is equal to this. Oh, this guillotine, shuddering as it was gripped by these murderers in their final moments. (*To Lecardon*) Doesn't it do anything for you? |
| LECARDON: | It tells me I should get out of here. |
| PALMYRE: | You're such a baby! (*To Millet*) He can be so childish. |
| LECARDON: | I'm really not in the mood. |
| PALMYRE: | Look, we haven't come here just to whisper sweet nothings to each other. (*Millet has sat down on the bench.*) |
| LECARDON | (*quietly*): What, in front of Millet? |
| PALMYRE | (*quietly*): We'll get rid of him when . . . |
| LECARDON: | But what about all the other people? |
| PALMYRE: | Just keep an ear open for the sound of footsteps. Quickly, kiss me. |
| LECARDON: | Millet, do you mind? |
| MILLET: | Go right ahead. |
| | (*Lecardon embraces Palmyre.*) |
| PALMYRE: | Do you not find this dungeon rather sensual as well, M. Millet? |
| MILLET | (*standing up*): Good God, Madame, I prefer something a little more comfortable. |
| PALMYRE | (*walking between the two men*): More comfortable? That's all very well for common or garden lovemaking (*to Lecardon*) but we prefer something different, don't we, dear? |
| LECARDON: | Just like this, in fact. |
| PALMYRE: | Come, make love to me! |
| LECARDON: | Let's go over here on the bench. |

PALMYRE:  No, there, in front of the guillotine. (*She turns around pensively.*) I've just remembered a little story about the guillotine. It happened just after the Revolution and an aristocrat and his lover were arrested together at the border and were to be guillotined at the same time. When the man, who was to be executed first, had his neck in the brace, the young woman escaped from the soldiers who were guarding her and, before the executioner had time to release the blade, she kissed her lover on the lips . . .

MILLET:  Brrr.

PALMYRE:  The judges were so impressed by this display of love that they granted her clemency.

LECARDON:  So much the better.

PALMYRE:  She became a famous courtesan and lived to a ripe old age. And shortly before she breathed her last, she told the nurse that of all the kisses she had given and received throughout her wanton life, the most disturbing and the most fulfilling was that one all those years ago when she tasted the mouth of her lover as he was decapitated!

MILLET:  Some women have some strange perversions, that's for sure!

PALMYRE:  Perversion? Come now! It appeals to the artist in me. (*To Lecardon*) You understand that, don't you?

LECARDON:  Yes, I understand! (*To Millet*) Leave it, eh?

PALMYRE:  Ah! Everything is in place for a sensual experience. You know what you now have to do?

LECARDON:  Leave?

PALMYRE:  No . . . you must put yourself in the machine, put your head through here (*indicates the neck brace*) and then offer me your lips.

MILLET:  What?

LECARDON:  Oh no, please!

PALMYRE:  You're not refusing me?

LECARDON:  But what do you expect to gain from all of this? For a start it would be a sham.

PALMYRE:  I have my imagination. I shall imagine that you are an aristocrat condemned to death, M. Millet will be the executioner and you must try to believe that the blade will actually fall.

LECARDON:  No, no, it's all too complicated.

PALMYRE:  Listen, don't refuse me, or else!

LECARDON  (*to Millet*): The acid! (*To Palmyre*) Can we go immediately afterwards?

PALMYRE:  Oh, all right then.

LECARDON  (*to Millet*): Do you think I should give in?

MILLET:  That would be my advice.

LECARDON  (*to Palmyre*): All right then, but let's be quick about it. I'll just put my head through here! (*He takes off his hat and places it on the bench, then lies down on the guillotine.*)

| | |
|---|---|
| PALMYRE: | Oh, you're so sweet! |
| LECARDON: | Brrr. (*He lowers himself in order to place his head in the neck brace, but he leans on the board by mistake, which wobbles and the neck brace shuts sharply on his neck.*) Ah! |
| PALMYRE: | Oh, this is perfect! A detachable collar! |
| MILLET: | The final cry! |
| PALMYRE: | That's exactly it! Oh, my darling. (*She kisses him on the lips.*) Oh, more . . . more . . . Imagine the blade is going to fall . . . I love you . . . I love you. |
| LECARDON: | Good, that's enough now. Millet, get me out of here. Press the button to release the neck brace. |
| MILLET: | The one on the left. (*He approaches.*) |
| LECARDON: | No, the one on the right. |
| MILLET: | No, old boy, I'm sure the curator said the one on the left. |
| LECARDON: | Don't touch it! That one's for the blade! |
| PALMYRE | (*smiling*): You really should have been listening, you know. |
| MILLET: | Perhaps if I pressed both of them. |
| LECARDON: | Stop messing about! |
| MILLET: | Come on, admit it, you're pulling my leg! |
| PALMYRE: | Isn't this exciting? |
| LECARDON: | Me pulling your leg!? That's a good one! What if the blade comes crashing down? |
| PALMYRE | (*taking hold of his head*): I'll catch your head. |
| LECARDON: | You're mad! |
| PALMYRE: | I'll never forget you. But I will have had the experience of a lifetime. |
| LECARDON: | This is what comes of stupid stories. Quick, go and fetch the curator. |
| PALMYRE: | Just stay there a moment. If only you knew how beautiful you look! (*To Millet*) Doesn't he look beautiful like that? |
| MILLET: | He certainly doesn't look bad! |
| LECARDON: | For God's sake! Get a move on! Aren't you going to look for the curator? Very well. (*He shouts*) Help! Help! |
| PALMYRE: | Oh, what a lot of fuss about nothing! |
| LECARDON: | Help! Help! |
| MILLET: | You've got no patience, that's your trouble. |
| CURATOR | (*entering from the right*): What's going on here then? |
| LECARDON: | Over here my good man! |
| CURATOR: | Right. Well you've got a nerve, interfering with the exhibits. |
| LECARDON: | It was an accident. |
| CURATOR: | That's what they all say. |
| PALMYRE: | I can explain, Monsieur . . . |
| CURATOR | (*approaching the guillotine*): I'm not interested in any excuses, love. (*To Lecardon*) Right, come on then, let's have you out of there. |
| LECARDON: | I can't. |
| MILLET: | The neck brace is locked. |

CURATOR:    The neck brace? Let's have a look then. (*He tries to open it by fiddling with the right-hand lever.*) You're right.

MILLET:    Open it then!

CURATOR    (*trying the lever*): Out of the question.

ALL:    What?

CURATOR:    You've made a right mess of things. The mechanism is completely buggered.

LECARDON:    What did you say?

CURATOR:    Just wait a moment.

PALMYRE:    Oh, he's not rushing off anywhere.

CURATOR    (*to Millet*): Look, since you're a friend of the condemned man, could you go and find the fellow who installed the machine. He's upstairs busy seeing to the Emperor of Russia who's started to crack up.

MILLET:    With pleasure. (*He exits left.*)

PALMYRE    (*wiping the sweat from Lecardon's brow*): Come on, calm down. You're making a lot of fuss about nothing.

CURATOR:    I ought to report you for this.

INTERPRETER    (*to the English tourists who are entering right*): And now, let us go to the first floor.

CURATOR    (*going to the left*): On the first floor, where we are now going, we have all the politicians.

INTERPRETER    (*approaching the Curator*): I see you've got an actor in.

CURATOR:    An actor? Oh, what a good idea!

PALMYRE:    An actor!

CURATOR    (*to the Interpreter*): Tell them there is a supplement of ten sous to see the torment of the condemned man as he awaits the executioner who has forgotten his handkerchief.

INTERPRETER:    Now you're talking! (*Taking his place in front of the tourists, he adopts a solemn air and takes off his hat.*) Hats down, please! (*Matthews and the tourists remove their hats. A deathly silence. Pointing towards Lecardon.*) That's a new and quite sensational sight. Here we see a poor fellow about to be put to death.

LECARDON:    What's he talking about?

INTERPRETER:    Shut up! Let me finish! (*To the tourists*) He is still waiting for the executioner who has forgotten his handkerchief. (*Changing his tone*) Ten sous supplement, if you please. (*The tourists pay.*)

LECARDON:    What's going on? This is simply too much! (*He gets worked up and they watch him.*) Are they paying to see me humiliated like this? That curator's an utter rogue! You idiots! Oh, just wait until I get out of here . . .

TOURISTS:    Bravo! Bravo! Encore!

MATTHEWS:    Bravo! Very funny!

KATE:    Yes, indeed.

TOURISTS:    Bravo! Hurrah!

LECARDON:    This is too much. I'm going to complain to the police!

INTERPRETER   (*in stitches, to the tourists*): <u>I'm sure you have never seen such a sight in England.</u>

CURATOR:   Ladies and Gentlemen. It is a sight seen nowhere else in the world.

PALMYRE:   Well no, it's quite unique!

TOURISTS:   <u>Bravo! Bravo! Encore! Hurrah! Hurrah!</u>

KATE:   <u>Excellent! Hurrah!</u>

PALMYRE:   Oh, what are you pulling such a face for?

LECARDON:   You, Curator! I'm going to inform the authorities about this.

CURATOR   (*turning towards him*): You don't say?! But it wasn't me who shoved you in there. You musn't touch the exhibits. The rules expressly forbid it.

LECARDON:   Are you going to let me out of here at all?

CURATOR:   You'll have to wait for the workman to arrive. Your friend can sort it all out. (*To the tourists*) Let us proceed to the politicians. (*He exits left, followed by the Interpreter and the tourists.*)

PALMYRE   (*moving to the left*): You know, that wasn't very polite of you.

LECARDON:   What? What wasn't polite?

PALMYRE:   Being so bad-tempered and grumpy like that.

LECARDON:   I see. You think it's funny that I'm like this?

PALMYRE:   Well, you couldn't say that it was boring. Just think, your neck is caught in the very neck brace that made Pranzini and Carrara squeak.

LECARDON:   I'm not exactly thrilled by the thought.

PALMYRE:   It's no wonder I get annoyed with you. Nothing excites you— you've got no imagination.

LECARDON:   No imagination?! Can you wipe my nose?

PALMYRE   (*wiping his nose with her handkerchief*): Yes. And this isn't the first time I've noticed it. Just the other day at the crematorium . . .

LECARDON:   There was a terrible burning smell.

PALMYRE:   Ah! I'm beginning to think that we're incompatible.

LECARDON:   Me too!

LECARDON
AND PALMYRE:   Oh!

ERNEST   (*entering left*): Good evening, Monsieur, Madame. (*To nobody in particular*) Your friend has gone to get my adjustable spanner from the caretaker. (*Noticing Palmyre*) My wife! What are you doing here?

PALMYRE   (*hiding Lecardon from him*): What about you?

ERNEST:   Well, they called me out to do some adjustments . . .

PALMYRE:   Do you know anything about this kind of thing then?

ERNEST:   Not really, but a locksmith is only a kind of mechanic and I know all about that.

PALMYRE:   You're not angry then?

ERNEST:   But you haven't told me your side . . . Well, you can tell me later. (*He is about to go the guillotine.*) I'd better free the victim.

PALMYRE    (*trying to prevent him*): There's no hurry.

ERNEST    (*getting past*): Fancy getting stuck in there. (*He bends down to see Lecardon's face.*) Good Grief! Lecardon!

LECARDON:    I'm afraid so.

ERNEST:    Lecardon! Now I get it! You've brought my wife to the museum . . .

LECARDON:    It's not true!

ERNEST:    Of course it is! I know all about it . . . you are Palmyre's lover!

PALMYRE:    Ernest, please . . .

ERNEST:    Shut up! (*To Lecardon*) Do you know what I'm thinking?

LECARDON:    I'll confess to everything, I swear.

ERNEST:    You see, I'm thinking that there is a god, after all!

PALMYRE:    Ernest!

ERNEST:    Oh yes, in the name of God, there is one! And he is great! And he is just!

LECARDON:    Why do you say that?

ERNEST:    Why? Because he has delivered you completely helpless into my hands. What a fine gentleman you are, physically fit and strong, every inch an ex-wrestler. You stole my wife, the woman I love, do you hear?

PALMYRE:    Ernest.

ERNEST:    Shut your trap! You took her from me and that's no laughing matter. I tell you, you're going to repay me for all I've suffered!

PALMYRE:    Ernest.

ERNEST:    Shut it! You see, I only have to press the lever here . . . (*He mimes it.*)

LECARDON:    Don't touch it! You'll cause an accident!

ERNEST:    Precisely. An accident, a little clumsiness. Punishment for you, exoneration for me.

PALMYRE:    You wouldn't do that?

ERNEST:    Who is there to stop me?

PALMYRE:    But Ernest, I can't believe you'd do such a thing—this is quite unlike you.

LECARDON:    I've got some money on me. Perhaps we could come to some arrangement?

PALMYRE:    Oh, the coward! He must be frightened if he's thinking of parting with his money.

ERNEST:    Keep your money, Monsieur! What do you take me for?

PALMYRE:    Well said, Ernest!

ERNEST:    I am not like you. (*Moving to stand in front of the guillotine*) I am a gentleman, Monsieur. Do you not believe me? (*He slaps him about the face.*) Ah! Do you insult me? (*He slaps him.*) You swine! (*Again*) Bastard! Look at you. Not much of a wrestler now, eh?

LECARDON:    Just wait till I get out of here!

ERNEST:    Really? Very well, in that case you will die. (*He puts his hand on the lever.*)

| | |
|---|---|
| LECARDON: | No! No! I'm sorry! |
| PALMYRE: | Don't be so spineless! |
| ERNEST: | He says he's sorry and he thinks that that's enough. But my life is ruined. You have stolen the heart of my wife! |
| LECARDON: | Me? I haven't laid a finger on her heart. We've just been fooling around a little together, that's all. |
| ERNEST: | Whatever you say! I know she doesn't love me anymore . . . |
| PALMYRE: | What makes you think that? |
| ERNEST: | Your behaviour. |
| PALMYRE: | Listen. I never really knew you. But certain things have happened that have made me realize that I've always loved you. |
| LECARDON: | There, you see! |
| ERNEST: | Lies! |
| PALMYRE: | No, it's the truth! I'd already realized that Lecardon was not the man I thought he was. |
| ERNEST: | Palmyre, you're having me on. If I forgave you, it would start over again next week. |
| PALMYRE: | I'm having you on? Watch this! (*To Lecardon*) Have you got all my letters with you? |
| LECARDON: | Yes. In the inside pocket of my jacket—on the right-hand side. |
| PALMYRE | (*taking them from the pocket and handing them to Ernest*): Here you are, Ernest. Here is proof of my infidelity. With these you could drag me through the courts. Take them and if I am ever unfaithful to you again . . . |
| ERNEST: | Very well, I must see these . . . |
| LECARDON: | I say, I'm a little uncomfortable down here . . . |
| ERNEST: | Wait a minute. I want to have a look at these. (*He reads the letters.*) Ah! How you thought you loved him! Those delicious little encounters you had together. |
| LECARDON: | Oh yes, quite delicious! |
| ERNEST | (*hand on the lever*): Exactly—delicious! (*Lecardon shuts up. To Palmyre.*) Why couldn't I have made love to you in the crematorium? |
| PALMYRE: | I didn't know you were into that sort of thing? |
| ERNEST: | You bet! That's really something! |
| PALMYRE: | Ah! If only I'd known before! And to think he used to get annoyed about it! |
| ERNEST: | Annoyed? What a swine! |
| LECARDON: | I say! |
| ERNEST | (*advancing towards him*): What? (*Hand on the lever.*) |
| PALMYRE: | I swear it's all been a misunderstanding. |
| ERNEST: | A terrible misunderstanding. |
| PALMYRE: | In that case, kiss me and let's be done with it. |
| ERNEST | (*passionately*): Palmyre! |
| PALMYRE | (*passionately*): Ernest! (*They embrace.*) |
| ERNEST | (*caressing her on the bench*): Together again! |
| LECARDON: | Watch my hat! |

| | |
|---|---|
| MILLET | (*entering left and approaching Ernest*): Here's your spanner! |
| PALMYRE: | Ah, M. Millet! Let me introduce you to my husband . . . M. Letocard. M. Millet, a friend. |
| MILLET | (*saluting*): Monsieur! |
| ERNEST: | Delighted to meet you! |
| LECARDON: | Millet! The spanner for god's sake! |
| PALMYRE: | You know, M. Millet, I have been reconciled with my husband. Lecardon—well, that was all a misunderstanding. |
| MILLET: | Ah! Really? |
| ERNEST: | Absolutely. (*He embraces his wife. They remain seated on the bench.*) |
| LECARDON: | All right, everybody's had a good laugh at my expense! Now, release me for god's sake! |
| CURATOR | (*returning from the left*): What, is he still shouting his mouth off? It's outrageous! |
| INTERPRETER | (*following closely behind the tourists, to the Curator*): Excuse me, old boy, there's a gentleman here who would very much like to see this gentleman's head cut off, and he's prepared to offer you one pound sterling for it. |
| CURATOR: | How much is one pound sterling? |
| INTERPRETER: | Twenty-five francs. |
| CURATOR: | It's a deal! (*To the tourists*) Gentlemen, you are now going to see an execution. |
| PALMYRE AND MILLET: | No? What!? |
| INTERPRETER | (*to the tourists*): <u>This man is going to be beheaded.</u> |
| TOURISTS: | <u>Really? How splendid! Capital!</u> |
| CURATOR: | Attention please, the blade is about to fall. One, two, three . . . (*The blade falls.*) |
| LECARDON: | Oh, my head, my head! |
| CURATOR | (*lifting the neck brace*): It's still attached to your shoulders, you idiot! The blade is made out of silver-coloured cardboard. (*Lecardon climbs out of the guillotine. Palmyre throws herself into his arms.*) |
| INTERPRETER | (*to the tourists*): <u>It is a joke, the knife is made out of cardboard.</u> |
| PALMYRE | (*to Lecardon*): Ah! My darling, for a moment you were in the grips of death, but from now on, we will live life to the full— together! (*The curtain falls on a scene of confusion. The Curator can be heard saying to the tourists, <u>'What about my twenty-five francs? What about my twenty-five francs?'</u> An argument follows. Palmyre passionately embraces a resigned Lecardon. Ernest is tearing out his hair, comforted by Millet.*) |

THE END

# Tics, or Doing the Deed

## (Après Coup! . . . ou Tics, 1908)

*by*

RENÉ BERTON

## Preface

René Berton's *Après Coup! . . . ou Tics* premiered at the Théâtre du Grand-Guignol on 28 April 1908 and was revived as late as 1939, and is an excellent example of a Grand-Guignol sex comedy. The desperate pursuit of adultery in a cosy country residence represents a ruthless satire on bourgeois morality. This is particularly highlighted when, although the middle-class husbands betray their wives and vice versa, the only true victims in the play are the servants. The play fulfils the formula of farce: the establishment of a situation that is complicated and finally resolved. Moreover, the play is fast-paced and makes significant use of innuendo and slapstick. The physical demands of the piece are very evident: the performers playing Doctor Martin, Monsieur Ernest de Merliot and Adrian need to master the tics, and all the characters need to make the entrances and exits slick and comical. A production of this play demands skills more associated with, for example, *commedia dell'arte* than horror theatre.[1]

Interestingly enough, *Tics* exploits the same kind of material as the horror plays. One of the central characters is a doctor, the most beloved professional of the Grand-Guignol.[2] In addition to the numerous doctors in horror plays, another comically unethical doctor is in Élie de Bassan's *Les Opérations du Professeur Verdier* (1907) where a surgeon has lost his prized golden tweezers and finds excuses to re-operate on numerous patients in the hope of retrieving them. The dysfunctional marriage of the Martins highlights the themes of jealousy and vengeance: qualities seen in other Grand-Guignol relationships. Even the tell-tale tics are

---

[1] Pierron argues that Grand-Guignol emanates, in part, from popular theatre traditions such as the commedia dell'arte (see Pierron 1995, XLVI–XLVIII) with its use of violence and the grotesque for comic and subversive effect. Certainly, elements of the medieval carnivalesque and Bakhtin's notion of 'grotesque realism' (Bakhtin 1984, 18) can be found within the Grand-Guignol.

[2] Berton himself, like Maurice Level, was a doctor before becoming a writer.

reminiscent of the recurrent madness that so often rises to the surface with such speed in horror plays in the repertoire. In addition, the anxieties revealed in the piece, the themes of betrayal, guilt, and the overall sense of violating moral laws (in that fine naturalistic tradition of human animals) belong to the same territory as the horror plays.

It is interesting that the author's other play included in this volume is a later work, *Euthanasia*, which also involves doctors and moral decisions: this time to do with the rights and wrongs of mercy killing, rather than whether to cheat on your spouse.

# TICS, OR DOING THE DEED

*(Après Coup! . . . ou Tics, 1908)*

*by*

RENÉ BERTON

---

Docteur Martin
Madame Henrietta Martin
Monsieur Ernest de Merliot
Madame Genevieve de Merliot
Adrian, the Martin's servant
Venus, the Martin's servant

---

*(The action takes place in the Martins' country residence.)*

*(Dr Martin sits in an armchair reading a newspaper while Mme Martin embroiders.)*

MME MARTIN: I think it's safe to say that our guests are not coming.

DR MARTIN: It's nearly five o'clock . . . but they still might get here.

MME MARTIN *(Sarcastic)*: I *do* hope it's not in the least *inconvenient* for you?

DR MARTIN: Well, I won't lose sleep over it.

MME MARTIN: No—just your temper.

DR MARTIN: Well to be honest it is rather taxing to arrange a meal and your guests don't turn up . . . I mean the Merliots did promise to join us this evening—oh they will, they will, they've probably just had a flat tyre or something. Automobiles are such *infernal* inventions, you can never be sure of arriving anywhere! *(Silence)*

MME MARTIN: What do you think of Monsieur de Merliot?

DR MARTIN: I think he's a most charming man.

MME MARTIN: The only thing you find charming about him is . . . his wife!

DR MARTIN: As if I would say such a thing!

MME MARTIN: I'm not worried about what you might *say*—I'm worried about what you might *do*!

DR MARTIN: My poor dear, you really are quite deranged.

MME MARTIN: I can see it only too clearly—you're besotted with her.

DR MARTIN: I find her rather enchanting, that's all.

MME MARTIN:    Enchanting!? She's common . . . she's vulgar . . . she's ugly . . . she plasters her face with make-up like an . . . an actress . . . Huh! I'd like to see her first thing in the morning! She'd be ever so pretty then—absolutely hideous more like!

DR MARTIN:    She's got beautiful hair.

MME MARTIN:    Give me two hundred francs and I'll get myself a lovely hairdo like that.

DR MARTIN:    Her mouth is extremely well formed—wouldn't you agree?

MME MARTIN:    Do you know what she was just before she got married?

DR MARTIN:    Engaged?

MME MARTIN:    Oh you fool . . . She worked down the market selling cotton! That's where that idiot found her—and if that wasn't bad enough—he married her, a count, a *count* no less marrying a silly little girl from down the market!

DR MARTIN:    Marriage is like fire—it purifies everyone, absolves one's past.

MME MARTIN:    Ha! Indeed!

DR MARTIN:    I have no interest in what Madame de Merliot did before marriage, but I know that her conduct now is absolutely beyond reproach.

MME MARTIN:    Beyond reproach? She cheats on him whenever his back is turned!

DR MARTIN:    There's a mean streak in you, spreading such rumours . . .

MME MARTIN:    One of their old servants told me . . . so it must be true—and it's obvious really.

DR MARTIN:    How come?

MME MARTIN:    It is very clear that she has one of those *temperaments* . . .

DR MARTIN:    Carry on.

MME MARTIN:    Obviously her husband doesn't notice a thing . . .

DR MARTIN    (*laughing*): Perfect!

MME MARTIN:    You think it's perfect, do you!?

DR MARTIN:    No . . . it's amusing . . . hilarious, in fact!

MME MARTIN:    I'm a fool to tell you these things—it only makes you more intrigued . . .

DR MARTIN:    I think you rather like the thought of that—

MME MARTIN:    If you ever tried anything on with her . . . I'd have to get my own back. It would absolutely disgust me of course, but I would *force* myself to—

DR MARTIN:    Henrietta, my dear, do calm down. I would never put you in the *appalling* situation where you'd be *forced* to commit adultery.

MME MARTIN:    Good. I should think not!

DR MARTIN:    But tell me, dearest Henrietta, you seem *terribly* well informed about all our neighbours . . . is there anything you *don't* know? (*Car horn honks in distance.*)

MME MARTIN:    There's, er, so little going on out here in the country that I . . . I think it's good to find out what everyone else is up to. (*Car horn honks again.*)

| | |
|---|---|
| DR MARTIN: | Here they are! |
| MME MARTIN: | Remember what I said—an eye for an eye! |
| DR MARTIN | (*laughing*): A hump for a hump—understood! |
| | (*The de Merliots enter.*) |
| DR MARTIN: | Hello my dear Madame, Monsieur . . . |
| MME DE MERLIOT: | Doctor, Madame . . . |
| MME MARTIN: | Welcome, welcome! |
| M. DE MERLIOT: | Hello, old boy! So sorry we're rather tardy. |
| DR MARTIN: | Did you break down? |
| MME DE MERLIOT | (*snidely between her teeth*): Very, very nearly— |
| M. DE MERLIOT: | Yes! A flat tyre, just a couple of miles away. |
| MME DE MERLIOT: | And he stalled the engine *three times*. |
| DR MARTIN | (*laughs*): Driving is obviously a most delightful pastime! |
| MME DE MERLIOT | (*charming*): We would've been *devastated* not to have dined with you. |
| DR MARTIN: | Please, please sit down—you must be quite worn out. |
| M. DE MERLIOT: | It'll be wonderful to sit down on something that's not moving! (*Sits on a rocking chair*) *Christ*! |
| DR MARTIN: | Please—sit on this chair instead. |
| M. DE MERLIOT: | I don't own an automobile—it's more like taking a ride in a bloody coffee grinder. (*He shakes for effect.*) |
| DR MARTIN: | Are the roads bad at the moment? |
| M. DE MERLIOT: | They are *atrocious*! My whole body's aching from the journey! |
| MME MARTIN: | Do you enjoy travelling by automobile, my dear? |
| MME DE MERLIOT: | I find it most agreeable. Of course, I don't drive myself, but I really do enjoy a jolly good *ride*. |
| MME MARTIN: | I'm sure you do. |
| M. DE MERLIOT: | So, Doctor, how are you—or more's the point, how are your patients! (*Roars with laughter.*) |
| DR MARTIN: | Actually, it's rather quiet at the moment—it's harvest time, so the peasants simply don't have time to be ill! |
| M. DE MERLIOT: | I must say you are the member of a most *fascinating* profession. I mean sometimes the job must be tedious and unhygienic even, but there must be some consolation . . . when you have to conduct a little examination, for instance . . . of, let's say, a beautiful young lady . . . what-oh, eh! |
| MME MARTIN: | Monsieur de Merliot! |
| MME DE MERLIOT: | Ernest! Do you mind!? |
| M. DE MERLIOT: | Sorry, Madame, just a little joke . . . All the same, it must be quite 'amusing' to be able to say to a woman without thinking twice 'Take your clothes off'! |
| DR MARTIN: | Well, it's not always . . . |
| MME MARTIN | (*indignant, to Mme de Merliot*): Would you like to freshen up, my dear? Why don't you come up to my room and powder your nose? |
| MME DE MERLIOT: | Yes please—let's leave these men to their *horrid* conversation. (*The women retire.*) |

| | |
|---|---|
| M. DE MERLIOT: | Your wife doesn't seem to find my sense of humour to her taste. |
| DR MARTIN: | She doesn't like me talking shop. |
| M. DE MERLIOT: | Does she get jealous? |
| DR MARTIN: | Only about as jealous as Othello. |
| M. DE MERLIOT: | Oh dear.<br>(*Enter Venus the maid, a grubby and rather uncouth country lass.*) |
| VENUS: | Madame de Merliot has sent me to find 'er little handbag what she has lost. |
| DR MARTIN: | It's over there. Don't just grab hold of it with your grubby hands—lift it up by the strap! |
| VENUS: | Ooh—I got one just like it m'self—I takes it to church wi' me. (*Exit*) |
| M DE MERLIOT (*disgusted*): | Is that your maid? |
| DR MARTIN: | She just comes over now and then to help the cook. |
| M DE MERLIOT (*horrified*): | She helps the cook . . .? |
| DR MARTIN: | Don't worry—she just does the washing-up! |
| M. DE MERLIOT: | She does the washing-up . . . |
| DR MARTIN: | Out here in the country you just can't get the staff. In fact, we were pleased to find Venus— |
| M. DE MERLIOT: | Venus!? |
| DR MARTIN: | Yes—Venus, as in Aphrodite, Goddess of Love, all that— |
| M. DE MERLIOT: | Thank God fashion sense has changed since those pagan days. If every woman looked like your Venus the human race would be facing extinction. |
| DR MARTIN: | Well that's just where you're wrong, old chap. Every fellow in the village is after her. |
| M. DE MERLIOT: | No!? |
| DR MARTIN: | I know you find her quite repugnant . . . but I don't know what it is—she seems to bewitch everyone . . . Adrian, my manservant, has even gone so far as to propose to her. |
| M. DE MERLIOT: | I suppose she might have some hidden charms. |
| DR MARTIN: | But where she's hidden them I can't imagine. |
| M. DE MERLIOT: | I honestly wouldn't know! |
| DR MARTIN: | Neither would I! |
| M. DE MERLIOT: | Tell me, dear boy, now we're on the subject and are . . . alone . . . I would like to ask for your professional opinion on something. (*Dr Martin is clearly irritated.*) Please don't think I'm abusing our friendship by trying to sneak in a little impromptu consultation—Heaven forbid!—but I'd like to tell you about a most bizarre, um, *condition* and I'm desperate to know what you think. |
| DR MARTIN (*resignedly*): | Very well—I'm all ears. |
| M. DE MERLIOT: | Good . . . it's about myself, and I think I should come straight out with it and not beat around the bush . . . but it's an extremely delicate matter . . . rather embarrassing to describe . . . |

| | |
|---|---|
| DR MARTIN: | Come on, man, out with it. |
| M. DE MERLIOT: | It's something very personal, very intimate—and I'm not sure how to put it into words . . . |
| DR MARTIN | (*smiles*): Oh I *see* . . . (*imitates a stalling engine and then cheerily declares*) Honk! Honk! |
| M. DE MERLIOT: | What? |
| DR MARTIN | (*winking*): A 'flat tyre'! |
| M. DE MERLIOT: | Are you alright? |
| DR MARTIN: | Yes . . . you've had a 'flat tyre' . . . you've stalled your engine . . . |
| M. DE MERLIOT: | I know I've had trouble with my automobile but we got here in the end. |
| DR MARTIN: | No, no—problems with shall we say *Venus*— |
| M. DE MERLIOT: | Venus!? That dreadful maid—how dare you! |
| DR MARTIN: | Cupid!? |
| M. DE MERLIOT: | I'll be damned if I know what you're talking about. (*Dr Martin whispers in his ear.*) |
| M DE MERLIOT | (*laughs*): Oh no, it's not that! Not that at all! But it is that sort of region if you know what I mean. But nothing like that—not that serious . . . just extremely embarrassing. |
| DR MARTIN: | I cannot possibly guess *what* the problem is. |
| M. DE MERLIOT: | Well, it's this . . . My God, it's so difficult to put it into words! It's this . . . I don't know how to make myself understood . . . well, it's . . . No! I can't say it. It's too embarrassing . . . you have no idea how embarrassing it is . . . I've never dared to see a doctor about it—ridiculous, eh? |
| DR MARTIN: | Well, old chap, sometimes consultations are more like confessionals. |
| M. DE MERLIOT: | Yes, quite. What I have to tell you is a confession. In short, this is it. I'm married, as you know, and naturally I sleep with my wife like everyone does— |
| DR MARTIN: | Eh? |
| M. DE MERLIOT: | What? |
| DR MARTIN: | Nothing—carry on. |
| M. DE MERLIOT: | Sometimes we . . . we chat . . . know what I mean? |
| DR MARTIN: | Perfectly. You often seem to stop mid-sentence—do you lose your train of thought? |
| M. DE MERLIOT: | Not at all! I am a perfect speaker . . . but if I try to speak after an act of *intimacy*, you know, after 'doing the deed', I don't know what happens—some attack of nerves or anxiety . . . I want to speak, but all I do is stutter. |
| DR MARTIN: | Eh? |
| M. DE MERLIOT: | I can't talk like I do normally . . . I just stammer, uncontrollably—please don't laugh. |
| DR MARTIN: | Sorry—do continue—I'll explain later . . . |
| M. DE MERLIOT: | It's such a bloody nuisance! When I'm with the wife it's not so bad—I just roll over and fall asleep . . . but when I'm with another woman, it is *most* embarrassing. |

DR MARTIN: I can understand that.

M. DE MERLIOT: And most women seem to have a bloody obsession with talking at that very moment! They decide to ask all sorts of questions . . . they ask if you're happy, if you enjoyed it. It's difficult to *ignore* questions like that.

DR MARTIN: Yes, of course—so what do you do?

M. DE MERLIOT: I become mute. I try and give them the impression that it was so absolutely marvellous I've lost the power of speech.

DR MARTIN: That's brilliant!

M. DE MERLIOT: But it's *so* embarrassing—I frequently change mistresses—but it always happens, without fail . . .

DR MARTIN: And how long does this affliction last?

M. DE MERLIOT: Precisely ten minutes.

DR MARTIN: How extremely bizarre.

M. DE MERLIOT: What's wrong with me?

DR MARTIN: Difficult to explain . . . an over-excitement of the nervous system . . . The very moment it's about to happen, put your feet into a bowl of hot water with some mustard in it.

M. DE MERLIOT: You expect me to have a foot-bath when I've just . . . How very convenient!

DR MARTIN: Well, wrap a mustard poultice around your thighs.

M. DE MERLIOT: Is that the best you can do?

DR MARTIN: I have to say that for such afflictions there is not a vast array of available treatments.

M. DE MERLIOT: Pah! That's typical of bloody doctors! They can cure colds and migraines—but when it comes to something a little more serious, they admit they're *impotent*!

DR MARTIN: If you were a little bit more impotent yourself, old chap, you'd be free of your little inconvenience.

M. DE MERLIOT: How dare you! I cannot be denied my pleasure—it's when I feel most like a man . . . despite my affliction.

DR MARTIN: I will study your case.

M. DE MERLIOT: It would be some consolation if I just didn't feel so dreadfully alone—

DR MARTIN: You're not. Rest assured. In fact, I know of someone else— that's why I was laughing earlier. He suffers with a similar affliction to you.

M. DE MERLIOT: Good heavens! And I thought I was the only one! Who is this fellow?

DR MARTIN: A friend of mine—a captain in the army. His case is very similar to yours except that rather than stuttering his right leg trembles uncontrollably.

M. DE MERLIOT: Good grief! And does he find it rather embarrassing?

DR MARTIN: Oh extremely. Happily it afflicts him worst when he's standing up—when he's sitting or lying down it's virtually imperceptible.

M. DE MERLIOT: Does it last a long time?

| | |
|---|---|
| DR MARTIN: | Rather like your case—ten to fifteen minutes. |
| M. DE MERLIOT: | I'd love to meet him. We could talk together—without any shame! A captain, eh? I'm sure he's a fine chap. |
| DR MARTIN: | I'll introduce you at the first opportunity. |
| M. DE MERLIOT: | I look forward to it. Anyway—nothing can be done for me? |
| DR MARTIN: | Not really. |
| M. DE MERLIOT: | Oh well—ssh! I can hear the wife! It's pointless trying to discuss the little infirmities of the human condition with her. |
| DR MARTIN: | Quite. |

(*Enter Mme de Merliot.*)

| | |
|---|---|
| MME DE MERLIOT: | Your wife sends her apologies—she's deep in conversation with the cook. |
| DR MARTIN: | Oh what a blessed nuisance servants can be! |
| M. DE MERLIOT: | You can say that again. |
| MME DE MERLIOT: | Really? Actually, Doctor, I wanted to ask you something— |
| M. DE MERLIOT: | No, no, my dear—I hope you're not going to pester our friend for an impromptu consultation—that'd be such an abuse of— |
| DR MARTIN: | I'd be delighted. |
| M. DE MERLIOT: | Oh come off it, old chap—you're exaggerating. I absolutely hate people who think that when they meet a doctor it's an excuse to prattle on about their pathetic little ailments. |
| MME DE MERLIOT: | I have no intention to ask for a consultation—I'm not ill, thank God! |
| DR MARTIN | (*aside*): What a shame . . . |
| MME DE MERLIOT: | But I do think that doctors are the most interesting people. |

(*Enter Adrian.*)

| | |
|---|---|
| DR MARTIN: | What is it? |
| ADRIAN: | The gentleman's chauffeur would like a word, sir. |
| M. DE MERLIOT: | Very well—would you excuse me? |
| DR MARTIN: | But of course. (*Exit M de Merliot.*) That really is a most enchanting dress, Madame. |
| MME DE MERLIOT: | Yes—not bad, is it. You know, Doctor, I can't discuss this in front of my husband, he'd mock me, but for some time I've felt a little bit under the weather. |
| DR MARTIN: | You don't look unwell. On the contrary, you look the very picture of health . . . vivacity— |
| MME DE MERLIOT: | Yes, so everyone tells me. But what upsets me is that I have a tendency to put on weight. I want to be slimmer. |
| DR MARTIN: | That *would* be a shame. |
| MME DE MERLIOT: | You see, Doctor, I want to have a figure— |
| DR MARTIN: | You do, Madame, believe me, you do . . . A terrific figure . . . and I know plenty a man who'd willingly—er, who'd agree with me. |
| MME DE MERLIOT: | Give me something to lose weight. |
| DR MARTIN: | A treatment? All you need is some exercise . . . some physical activity . . . |

| | |
|---|---|
| MME DE MERLIOT: | Exercise? |
| DR MARTIN: | Yes, like walking. |
| MME DE MERLIOT: | I'm always walking—I walk as much as I can possibly bear—I walk from the bedroom to the lounge, to the garden . . . I'm always walking, walking, walking. |
| DR MARTIN: | And how do you feel afterwards? |
| MME DE MERLIOT: | Horribly tired. My legs get worn out, my back aches. |
| DR MARTIN: | Well you should give your legs—and your back—a good firm rub. Every fatigued part of you . . . rub it. Massage is excellent. But of course men do it best. They're stronger, more . . . vigorous. Especially when you're in expert hands—like a doctor's for instance . . . If you like, Madame, I could demonstrate the correct technique you should use for rubbing yourself . . . |
| MME DE MERLIOT: | You're really too kind. There's another thing. I sometimes get a little palpitation in my heart. |
| DR MARTIN: | Shall I get my stethoscope? Or I could simply press my ear against your chest . . . (*He does so.*) |
| MME DE MERLIOT: | Ooh—you're pressing rather hard—you'll squash me! |
| DR MARTIN *(aside)*: | Good God, they're firm. |
| MME DE MERLIOT: | Well? |
| DR MARTIN: | Well what? Oh yes—it sounds fine. |
| MME DE MERLIOT: | Seriously Doctor—is there anything wrong with my heart? |
| DR MARTIN: | Nothing, Madame—nothing at all. |
| MME DE MERLIOT: | Oh God, and I've been so worried! |
| DR MARTIN: | You have no idea how happy I am to be alone with you, what pleasure it gives me just to look at you, to hear the sound of your voice! Madame, you are a most exquisite creature! |
| MME DE MERLIOT: | An exquisite creature with a few little maladies—I find digestion rather difficult . . . |
| DR MARTIN: | Have a glass of water with Epsom salts before you go to bed . . . If only you knew how I have to put up with so many ugly and vulgar people—imagine how I feel looking at you! |
| MME DE MERLIOT: | One glass a night you say? |
| DR MARTIN: | Yes, one glass . . . I want to make you understand . . . |
| MME DE MERLIOT: | What about food? Is there anything I should avoid? |
| DR MARTIN: | Yes, yes, I'd recommend you avoid a few things . . . You are so tantalising, so exquisite . . . no one can match you, no one can touch you! |
| MME DE MERLIOT: | Potatoes, for instance . . . I've been advised against them; I adore them as they are, with nothing on. |
| DR MARTIN: | You eat them with nothing on, you say? |
| MME DE MERLIOT: | I had some this morning and I knew I'd be in trouble—and sure enough my stomach swelled up. |
| DR MARTIN: | Your stomach . . . May I? (*Puts his ear to it*) Yes, it is a bit swollen . . . |

| | |
|---|---|
| MME DE MERLIOT: | What should I do? |
| DR MARTIN: | I must have a look—I must examine you most thoroughly . . . but here's not the best place . . . Come to my study . . . I'll give you a complete physical and you can tell me *all* your problems . . . |
| MME DE MERLIOT: | You really think I need a complete physical? |
| DR MARTIN: | Perhaps we'll find something serious—come along for your own sake . . . (*aside*) and mine! (*Adrian enters just as the Dr Martin and Mme de Merliot are entering the study.*) |
| ADRIAN: | Sir! |
| DR MARTIN: | What the hell is it? |
| ADRIAN: | It's about the wine for supper, sir. |
| DR MARTIN: | I am about to commence a consultation so please . . . *bugger off*! (*Slams the study door.*) (*Enter Mme Martin.*) |
| MME MARTIN: | What do you want? |
| ADRIAN: | What wine would you like served at table this evening? |
| MME MARTIN: | I don't know about that sort of thing—ask my husband. |
| ADRIAN: | The master's just commenced a consultation. |
| MME MARTIN: | Where? |
| ADRIAN: | In his study. |
| MME MARTIN: | Did a patient turn up? |
| ADRIAN: | The lady who arrived this afternoon. |
| MME MARTIN: | Madame de . . .? I see. Very well—wait until he's finished. |
| ADRIAN: | Right you are, Madame. (*He exits.*) |
| MME MARTIN: | Ha! A 'consultation' indeed! With that little slut! (*Enraged*) Typical! Well just you wait, my dear—you'll see . . .! (*She looks out the window.*) Ah, Monsieur de Merliot! (*She undoes the top of her dress and sits in the rocking chair with her legs revealed.*) |
| M. DE MERLIOT: | Hello, Madame. How come you're alone? |
| MME MARTIN: | I'm not—now that you're here. |
| M. DE MERLIOT: | There's a most impressive view from here. |
| MME MARTIN: | Yes . . . beautiful. (*Silence*) |
| M. DE MERLIOT: | It's very warm . . . |
| MME MARTIN: | Yes, stifling . . . That's why I've put my feet up as you can see . . . Please excuse me . . . |
| M. DE MERLIOT: | Oh Madame, I insist . . . |
| MME MARTIN: | Ah! |
| M. DE MERLIOT: | What is it? |
| MME MARTIN: | Something fell down the back of my dress! A caterpillar—oh it's horrible. |
| M. DE MERLIOT: | Probably just a sycamore seed—they're coming down at the moment and no doubt the wind . . . |
| MME MARTIN: | I don't know what it is but it's ghastly . . . it's so itchy . . . I don't know how to get at it . . . |

| | |
|---|---|
| M. DE MERLIOT: | If I may, Madame, I could get it out for you—it'd be very easy . . . |
| MME MARTIN: | Oh yes, yes, please do. (*He obliges.*) There—in the middle . . . lower . . . Haven't you got it? |
| M. DE MERLIOT: | No . . . oh yes . . . I do believe I have . . . Good heavens! It really is low down—in fact it's pretty much stuck! |
| MME MARTIN: | Agh! That hurts! You're yanking on something but it's not a sycamore seed! |
| M. DE MERLIOT: | Terribly sorry, Madame—I thought it was what we're after! |
| MME MARTIN: | Ooh! It's slipped—it's right down my corset now! |
| M DE MERLIOT | (*suddenly rather excited*): Your *corset*? If you want I could continue my search there . . . |
| MME MARTIN: | It's alright thank you very much—I'll get it later . . . tonight, when I slip my clothes off I'm sure it'll just pop out! |
| M. DE MERLIOT: | (*flustered*): When you slip your clothes off . . . (*His whole body jerks.*) |
| MME MARTIN: | My God, you're agitated—what's wrong? |
| M. DE MERLIOT: | Wrong? I'm a little . . . a little nervous . . . (*abruptly*) Where's my wife? |
| MME MARTIN: | I do believe Madame de Merliot's gone for a stroll in the garden . . . |
| M. DE MERLIOT: | I'll join her. |
| MME MARTIN: | And leave me all alone? |
| M. DE MERLIOT: | I really, really must talk to my wife. |
| MME MARTIN: | I'll call Adrian—he can convey your message for you. |
| M. DE MERLIOT: | No, no! Only I can say what I have to say to, er, my wife. |
| MME MARTIN: | Surely it can wait until my husband's finished his consultation. |
| M. DE MERLIOT: | The Doctor's busy? Will he be long? |
| MME MARTIN: | Very, very long. |
| M. DE MERLIOT: | Oh my God. (*He hastens across the room and looks out the window.*) Is that your greenhouse? |
| MME MARTIN: | There? Yes. |
| M. DE MERLIOT: | Is it good? |
| MME MARTIN: | Marvellously humid. |
| M. DE MERLIOT: | I'm sure that you grow quite wonderful flowers there. |
| MME MARTIN: | Indeed. At the moment I have a truly superb collection of peonies. |
| M. DE MERLIOT: | Oh, Madame, I absolutely *adore* peonies. |
| MME MARTIN: | Come on then—I'll show you (*They dash out. The study door opens and the Doctor sticks out his head and looks around.*) |
| DR MARTIN: | My wife's not around . . . Perfect! Come on, my darling! (*Mme de Merliot enters, adjusting her dishevelled hair. The Doctor's right leg shakes.*) Well, my dearest? (*Silence*) Aren't you going to say anything? |
| MME DE MERLIOT: | You monster! |

| | |
|---|---|
| DR MARTIN: | Oh I'm a monster now am I? |
| MME DE MERLIOT: | You took advantage of a vulnerable young woman . . . |
| DR MARTIN: | You are *so* gorgeous I just had to—(*His right leg goes wild.*) |
| MME DE MERLIOT: | Is that some sort of tic? |
| DR MARTIN: | What? Oh *this*? Yes, yes, a tic . . . it's nothing really . . . |
| MME DE MERLIOT: | Are you quite sure? |
| DR MARTIN: | Nothing at all (*stamps his foot aggressively*). You see—it's stopped now. Everything's fine now. (*It starts again worse than ever.*) |
| MME DE MERLIOT: | Quite . . . Why not walk around a bit—maybe that would help? |
| DR MARTIN | (*sits*): If it's alright by you, I'd rather sit down. (*Aside, looking at his watch*) Ten minutes! I'll be fine in ten minutes! What a drag! Genevieve, please, sit down. (*She sits.*) You can rest assured that I will never forget that moment of passion—it was over too quickly, alas! |
| MME DE MERLIOT: | At least it's calmed down now. |
| DR MARTIN: | What? Oh—my leg? Yes, yes, it's fine now. I will never forget that *encounter* . . . |
| MME DE MERLIOT: | Was it good for you? |
| DR MARTIN: | How can you even ask? It was so good I'm literally wild with—(*He stands and his leg shakes madly.*) |
| MME DE MERLIOT: | Agh! It's back! |
| DR MARTIN: | Sorry! (*Sits down*) I'm like a ravenous man in a tremendous restaurant—I've had a delicious *hors-d'oeuvre* and then I'm dragged, screaming, from the table! |
| MME DE MERLIOT: | You fancy your main course? |
| DR MARTIN: | Main course, dessert, cheese and crackers! |
| MME DE MERLIOT: | You've got a big enough appetite for all that? |
| DR MARTIN: | I have an *enormous* appetite—I am, as they say in Italy, a very good *fork*! |
| MME DE MERLIOT: | That really is most interesting . . . let's continue our little supper— |
| DR MARTIN: | At once, Madame! |
| MME DE MERLIOT: | No—later. Could you pass my handbag please? |
| DR MARTIN: | Your bag? |
| MME DE MERLIOT: | Yes, it's on the table behind you. |
| DR MARTIN | (*anxious*): With pleasure . . . (*He stands up and his legs shake so much he is forced to sit down again. He tries to clamber over the back of the sofa—he reaches it and passes it to Mme de Merliot.*) |
| MME DE MERLIOT: | Are you in training for an assault course? |
| DR MARTIN: | Yes, that's right! And here I am—back in one piece! Ha! (*Enter Adrian.*) What is it!? |
| ADRIAN: | What wine would you like served at table this evening, sir? |
| DR MARTIN: | Wine? Some burgundy and champagne . . . always champagne . . . But you don't have the key to the cellar . . . I'll come with you. (*He stands and his leg shakes.*) |

|  |  |
|---|---|
| ADRIAN: | Is your leg alright, sir? |
| DR MARTIN | (*enraged*): *Will you bugger off*! |
| MME DE MERLIOT: | Why don't you support yourself on my arm? |
| DR MARTIN: | Oh thank you, Madame. |
| MME DE MERLIOT: | What *is* wrong with your leg? As a doctor you must— |
| DR MARTIN: | I don't know—it's simply idiotic! It suddenly came upon me again just then. I must have bashed my knee or something. (*Dr Martin exits on Mme de Merliot's arm. Adrian remains, watching the Doctor with fascination. Enter Venus with some flowers. Adrian grabs her from behind.*) |
| VENUS: | You gave me a fright! |
| ADRIAN: | You're gorgeous—I love you! |
| VENUS: | Ooh, you ain't half a sweet talker! |
| ADRIAN: | I don't know what it is but something's in the air today—it must be love! Venus, my sweetheart, I love you! Come on . . . (*Tries to drag her away.*) |
| VENUS: | You old rogue—you just want a bit of how's-your-father! |
| ADRIAN: | Come on, Venus—I promise I'll marry you after harvest time! |
| VENUS: | You're always saying that! But you'll change your mind soon enough! |
| ADRIAN: | I swear—I *will* marry you! |
| VENUS: | Oh, my lover! |
| ADRIAN: | Oh, my Venus! (*They rush off.*) (*Mme Martin enters, rearranging her hair. M de Merliot comes on a moment afterwards looking very sheepish. He looks at his watch desperately.*) |
| MME MARTIN: | Well? (*M de Merliot busies himself to avoid speaking.*) Cat's got your tongue? That's not very nice of you, is it. |
| M. DE MERLIOT: | Bu- bu- bu- |
| MME MARTIN: | What? |
| M. DE MERLIOT: | Bu- bu- bu- |
| MME MARTIN: | What nonsense is this? |
| M. DE MERLIOT: | No- no- no- |
| MME MARTIN: | What on earth is wrong with you? You're speechless? Oh I see! My poor, poor boy . . . You must be in such suffering . . . How about a little word with my *husband* . . . He could give you something to calm you down. (*M de Merliot shakes his head desperately.*) No? Are you sure? On your own head be it. (*Unperceived Dr Martin enters, his leg shaking wildly, and dashes to the rocking chair and immediately acts nonchalantly. He coughs and Mme Martin and M de Merliot turn in shock.*) |
| MME MARTIN: | Ah, my dear! You're here. |
| DR MARTIN: | As you can see. |

(*M de Merliot looks for somewhere to hide—he heads with resolve towards the garden.*)

MME MARTIN: I thought I would go for a little stroll around the garden.

DR MARTIN: By all means, my dear. I'm going have a little rest myself . . . I'm a little tired . . . Wild horses couldn't tear me away from my favourite chair! Haha! (*He reaches over and grabs M de Merliot.*) Where you going, old chap? (*M de Merliot sits down solemnly and looks at his watch.*) Cigarette?

MME MARTIN: No! smoking disagrees with Monsieur de Merliot—he doesn't like the taste.

DR MARTIN: Doesn't like the taste? On the contrary, he is an extremely heavy smoker! (*M de Merliot looks at Mme Martin desperately then sags back into the chair.*) Speechless, eh? (*Enter Venus, her hair wildly disarrayed.*)

VENUS: Do you want your tea 'ere or in the lounge?

MME MARTIN: In the lounge . . . And please, my girl, do *something* with your hair . . . Have a bit of *grace*.
(*Exit Venus. Mme Martin follows her.*)

DR MARTIN (*watches Venus exit*): I see . . . Honestly old chap—you have no taste at all! Doing it with that common little scrubber! You really do have a *voracious* appetite to resort to dear old Venus! (*He leaps up, slaps a relieved-looking M de Merliot on the shoulder. M de Merliot relaxes and laughs and then notices the Doctor's leg. Momentarily M de Merliot's own leg shakes and he points at the Doctor's.*) What? Oh it's nothing. (*Doctor flings himself into the chair.*)

M. DE MERLIOT: Y- y- you f- f- fraud! *You're* the c- c- captain!

DR MARTIN: What captain? Oh, yes alright—*I am* . . .

M. DE MERLIOT: Who w- w- were you with in in in your st- st- st-

DR MARTIN (*embarrassed*): Who?

M. DE MERLIOT: Y- y- yes—wh-

DR MARTIN: With . . . with Venus!

M. DE MERLIOT: Th- th- th- that's *disgusting*!

DR MARTIN: Well, old chap—hidden charms! But I do believe the ladies are waiting for us in the lounge . . . Let's partake of a little tea.

M DE MERLIOT (*looking at his watch*): W- wait—t- t- two minutes!

DR MARTIN: I'll find out if it's ready (*Considers standing but then stays put*) Adrian! (*Silence*) Where is he? (*Dashes across room from chair to chair and rings the bell. Enter Adrian.*)

DR MARTIN: Is tea being served? (*Silence*) Is tea being served? (*Silence*) Answer me when I'm addressing you!

ADRIAN (*into his handkerchief*): Woof! Woof!

DR MARTIN: You're barking like a dog—stop this horseplay!

ADRIAN: Can't, sir, woof! Woof!

DR MARTIN: I order you to stop this impertinence at once!

ADRIAN: It's not impertinence, sir, it's a tic! Woof!

DR MARTIN: A tic? What nonsense are you talking about?

ADRIAN: When my mother was pregnant with me she was attacked by a rabid dog—woof, woof—and whenever I've been doing the deed—woof, woof—I bark—woof, woof!

M. DE MERLIOT: That's very fu- fu- funny!

DR MARTIN: Do you mean to tell me you've been doing the deed-

ADRIAN: Yes sir, just now woof, woof . . . but I've promised to marry her woof, woof!

DR MARTIN: Who did you—

ADRIAN: Venus, woof, woof!

DR MARTIN: Venus!? That's absolutely disgusting! I give you a week's notice. (*To M de Merliot*) Can you believe it? Under this very roof!? It is nothing short of an outrage! (*Enter Venus.*) You too—you're fired!

VENUS (*bursts into excessive tears*): Oh God, oh God!
(*Enter Mme Martin and Mme de Merliot.*)

MME MARTIN AND
MME DE MERLIOT: What *is* going on!?

DR MARTIN: Nothing! Nothing at all! Please—how about we all have a nice cup of tea! (*Dr Martin stands and his leg goes wild, M de Merliot stammers, Adrian barks and Venus howls with tears.*)

THE END

# In the Darkroom

## (Sous la lumière rouge, 1911)

*by*

### MAURICE LEVEL AND ÉTIENNE REY

## Preface

Maurice Level and Étienne Rey's *Sous la lumière rouge* was first performed at the Théâtre du Grand-Guignol on 9 May 1911, but had previously existed as a short story by Level (translated by Alys Eyre Macklin as 'In the Light of the Red Lamp' in *Crises: A Volume of Tales of Mystery and Horror* (1920)). The theme of premature interment has been a recurrent motif in classical culture (see Steiner 1984) and is a theme that has had a special place in both traditional ghostlore and the literary horror tale. It is, of course, a recurrent obsession for Edgar Allan Poe in tales like 'The Premature Burial', 'The Fall of the House of Usher' and many others.

Level's short story is a much more succinct and simplified version. Like many other of Level's short stories, there is a single climax to the piece: a specific and calculated moment of horror, almost like a punch-line. While the play tells the tale of Thérèse's death, the taking of the death-photograph, the realization that she has been buried alive and the subsequent exhumation which ultimately confirms their suspicions, the short story itself ends with the developing of the photographic negative, showing Thérèse with her eyes wide open. This is important as it makes a vital switch in where the horror is actually focused. In the short story, the fact that the reader is left with the closing image of Thérèse's open eyes means that the horror is focused on her as the victim and the terrifying fate that she is enduring at that very moment. By bringing the short story to closure at that point of realization, Level places the reader in Philippe's position. In the play the audience is distanced from Philippe by being transformed into observers of *his* torment. The horror is focused on Philippe and his ordeal, rather than on Thérèse who is at the end of the play revealed to be beyond help. This is typical of the Grand-Guignol which often focuses upon the psychological horrors of those onstage rather than the physical horrors endured by those offstage. This is another case of the importance of the centrality of the witness and is not dissimilar to the techniques used in *Au téléphone*. Just as in *Au téléphone* the horror is embodied within Marex having to 'witness' the brutal murder of his family at the other end of the telephone, so is the horror in *In the Darkroom* embodied within Philippe's torment as he waits for his suspicions to be confirmed. There are further similarities between the two plays. Both display a sense of modernist technophobia that has become a staple element in horror ever since.[1] In the same way that Marex is undone by his obsession with the telephone, so is Philippe's fate sealed by his unquestioning attachment to his camera and dark room. Both protagonists seek comfort, consolation, and even pleasure, in their 'mod cons'. Both characters, in this sense, are victims of modern technology and in both plays that technology acquires a central role in the proceedings, adopting the importance and status of a character in its own right, influencing or determining the course of events within the play. These events occur within a similar developmental structure, beginning in the domestic security of the main protagonist and then later transferring to a different location where he is 'distanced' from the physical horror.

In *Au téléphone* the milieu of the play is undeniably middle-class and underpinning the play is a critique of bourgeois values. The same could be said of *In the Darkroom*. Once again the setting is one of bourgeois domesticity, and the values the characters espouse reflect this. Although his profession is never revealed, there is little doubt that Philippe is a man of means, as is his friend, Didier. Apart from the gravediggers in the final act, the only working-class character in the play is that of Thérèse herself and it is this relationship between Philippe and Thérèse that is particularly revealing.

Thérèse is a minor actress whom Philippe has introduced to the comforts and securities of a middle-class lifestyle, even though there is a strong sense of irony that these bourgeois trappings cannot rescue her from her terrible fate. The many references to her youth[2] and her child-

---

[1] Noteworthy examples of films that use telephones for horrific effect include Wes Craven's *Scream* series (1997 onwards) or *Rabid* (David Cronenberg 1976) where a latter-day Marex similarly hears his wife murdered at the other end of a telephone. Another example in recent film is Mike Tarnower's controversial *15 Minute Tape* (1999). The majority of this short film is presented—like *The Blair Witch Project* (1999)—as 'found footage' which has inadvertently recorded a rape and murder of a pregnant woman in her own home. Tarnower's film is a conscious tribute to the Grand-Guignol form in its duration and in its disturbing mixture of the violent, the erotic and even, in the film's last few moments of ironic self-deconstruction, humour. Perhaps the greatest achievement of the film, however, is the way in which it taps into contemporary technophobia: not only does the private nature of the camcorder footage leave the viewer with an uncomfortable feeling of voyeurism and collusion, but we feel a sense of horror at the indifference of the camcorder as it impassively chronicles the death of its 'owner'.

[2] According to Philippe, when giving the information to the doctor in Act 1, Thérèse was aged twenty, although according to the nameplate on her coffin (Act 3) she was merely nineteen.

like qualities suggest that Philippe is a much older man and although there is no firm evidence to suggest that she has prostituted herself to him, or that their love for each other is anything but genuine (Philippe's obsession with Thérèse is certainly without ambiguity), there is perhaps suggested an inequality in their relationship which borders on the pornographic. It is a suggestion that is further enhanced by the continual references to photography throughout the play, from the costumed photographs of Thérèse that Philippe keeps in a drawer to his description of their excitement at developing their holiday pictures. Even the death-photograph has a manipulative and voyeuristic feel to it. The macabre sexuality of the play can be further highlighted if we remind ourselves of the central horrific event in the play and then turn to Sigmund Freud:

> To some people the idea of being buried alive by mistake is the most uncanny thing of all. And yet psychoanalysis has taught us that this terrifying phantasy is only a transformation of another phantasy which had originally nothing terrifying about it at all, but was qualified by a certain lasciviousness—the phantasy, I mean, of intra-uterine existence.
>
> (Freud 1985, 366–67)

In Level and Rey's play, Thérèse, the object of Philippe's lasciviousness and sexual fantasy, is transformed into the object of the most uncanny and terrifying fantasy imaginable. The transformation of Thérèse, combined with Philippe's journey from unthinking lust (virility) to knowledgeable impotence (castration), gives an increased resonance to his display of inconsolable guilt.

The idea of the photograph, or at least the still image, as an agent of revelation of horrific events, is one that has a long history in horror writing, as in M.R. James's short story 'The Mezzotint' (1904) where an antique engraving changes its composition to reveal a tragic series of events, or Oscar Wilde's classic *The Picture of Dorian Gray* (1891). It is also an idea that is echoed in the film *Dead of Night* (Robert Hamer et al. 1945), in which the characters in the film retell a series of ghost stories (structured in a distinctly *douche écossaise* pattern *à la* Grand-Guignol), one of which concerns a haunted mirror that reflects the scene of a horrific murder. When it comes to the specific use of photography for uncanny effect in film we may also think of *Les Diaboliques* (Henri-Georges Clouzot 1954) where a photograph reveals the face of the presumed dead Delassalle (Paul Meurisse). Such examples exploit the supernatural potential of 'imaging', most immediately recognizable in the form of photography: from the Cottingley Fairies to the present day, there have been many examples of the camera (that ultimate tool of realism) revealing 'unexplained' images.

At the end of *In the Darkroom* there is a concerted effort to prove to Philippe that his photograph is such an example of the inexplicable. Level's intention, however, is to demonstrate that the camera does indeed never lie and the horror of his story is that the photograph captures, with dreadful accuracy, the terrible *fact*. A later example of the manipulation of photographic horror is *Blow-Up* (Michelangelo Antonioni 1966) where a photographer (David Hemmings) only realizes in the darkroom that his idle snapshots in a city park have, in fact, captured a murder. As fine a thriller as Antonioni's film is, it is not as disturbing as the original short story it is based on (Julio Cortazar's 'Las babas del diablo', 1959) where the photographer realizes that the three figures incidentally caught on his camera are not, as he thought, two parents and their child but rather two paedophiles and their victim. The story leads us through the central character's horror in the darkroom (the moment, like Philippe's, of realization), and the subsequent psychological journey through guilt and remorse (like Philippe's failure to notice at the time). Ultimately this becomes fear, most acutely in the male paedophile's gaze directly into the camera ('the man . . . was looking at me with black holes he had in place of eyes, surprised and angered . . . wanting to nail me . . .' (Cortazar 1967, 130)). The paedophile—like Thérèse—is frozen for eternity in a snapshot. But such a gaze works both ways: they similarly trap or 'nail' the viewers in what Jean-Paul Sartre would call the petrifying gaze of the Medusa. Both Cortazar and Level's protagonists are trapped forever as unconscious—and thus impotent (to think of Freud once more)—witnesses.

*In the Darkroom* is also interesting for the way it portrays the medical profession, a common concern of many Grand-Guignol plays. Here, although his actions lead directly to the death of Thérèse, the doctor is neither the psychopathic sadist of the stage versions of *Le Cabinet du Dr Caligari* (1925) or *Les Yeux sans visage* (1962), nor the deluded, obsessed scientist of *L'Horrible Expérience* (1909). Rather he is merely guilty of the same kind of bourgeois arrogance and self-righteousness as displayed by Leduc in *The Kiss of Blood*. In fact, although Legeron is clearly guilty of professional negligence, there are, he claims, mitigating circumstances. His protest that the sheer volume of work expected of him by the state prevents him from conducting thorough examinations of corpses seems to carry a degree of social comment that would have resonance today: when members of the medical profession are overworked, then mistakes which lead to tragedy are the inevitable consequence. Although there is no suggestion that Legeron is exonerated by this, there is still a certain degree of sympathy for a man whose professional career has been ruined. It is a tribute to the dramatic irony of the play that at the end of the piece one is not sure whether the lie told to Philippe is cooked up in order to protect him from the truth of his lover's demise or is a cover-up to protect the medical and bureau-cratic establishment. One of the criticisms levelled at Legeron by the pathologist is that he confirmed Thérèse's death a mere five hours after it had been reported and that this may have been a contributory factor in the tragedy. It is suggested that, had he waited longer, Thérèse may have naturally woken from the comatose state in which she lay. His claims that due to overwork he always visited first those cases closest to his own home betrays a delicious irony. Thérèse, it would seem, was visited so early because Philippe's home lay in the same middle-class neighbour-hood as the doctor's. Had Thérèse been living in a working-class district, then her life might well have been saved by the late arrival of the doctor. Philippe's Pygmalionesque installation of Thérèse into a middle-class environment not only failed to prevent her death, but may have actually contributed to it.

It is evident that the changes which were made to the story during its adaptation to the stage have the effect of dramatically changing its meaning, with an increased level of social commentary and a shift in focus towards Philippe's horrific ordeal. These changes may have been made for largely pragmatic reasons, since the lengthening of the story makes for a more engaging piece of drama that exploits the pace and patterns of horror. The twists and turns in the dramatic plot transform Level's fine and yet one-trick story into a more complex narrative, ideal for theatrical exposition where the suspense ebbs and flows. This shift in focus may make greater demands on the actors, but is less demanding on the technical designer. This is not to say that design plays no role in the play. In fact, according to Pierron the opposite is true (1995, 440). The resources of the technical department were, it seems, concentrated on the set and lighting design. Pierron quite rightly points out that 'special effects at the Grand-Guignol are not just a matter of haemoglobin, liquid carmine or redcurrant jam. It is also about the choice of colour in the décor and the use of lighting' (ibid.).

# IN THE DARKROOM

*(Sous la lumière rouge, 1911)*

*by*

MAURICE LEVEL AND ÉTIENNE REY

---

Philippe
Didier
Doctor Legeron
The Pathologist
The Police Superintendent
The Undertaker
The Warden of the Cemetery
Gravediggers
Suzanne
Gertrude
Woman

---

## ACT 1

*(A study. Downstage right, a table covered in papers and books. In one corner of the table, a box camera. Stage left, a door with a curtain across it, a mirror over the chimney breast and a sideboard with the doors open. At the back, a heavy-curtained window and a double door. When the door opens, a bed can be seen with a figure stretched out on it, although everything is rather indistinguishable, being lit faintly by candles.*

*Next to the chimney, an armchair, in front of which is a small table with various knick-knacks and a vase of flowers. There are also flowers on the mantelpiece. Although the setting is sombre, the details of the room betray a woman's touch.*

*As the curtain rises, the stage is empty. The piano is being played softly, apparently coming from upstairs.*

*A bell rings. Suzanne enters by the door at the back and moves downstage a little. At the same time Gertrude, the maid, appears in the door on the left.)*

|                |                                                                                                             |
|----------------|-------------------------------------------------------------------------------------------------------------|
| SUZANNE:       | Go upstairs and ask if they'll stop playing . . .                                                           |
| GERTRUDE:      | Yes, mademoiselle. (*Holding out a silver plate*) Some letters which have just been delivered.               |
| SUZANNE        | (*putting the letters on the table*): Could you also leave the door open, so that nobody else need ring the bell. |
| GERTRUDE:      | Of course, mademoiselle. (*She exits. At the same moment a bell rings.*)                                     |
| SUZANNE        | (*irritated and going towards the door*): Who on earth is that?                                              |
| GERTRUDE       | (*reappearing*): There's a gentleman, who . . .                                                              |
|                | (*Before the maid gets a chance to finish what she was saying, the Undertaker enters.*)                      |
| UNDERTAKER:    | Madame, I would like to speak to M. Philippe Garnier.                                                        |
| SUZANNE:       | M. Philippe Garnier is not able to see anybody at present.                                                   |
| UNDERTAKER:    | It's a matter of great urgency.                                                                              |
| SUZANNE        | (*uncertain*): What is it about?                                                                             |
| UNDERTAKER     | (*presenting his card*): I am from Nicard and Faverot, Funeral Directors.                                    |
| SUZANNE:       | But somebody came half an hour ago.                                                                          |
| UNDERTAKER:    | Oh, not from Nicard and Faverot, Madame.                                                                     |
| SUZANNE:       | Quite possibly, I didn't take any notice . . .                                                               |
| UNDERTAKER:    | We are the premier undertakers in the whole of Paris and, if it were not for circumstances beyond our control, we would have been here two hours ago. |
| SUZANNE        | (*showing him to the door*): Monsieur, the deceased did not pass away until gone five . . .                  |
| UNDERTAKER     | (*obsequiously, but without moving*): I realize that, Madame, I realize that. The deceased passed away at twenty past six— we are precise about times at Nicard and Faverot. As I said, normally we would have been here before seven. |
| SUZANNE        | (*leading him to the door*): As I said, Monsieur, somebody has already been and . . .                        |
| UNDERTAKER:    | Ah, that's always so annoying . . .                                                                          |
| SUZANNE:       | Please, Monsieur, if you wouldn't mind . . .                                                                 |
| UNDERTAKER     | (*on his way to the door*): Of course, Madame, you have our card and if you change your mind, we would be happy to be at your service . . . |
|                | (*Suzanne accompanies him to the door. The Undertaker is heard saying 'Excuse me, Monsieur' and another voice replies, 'Excuse me', then the Doctor arrives in the doorway.*) |
| SUZANNE:       | Monsieur?                                                                                                    |
| DOCTOR:        | I am the doctor. The civic registrar.                                                                        |
| SUZANNE:       | Please, come in.                                                                                             |
| DOCTOR:        | I've just come to certify the death. Are you a relative of the deceased?                                     |
| SUZANNE:       | No, doctor. I'm just a friend.                                                                               |
| DOCTOR:        | Would you mind showing me to the body straight away? Might I also be able to speak to a member of the family? |

SUZANNE:    There's nobody here but her fiancé and myself. If you would care to take a seat for a moment, we'll just wash the body . . .

DOCTOR    (*very detached*): Oh, there's no need for that. I'm in something of a hurry.

SUZANNE:    I'll just go and tell her fiancé.

DOCTOR:    But please . . . it's a mere formality, very quick and straightforward.
(*Suzanne has opened the door at the back and said a few words to Philippe who can be seen sitting at the foot of the bed. She then re-enters.*)

SUZANNE:    Would you care to come in, doctor?
(*The Doctor goes in. The door is now wide open and the bed with the body on it can now be fully seen. The faintly burning candles throw a flickering light on proceedings.*)

DOCTOR    (*bending over the deceased*): Natural causes, I presume?

PHILIPPE:    Yes.

DOCTOR    (*pulls back the sheet, presses his fingers on her eyes, rests his head on her breast to listen, raises and then lets fall her arm*): Yes. One second. Monsieur, there is some paperwork . . . (*He returns into the study, followed by Philippe. He speaks to Suzanne as she begins looking for paper and a blotter.*) No, no, mademoiselle, we're in something of a hurry, just a pen will be fine. (*He produces a sheet of paper from his pocket and sits down.*) Name?

SUZANNE:    Thérèse Vaugeois.

DOCTOR:    Age?

PHILIPPE:    Twenty.

DOCTOR:    Profession?

PHILIPPE:    None.

DOCTOR:    Married?

PHILIPPE:    No.

DOCTOR:    When was she taken ill?

SUZANNE:    Two days ago.

DOCTOR:    And what's the name of the doctor she was under?

PHILIPPE:    I don't know . . . we just asked somebody from the local practice to come as quickly as possible.

SUZANNE    (*placing a sheet of paper on the table*): Here's the prescription he left.

DOCTOR    (*peering at the signature*): Ah, thank you. (*Whilst writing*) So, a very short period of illness . . . did the doctor tell you what she died of?

SUZANNE:    A form of meningitis.

DOCTOR:    And death occurred at?

PHILIPPE:    At six o'clock. This morning.

DOCTOR:    Very good. Right, I'll arrange for a coffin to be brought around tomorrow morning at about seven o'clock.

SUZANNE:    So soon?

DOCTOR:    The funeral itself can then take place at around midday. (*He rises.*)

PHILIPPE   (*very emotional*): So soon?!

DOCTOR     (*taking his hat*): It's for the best.

PHILIPPE:  But, Monsieur, why all the hurry?

DOCTOR     (*ready to leave*): Are you waiting for relatives?

PHILIPPE:  No, but . . .

DOCTOR:    Well, then, it will be for the best.

SUZANNE:   But he would like the body to stay here for a while . . .

DOCTOR:    No, Mademoiselle, absolutely not. We are in the grip of an epidemic. (*Pointing to the bedroom*) You see. In your own interests, in the interests of the whole community, we can't leave bodies unburied any longer than necessary. It's nothing unusual. I've been saying the same for every death I've had to deal with in the last couple of days and, God knows, there have been quite a few. Mademoiselle. Monsieur. (*Exits.*)

PHILIPPE   (*throwing himself into a chair*): Now they want to take her away from me.

SUZANNE:   It'll all be for the best . . .

PHILIPPE:  You as well!

SUZANNE:   But it's necessary . . .

PHILIPPE:  I won't have her any more! They'll take her from me! (*He goes towards the bedroom, stops, and turns back.*) I don't want to see anyone at the moment. There's only a few hours left.

SUZANNE:   And what if any of your friends come?

PHILIPPE:  Look after them, will you? But I don't want to see anyone. Besides, nobody will come.

SUZANNE:   But what about your friend Didier who you asked me to send the telegram to?

PHILIPPE:  Yes, there's him. But do you think he'll come? Is he even in Paris? No, Suzanne, nobody will come . . . (*A pause*) Just think, tomorrow after they've laid her to rest in the ground, I'll have to go out in the evening. And if I go out, then I'll have to come home, all alone, to an empty house. So you see, I want to look at her, to give her my complete attention, whilst she's still here!

SUZANNE:   I understand.

PHILIPPE   (*taking from the mantelpiece the letters that Gertrude brought in earlier, skims through them, then reads out loud, trying to stop himself from shaking*): 'My dear Thérèse. I shall come and pick you up next Thursday after lunch. We can go shopping and after that we'll go for a walk in the woods. Agreed? Gaby.' (*He sits down, crying.*)

SUZANNE:   Poor Philippe.

PHILIPPE:  Oh, it's all so unfair! (*All of a sudden, aggressively*) It's all my fault! I should never have left her for a moment and I should never have let her go and stay with you in the country! That's how she caught cold in the first place!

SUZANNE: But I looked after her as if she were my own sister . . .

PHILIPPE: I'm sorry. I'm just upset, that's all . . .

GERTRUDE: (*entering left*): Monsieur, it's . . .

PHILIPPE: (*interrupting her mid-sentence*): Nobody! I don't want to see anyone!

SUZANNE: (*to Gertrude*): Who is it?

GERTRUDE: Monsieur Didier.

PHILIPPE: (*lifting his head and with passion*): Didier? Ah, let him in! Let him in!

SUZANNE: You see, he hasn't let you down. I'll leave the two of you and go and sit by her. (*She exits at the back. At the same time Didier enters from the right.*)

DIDIER: My dear friend! (*They embrace.*)

PHILIPPE: It was good of you to come! I feel just awful . . .

DIDIER: It's terrible . . . I never thought for one moment . . . I was about to leave . . . When did it happen?

PHILIPPE: This morning at six.

DIDIER: But how? What was wrong with her?

PHILIPPE: I don't know. Nobody seems to know . . .

DIDIER: But last week, when we had dinner together, she didn't seem ill . . . a little tired, perhaps . . .

PHILIPPE: Her health was never wonderful, but to deteriorate like that in the space of forty-eight hours!

DIDIER: It's terrible. Quite terrible.

PHILIPPE: The funeral will be tomorrow. Three days ago we were making all kinds of plans . . . and now! It's not possible, just not possible! And her presence is all around the place! The flowers that she arranged, the book she was reading . . . there's her perfume . . . I can hear the sound of her dress rustling, her footsteps and her laughter, her childlike laughter. Oh, if you only knew how wonderful she was!

DIDIER: I know.

PHILIPPE: No, you can't possibly know, even knowing her as you did. You had to live with her to understand the happiness, the youthfulness, the joy she brought with her! When she walked into a room, all the joys of life came in with her . . .

DIDIER: That's right, I never once saw her in a bad mood.

PHILIPPE: Never. You see, we weren't like other lovers. There were never any quarrels or tears here. We hadn't a care in the world, a life full of joy and tenderness. We were so happy just spending time here together talking, as if we were an old couple, who'd loved each other all our lives, reminiscing . . .

DIDIER: And you were only together for two years . . .

PHILIPPE: But what a two years! How her life changed. And mine!

DIDIER:   True! She was no longer the young actress you saw that evening.

PHILIPPE   *(becoming perceptibly worked up as he remembers her, his voice becomes clearer, his gestures more precise, as if any second she will walk right in)*: Do you remember that evening? I can just see her in her red sequined dress, amongst all those ugly women. And her singing! Those harsh songs which she sang so beautifully!

DIDIER:   What a delicious little thing she turned out to be. How I envied you! I often said to you, 'Find me a little Thérèse of my own!'

PHILIPPE:   There are no other little Thérèses.

DIDIER:   So true! It was a month ago that I came here, depressed. You came back from the country.

PHILIPPE   *(pacing up and down as he speaks)*: I remember. She put flowers everywhere. When you came in she was sitting over there in the armchair. She didn't want you to go, you remember. She wanted to make you up a bed on the couch. She pretended to be one of those cabaret singers to make you laugh.

DIDIER:   And by the end I was laughing.

PHILIPPE:   How could anyone resist her infectious sense of fun? She was so full of life. She found fun in everything. Nothing was left untouched by her, no stone unturned. She turned everything upside-down.

DIDIER:   She was always at something.

PHILIPPE:   But she was so gentle with it. She couldn't keep still for one minute. She would come, she would go, one minute she was sitting down, the next she was by my desk. Then from the desk to the piano to the mirror, then back to me at the desk. *(With this last sentence he finds himself next to the door at the back, which he opens. The bed is visible.)* She's now still for the first time in her life. *(Pause)* Poor child! Look at her ... *(Didier approaches. For a moment they both stand still.)*

DIDIER:   She's so beautiful!

PHILIPPE:   Isn't she?

DIDIER:   And so young!

PHILIPPE:   Nothing but a child. Nothing but a small child.

DIDIER:   She's at peace. She's not suffering any more.

PHILIPPE   *(closing the door)*: Who knows for sure? *(He goes back towards the desk.)* What I'm going to say to you may seem terrible, but I'd rather she was ill for months than this.

DIDIER:   You don't mean that!

PHILIPPE:   Oh, but I do. If you have to watch the one you love suffering, you get used to the thought of their passing. You can at least say to yourself that they won't be in any more pain. But this ... in the fullness of life!

DIDIER:     It was all so unexpected.

PHILIPPE:   Exactly. And I always used to make such a fuss of her. I loved her, you know, like a husband loves his wife and as a father loves his child. I loved her because she was so vulnerable, I loved her because of all the worries she gave me, I loved her because she was my youth, my reason for living, my whole life . . . I loved her because I loved her! (*Voices can be heard in the corridor.*) What's going on out there?

GERTRUDE:   (*opening the door*): A package has been delivered.

PHILIPPE:   Give it here.

GERTRUDE:   (*embarrassed*): It's not for you, Monsieur. It is for . . . erm . . .

PHILIPPE:   For Madame? Give it to me. Here. (*Holding the package between his fingers*) A letter . . . there you are, you see, there are people who think she's still alive! (*He opens the package and takes out some lace collars, which he looks at for a while and then puts them back.*)

DIDIER:     (*to Gertrude*): Take them away.

PHILIPPE    (*to Gertrude*): No, leave them. (*To Didier*) I just want to be surrounded by her things. Nothing will bring her back, but just anything that will help me remember her. One can never forget the sad times, but the good times leave behind so few mementoes. Her memory is already becoming blurred. If I close my eyes I can scarcely see her. Later on, before very long, who's going to help me remember her?

DIDIER:     Everything will remind you of her. Your heart will remind you. When we speak about her, when you look at her photograph.

PHILIPPE:   I don't have any . . . at least only bad ones. (*He opens a drawer.*) This was her drawer. (*He unfolds a sheet of paper.*) The poor child . . . her last engagement. Newspaper cuttings . . . (*He reads.*) 'The young Yette—Yette was her stage-name—was the joy of this play . . .' (*Taking another cutting*) Maybe she wasn't hugely talented, but she was so alive . . . Oh, my God! (*He throws down the cuttings.*) These photographs . . . that's not her . . . that's not her. The least bad one . . . I didn't show it to her, it would have made her furious. She thought they made her so ugly . . . (*He puts them back into the drawer.*) In all of them she's in a stage costume. They're all so old.

DIDIER:     But I think they're very pretty.

PHILIPPE:   No . . . no, it's not her. What I would like . . . what I want, is her, just as she was at the end, just as she is now, her true self, in our house, in *her* house. Do you understand?

DIDIER:     But . . .

PHILIPPE    (*after a momentary pause*): Listen, and don't tell me I'm wrong. The idea had been tormenting me for the last three hours and normally I wouldn't dare even think it. A moment ago I was still uncertain. But now, having seen all those photographs again, and not seeing the real 'her' in a single one, I'm now quite sure. To have one like this (*showing a photograph*) is the same as not having one at all.

DIDIER: But it's a lovely picture . . .

PHILIPPE: It might have been yesterday, but not today. I want to see her as she is now, do you understand?

DIDIER: Yes, yes, I understand. But it will be such a morbid memento.

PHILIPPE: No.

DIDIER: So, you want somebody to come here and take a photograph?

PHILIPPE: Oh, there's no need. I have everything I need here . . . (*He points to the sideboard on the left.*) I simply need you to give me a hand. (*Pleadingly*) Will you?

DIDIER: All right, but let's be quick about it.

PHILIPPE: Yes, of course. We'll make sure we're not disturbed. Lock the door.

(*Didier locks the door.*)

DIDIER: You've got everything?

PHILIPPE: Everything.

DIDIER: The black cloth?

PHILIPPE (*who has opened the sideboard*): Here it is.

DIDIER: Flashpowder?

PHILIPPE: Yes.

DIDIER (*by the door at the back*): Ready?

PHILIPPE (*picking up the camera*): Open it.

(*Didier opens the door of the bedroom. Philippe enters it and positions the camera at the foot of the bed. Only Didier is visible.*)

DIDIER (*in hushed tones*): You will tell me . . .

PHILIPPE (*likewise*): Yes. Lift up the curtain. We need to create a shadow.

DIDIER: Like this?

PHILIPPE: Yes. And get rid of the flowers so that she doesn't look as if she's dead. Put out the candles . . . are you ready?

(*Didier removes the flowers and puts out the candles. A short silence.*)

DIDIER (*lighting a match and holding it to the flashpowder*): Ready.

PHILIPPE (*bending over, he takes a look at the corpse, then straightens up. Then in a dry, almost hard, voice*): Take it!

(*The room is lit with a bright flash of magnesium. The curtain falls very quickly.*)


## ACT 2

(*The same as in Act 1. As the curtain rises, the stage is empty. The day is ending and the stage room is dim. The door on the right opens and Philippe enters, followed by Didier and Suzanne. They have returned from the funeral.*)

*Philippe goes to sit down in an armchair. He is crying, his face in his hands. Didier and Suzanne silently watch him.)*

DIDIER    (*approaching him*): Philippe, my friend, be reasonable.
PHILIPPE: Reasonable? When she is down there, beneath the earth?
DIDIER:   You must be brave.
SUZANNE   (*to Didier*): He's exhausted. He hasn't had a thing for two days . . .
DIDIER    (*to Philippe*): You must eat something.
SUZANNE:  Have a bowl of soup . . .
PHILIPPE: In a moment . . . I'd just like to be alone for a little while. (*He takes off his overcoat.*)
SUZANNE:  I'll go and find you a change of clothes. (*She takes a step towards the bedroom door.*)
PHILIPPE  (*getting up*): I'll go myself.
SUZANNE:  Stay there, I'll . . .
PHILIPPE: Why?
SUZANNE   (*with some hesitation*): Nothing . . . it's just that room . . .
PHILIPPE: I'm going to have to go back in there sooner or later, aren't I? (*He pauses briefly in front of the door.*)
SUZANNE:  In any case, you're going to stay over at my place tonight.
PHILIPPE: No.
SUZANNE:  You're not staying here.
PHILIPPE: Yes, I am staying here. (*He exits into the bedroom.*)
SUZANNE:  He's a little calmer now.
DIDIER:   That's what worries me.
SUZANNE:  What do you mean?
DIDIER:   You never know what that calmness may be hiding.
SUZANNE   (*emotional*): Oh, you don't think . . .? Perhaps I'd better keep an eye on him.
DIDIER:   Yes, go and have a look.
          (*Just as Suzanne is about to enter the bedroom, Philippe appears in the doorway. He is carrying a jacket. He stops, very pale.*)
PHILIPPE: What are you looking at me like that for?
SUZANNE:  But . . . no . . . I'm not looking at you like anything . . .
PHILIPPE: It looked to me as if you were. (*He goes to the desk and rearranges the things, then sits down and opens one or two drawers. Didier and Suzanne watch him constantly.*)
DIDIER:   What are you looking for?
PHILIPPE: Nothing. (*He goes over to the sideboard, picks up one or two of the small medicine bottles, examines them and then puts them back.*)
DIDIER:   Do you want anything?
PHILIPPE: No, thank you.
SUZANNE:  Perhaps you should try and get some sleep?
PHILIPPE: Later. Please, I'd just like to be left alone for a short while.

DIDIER: Why do you want to be alone?

PHILIPPE: I just want to be alone.

SUZANNE: I don't think that's a good idea.

PHILIPPE *(nervously)*: Why not? I'm fine. You see, I'm perfectly calm.

DIDIER: I'm leaving Paris tomorrow. At least let me spend today with you.

SUZANNE: We'll all have dinner together here and then we'll leave you alone.

PHILIPPE: But . . .

DIDIER *(moving towards the door)*: I'll just send a message home that I'll be late.

PHILIPPE: Go on then.

DIDIER: Straight away. *(He leaves.)*

PHILIPPE: Tell me, who was that man who said hello to us as we came in just then?

SUZANNE *(innocently)*: I think he's a doctor.

PHILIPPE: Oh, no!

SUZANNE: I don't mean the doctor, but the one who came yesterday.

PHILIPPE: Ah yes, you mean the civic registrar. *(Pause)* Thank you, Suzanne. Could you go and see what the maid is up to or something.

SUZANNE: Is there anything you want?

PHILIPPE: No . . . I'm going to read . . . or perhaps sleep a little. *(Suzanne exits. Philippe, alone, slowly walks up and down. He looks all around him, opens a book, then closes it again. He takes a mirror from the table next to the armchair and looks at it for a long time.)* If only she was able to look into this mirror again! *(He replaces the mirror and opens the door at the upstage. The bedroom is tidy. He pauses briefly, motionless.)* What a sad place this is! *(He closes the door again and goes and stands by the fireplace and looks at the clock.)* So now you can count out the sad hours ahead! *(He picks up a photograph from the table and reads aloud the dedication.)* 'Yesterday, tomorrow, always.' Always! Look at me! That's not you . . . *(He drops the photograph.)* How things were different yesterday! *(He slowly goes towards the door, looks out, then closes the door. He then opens the window, closes the shutters and carefully closes the curtains. He goes over to the small sideboard, stage left, and takes out some basins and bottles, which he puts on the table. He takes out a desk lamp and plugs it in. The scene is only lit by the red bulb of the lamp which illuminates the table. Suddenly there is a knocking. Philippe stays completely still. The knocking continues and Philippe remains motionless. The sound of the door being tried and then the anguished voice of Didier.)*

DIDIER *(offstage, from behind the door)*: Philippe! Philippe! Open the door!

PHILIPPE:  Oh, it's you! (*He open the door and Didier rushes in.*) Shut the door.

DIDIER:  What are you doing? Look at me and tell me what you're up to.

PHILIPPE  (*in a strange tone*): I want to see her again. I need to.

DIDIER:  What are you saying?

PHILIPPE:  I want to see her again. I've been thinking of nothing else since yesterday . . . since I had the idea of preserving her image. The idea has been haunting me, I've been obsessed by it. I'm going to tell you something terrible. Already I can't see her face in my mind, I can't make out her features . . .

DIDIER:  You're tired . . . it's an emotional time.

PHILIPPE:  You can't imagine how quickly the dead leave us. She's fading away . . . fading away . . . her eyes . . . her mouth . . . her expression . . . it all eludes me. It's like being bereaved all over again. Even that picture over there doesn't seem to be her. It's as if it's a photograph of a complete stranger.

DIDIER:  Wait a while first before . . .

PHILIPPE:  Wait for what? Every second that passes is robbing me of her image. One minute she's there in front of me and then suddenly she's vanished! No, that's not what I want. This void, this darkness, it's horrible. I want to see her whenever I want, whenever I feel like it, every single day if I wish . . . (*lower*) I want to see her right now, just as I saw her on the bed, for the last time. I don't need that photograph or any of the others, but just the one which we took yesterday.

DIDIER:  Don't do it now, not whilst you're in this state.

PHILIPPE  (*forcefully*): I will.

DIDIER:  Listen to me!

PHILIPPE:  Why? You're not going to persuade me otherwise. Look, I've got everything ready . . .

DIDIER:  This is madness!

PHILIPPE:  On my own, yes, I admit that it may have been terribly painful, but now that you're here!

DIDIER:  I promise you, later . . .

PHILIPPE:  But later you won't be here. This has to be done now. I've got everything ready. The bowls, the trays, the lamp . . .

DIDIER:  But why torture yourself?

PHILIPPE:  This isn't going to increase my pain, it will reduce it, I promise you.

DIDIER  (*sensing that any further discussion would be useless*): All right then! Is it dark enough?

PHILIPPE:  Yes. We often used to develop our negatives here after we'd been on a trip. The shutters are solid and the curtains are nice and thick.

DIDIER:  Have you got everything?

PHILIPPE:  Did you close the door?

DIDIER:   Yes. Hurry up!

PHILIPPE   (*opening the camera and removing the negative plate*): Here she is!

DIDIER   (*holding out his hand*): Give it me, my friend,

PHILIPPE:   No. This is her! This is her!!

DIDIER:   Let me do it. You sit down.

PHILIPPE:   Oh no, I'm the only one allowed to touch this . . . (*He plunges the plate into the tray and tips it gently backwards and forwards.*)

DIDIER:   Can you see anything?

PHILIPPE:   Nothing.

DIDIER   (*bending over Philippe's shoulder*): The edges are getting darker.

PHILIPPE:   Yes.

DIDIER:   Do you think that the developer might be too weak?

PHILIPPE:   A little.

DIDIER:   Do you want me to add a drop more?

PHILIPPE:   No. Don't touch anything. Now the whites are beginning to appear . . . slowly.

DIDIER:   Can I have a look?

PHILIPPE:   Wait a moment. Don't lean on me like that, you're shaking.

DIDIER:   Sorry.

PHILIPPE:   Something's happening. Look. This dark rectangle, that's the bed. And there's the pillow. And this lighter bit here that's still a bit vague, that's her, my darling. I'm frightened. (*As he steps back he knocks something over and shudders.*) What was that?

DIDIER:   Nothing. Nothing at all. Carry on.

PHILIPPE:   Oh, this is dreadful. The details are becoming clearer . . .

DIDIER:   Let me see.

PHILIPPE:   Look, her hair . . . oh, she was so proud of her hair . . . and her hands, her beautiful hands. It's as if she's coming back to me, it's as if I'm really looking at her.

DIDIER:   Don't you think it's been in the developer long enough?

PHILIPPE:   Not yet. It's very slow. It'll be better like this. (*Takes the plate out, looks at it, pauses, then suddenly stops*) But . . .

DIDIER:   What?

PHILIPPE   (*putting the plate back into the tray*): Nothing.

DIDIER:   Still not enough?

PHILIPPE   (*very emotionally*): No . . . no, no.

DIDIER:   I'm sure . . .

PHILIPPE:   No, some of the details are still too vague. Another three or four seconds. (*Pause*) Now it'll be enough.

DIDIER:   Yes. If you're not careful, you'll ruin it.

PHILIPPE   (*looking at the plate*): But . . .

DIDIER   (*alarmed*): What?

PHILIPPE:   But it's not possible . . .

DIDIER (*unnerved*): What? What's not possible?

PHILIPPE (*distraught*): I'm going mad!

DIDIER (*in anguish*): I knew it!

PHILIPPE (*straightening up and with the look of a man who doesn't want to submit to an hallucination*): Wait a minute! Look! I'm losing my mind. Do you remember exactly how she was when you last saw her?.

DIDIER: Yes. Why?

PHILIPPE: How was she? Describe her.

DIDIER: Well . . . stretched out . . . her hands crossed.

PHILIPPE: That's not what I mean. Her eyes, can you remember her eyes?

DIDIER: Her eyes?

PHILIPPE: Yes. Were they open or closed?

DIDIER: Closed.

PHILIPPE: Are you sure?

DIDIER: Yes, quite sure. I remember.

PHILIPPE (*crying*): Well here they are open. Do you hear? Open! (*Didier takes the plate and holds it underneath the light.*)

DIDIER (*with a cry a fear*): Ah!

PHILIPPE: Her eyes are open!

DIDIER: But how could that happen?

PHILIPPE: She must have opened them when the flashpowder went off . . .

DIDIER: But that means . . .

PHILIPPE (*shouting*): She wasn't dead! She wasn't dead! (*Curtain*)


## ACT 3

(*The office at the cemetery. Stage right, a counter behind which is sat the Chief Warden. Along the walls are racks of pigeon-holes for all the registration documents and police records, and also a map of the cemetery. Stage left, a door which leads into another room. Stage right is the entrance door. At the back is a French window through which can be seen a path through the cemetery and some tombs. As the curtain rises, the Warden is alone. The tolling of a bell is heard and through the window can be seen a passing cortège. Through the door on the right a woman enters carrying some flowers in her arms.*)

WOMAN: Excuse me, Monsieur. Could you tell me how to find the grave of M. Jean-Baptiste Delarue?

WARDEN: Do you know when he died?

WOMAN: 27 July 1908.

WARDEN: Delarue, Jean-Baptiste. 27 July 1908. No. 3026. Turn right out of the door, take the third path on your left and another warden will take you from there.

WOMAN: Thank you, Monsieur. (*She exits. The Doctor enters.*)

WARDEN: Can I help you, Monsieur?

DOCTOR: I am the Civic Registrar and I'm after some information.

WARDEN: About what?

DOCTOR: Is it true that you have received an exhumation order for one Thérèse Vaugeois, who was interred yesterday?

WARDEN: Yes, I received it a quarter of an hour ago.

DOCTOR: Ah! And when will the body be exhumed?

WARDEN: As soon as the Police Superintendent and the Pathologist arrive.

DOCTOR: They just told me at the Police Station and I couldn't believe it. It's incredible!

WARDEN: Ah! It's quite unheard of. In the twenty years that I've been here, I've never seen anything like it. (*Enter Superintendent.*) Ah! The Police Superintendent!

SUPERINTENDENT: Good morning. Good morning, doctor. (*Introducing everyone*) Doctor Legeron, who confirmed the death. Doctor Naudet, pathologist.

DOCTOR: Pleased to meet you!

PATHOLOGIST: Delighted! (*They shake hands. Addressing the Superintendent and the Warden*) Are the family going to be here?

SUPERINTENDENT: They'll be here shortly. M. Garnier would not have been informed until after us. (*To the Warden*) Are your men in place?

WARDEN: Yes, sir.

SUPERINTENDENT: Then please make sure that everything is ready.

WARDEN: Everything is prepared.

SUPERINTENDENT: Will it take long?

WARDEN: Not at all. The tomb has not yet been sealed.

SUPERINTENDENT: Perfect. (*To the Pathologist*) So that we don't waste any time, I would like to retrieve the coffin from the vault straight away. Is it to be brought here?

PATHOLOGIST: Indeed, please do that.

SUPERINTENDENT (*to the Warden*): Show me the way. (*They exit.*)

PATHOLOGIST: Tell me, now that we're alone, you realize that this is an extremely serious business? The fact that I've been called in makes this anything but a simple formality. This M. Garnier has requested the presence of a pathologist because he has lodged a formal complaint against you.

DOCTOR (*stunned and unnerved*): A complaint? Against me?

PATHOLOGIST (*with an affirmative nod*): And an investigation has been opened.

DOCTOR: They can investigate all they like. I've nothing to hide.

PATHOLOGIST: I don't doubt it. But this gentleman has accused you of drawing up the death certificate (*hesitating and searching for the word*) with culpable negligence.

DOCTOR:   That's quite wrong!

PATHOLOGIST:   Well, what would you say was the cause of death?

DOCTOR:   But you know as well as anyone that it's not my job, as a Civic Registrar, to confirm the cause of death. At least it's not our role in the majority of cases, when you only get to examine the body for a couple of minutes . . .

PATHOLOGIST:   Why do you only examine a body for a couple of minutes?

DOCTOR:   Because we haven't the time to do it for any longer. It's the same as asking a military doctor, who has to see 150 men in an hour and a half, why he doesn't spend more than a few seconds with each. Do the sums for yourself and you'll see. The morning when I was called to this woman's house, I had another sixteen deaths to register that same day in all four corners of the district.

PATHOLOGIST   (*without conviction*): I'm sure, I'm sure.

DOCTOR:   Of course, when there's a suspicion of violent death or foul play, then it's a different matter altogether. But in this case, there wasn't a trace of violence or poison. All I saw was a cold body without any tension in the joints. There were no signs of breathing, no pulse, no heartbeat, and this was all after the doctor who was treating her had already confirmed death. In Paris it's not like it is in the country. There are only the two of us—him and me.

PATHOLOGIST   (*becoming irritated and with a certain authority*): Nevertheless you must never forget that you are there not simply to confirm the diagnoses—or in this case the death—as stated by the visiting doctors, but to monitor them. Why, if you all went round protecting each other . . .

DOCTOR:   Look, this woman was dead, well and truly dead, I give you my word. And if I had had the slightest shadow of a doubt, I would not have issued the burial certificate.

PATHOLOGIST:   Of course. (*Troubled, but not wanting to let it show*) But you hear all kinds of stories circulating about premature burials, and one must exercise great care.

DOCTOR:   I am as careful as it is possible to be and these cases that you allude to are extremely rare and the truth of these stories is debatable.

PATHOLOGIST:   Perhaps less rare than we think.

DOCTOR:   One case in fifty years.

PATHOLOGIST:   You think so? There are some terrible statistics. And remember that these statistics only include those cases where the mistake has been noticed in time. You see, there can be no argument when they are dead and buried. Two or three years ago I gave a lecture and in it I quoted, amongst others, from the notes of Legueru. From 1833 to 1846, in France alone,

there were 94 premature interments, where pure chance—
such as the coffin being dropped or a delay in preparing the
corpse—was the only thing that prevented disaster. And one
considers that after suffering a blackout, a person might not
recover consciousness for several hours after they have been
placed in their coffin!

DOCTOR    (*becoming increasingly worried*): You surely don't believe
that!

PATHOLOGIST:    No . . . No . . . Nevertheless . . . (*He pauses.*) There were no
reflexes?

DOCTOR:    None at all.

PATHOLOGIST:    The body was rigid?

DOCTOR    (*after a momentary hesitation*): Yes.

PATHOLOGIST    (*firmly*): Well, yes or no?

DOCTOR:    Well, not completely. After all I was there only five hours
after death had occurred.

PATHOLOGIST:    Five hours? Is that all? That's barely legal!

DOCTOR:    As I've already told you, I had seventeen deaths to record and
I began with those closest to where I live.

PATHOLOGIST:    The terrible thing is that one can display all the signs of death
. . . There's the research of Icard from Marseilles. You're
familiar with fluorescine? But you didn't think to administer
it?

DOCTOR:    It's never given, except on the specific request of the family.

PATHOLOGIST:    And what if the family is unaware that they're able to request
it? Look, you need to have procedures like they do in
England and in Bavaria, I believe, as well. At the cemetery
they have a place where all the bodies—whether they're
suspect or not—are laid to rest until decomposition begins to
set in. It's very peaceful there. It's because that is a sign, the
only sign that can't be misread. But come on, how can you be
sure after only five hours? Well, it's a tricky one . . . (*Pause*)
You closed her eyes, didn't you?

DOCTOR:    Yes.

PATHOLOGIST:    And you know all about this photography business that has
led to all this?

DOCTOR    (*a little worried*): Yes, yes.

PATHOLOGIST:    So how do you explain that in this photograph the eyes
appear to be open?

DOCTOR:    Were they really?

PATHOLOGIST:    I assume so, since the police . . .

WARDEN    (*entering through the door stage right*): This is Monsieur
Garnier, the gentleman who has requested . . .
(*Philippe, very pale, enters behind him. He is followed by
Didier.*)

PHILIPPE:    We have come for the exhumation . . .

WARDEN:    This is the Pathologist.

(*Philippe greets him and recoils as he catches sight of the Civic Registrar.*)

DIDIER    (*approaching the Pathologist*): You can understand that this is most distressing for my friend. If this sad business could be carried out as quickly as possible . . .

PATHOLOGIST:    The Superintendent has already gone over there.

PHILIPPE    (*angrily*): Then we must go and join him!

PATHOLOGIST:    There's no need, Monsieur. The coffin will be brought to us here.

PHILIPPE    (*with surprise and anguish*): Ah!

DIDIER:    Here?

PATHOLOGIST:    Well, no, into the next room. Legally, it's in there that we have to open it. If you would just wait a few moments.

PHILIPPE    (*violently*): Wait!? Wait!? Do you want to drive me mad? I've had to wait at the police station, at the prosecutor's office, everywhere. Then there were all the procedures and the petitions . . .

PATHOLOGIST:    But, Monsieur, normally it takes eight days to arrange an exhumation. You have been granted this authorization in an extraordinarily quick time.

PHILIPPE:    But, think, every minute could be important. A human being could be dying while we're standing around here!

PATHOLOGIST:    No, Monsieur, no, believe me . . .

PHILIPPE:    Ah! You don't want to believe that she's been buried alive! But I tell you it's true! I can feel it . . . I'm sure of it! She has only been buried for a few hours, perhaps all is not lost . . . Save her, I beg of you, save her! (*He slumps into the chair and sobs, his head in his hands.*)

PATHOLOGIST    (*to the Warden*): Go and tell the Superintendent to hurry up. (*The Warden leaves. The Pathologist leads Didier to the other side of the room and talks to him in a low voice.*) Tell me, Monsieur, have you been with your friend for all of the past couple of days?

DIDIER:    I haven't left his side.

PATHOLOGIST:    Good, then you can tell us whether there is any truth in this story of the photograph.

DIDIER:    Only that when we were with the body the eyes were closed, but the negative showed them open.

DOCTOR    (*at first in hushed tones, but getting more animated*): But that's impossible! Your memory's playing tricks on you! Or perhaps there was something wrong with the plate that has made you think . . . and on the basis of this rather scanty evidence you've brought in the Public Prosecutor and arranged for an exhumation? It's insane, quite insane! (*Philippe who has suddenly lifted his head, gets up and approaches the Doctor.*)

PHILIPPE    (*menacingly*): What did you say?

DOCTOR *(very nervously)*: I . . .

PHILIPPE: You think I'm mad, that I've been hallucinating, don't you?

DOCTOR: I didn't mean that at all.

PHILIPPE: Then what did you mean?

DOCTOR: Nothing .. Just that under such circumstances even the calmest of men can lose his sense of reality.

PHILIPPE: I have a perfect grip on reality. A less rational person would have been astounded by the ferocious haste with which you arranged the funeral and had the body whisked away.

PATHOLOGIST *(trying to calm things down)*: There was no undue haste . . . every precaution was taken, every check made . . .

PHILIPPE: Come off it! This gentleman hardly even looked at the body. He laid his hand on her, lifted up her arm and let it fall . . . but nothing more than that. I was there.

PATHOLOGIST: I'm not even going to discuss it any more.

PHILIPPE: Very well. *(Threateningly)* But if through your fault something terrible has happened . . .

DOCTOR: Are you accusing me?

PHILIPPE: Don't you think I have the right?

DOCTOR: If you have any doubts whatsoever . . .

PHILIPPE: It's your job, not mine, to have the doubts, but I certainly have them now, and you know exactly why! I have doubts because, you see, I have seen that negative and the eyes of my poor darling are wide open and he *(pointing to Didier)* has seen it as well. And because I closed those eyes that morning with my own hands and saw them still closed after the photograph had been taken, those eyes which I touched, kissed and thought closed for ever, were looking at me with a vivid and terrible stare for a few seconds in that darkroom.

DOCTOR: I assure you, I followed all the legal procedures.

PHILIPPE: No. What are worthless procedures compared to this. Eyes wide open! Eyes wide open! Do you not realize how much horror is contained in those three words? Are you not terrified yourself by the very idea of what might have happened down there? But of course not, you're in no rush, you're not in such a hurry anymore. It's only when the death has to be registered that everything has to be done quickly. You came in, threw your orders about and then left! You're only bothered about getting them buried, you don't give a thought to them after that! But we do, we think about those we have lost! At night time we see them again, we see them as they are, as they have become, as they might be . . . if even once you have been wrong! *(He fixes his gaze on the Doctor.)* Ah, you're afraid as well now. You're afraid, like me! You can see her, in her coffin, that poor, pathetic figure, tightly packed into that wooden box!

(*At that moment the door opens and the Gravediggers enter, carrying the coffin and followed by the Superintendent. There is a sudden silence. Philippe steps back and Didier takes his hand. The Gravediggers slowly cross the stage and enter the room at the back. They can be seen placing the coffin on the ground. The Superintendent and the Doctor follow them through the open door. In the doorway, the Pathologist turns to Philippe.*)

PATHOLOGIST: Your agony will soon be over, Monsieur.

PHILIPPE: (*going to follow him*): I'm coming with you.

PATHOLOGIST: No, Monsieur, it's not necessary. (*He enters the room.*)

PHILIPPE: I insist on it!

DIDIER: (*stopping him*): For God's sake, Philippe, don't go in!

PHILIPPE: (*distraught*): Why not? Do you think I'm going to see something worse than I've already imagined?

DIDIER: Whatever, but you mustn't go in there!

PHILIPPE: But what if she's still alive?! No, it's not possible . . .

DIDIER: (*pleading*): My friend . . .

PHILIPPE: (*terrified*): But what if they've killed her . . .
(*The Superintendent's voice can be heard through the open door.*)

SUPERINTENDENT: (*reading the nameplate on the coffin*): Let's just check the inscription . . . Thérèse Vaugeois, born November 15th 1890, died February 25th 1910.

PHILIPPE: (*falteringly*): I can't bear it any longer, I can't bear it!

DIDIER: (*taking him towards the door stage right*): Don't stay in here, go outside, just for a moment . . . (*He leads him out and closes the door behind him. He then goes and stands in the doorway of the room where the coffin is being opened and watches the proceedings, full of anguish. Apart from him, nobody else can be seen. Only their voices can be heard.*)

SUPERINTENDENT: Come on now, hurry up!

PATHOLOGIST: What's the matter?

GRAVEDIGGER: One of the screws seems to be stuck.

SUPERINTENDENT: Then use your crowbar.
(*The sound of splintering wood can be heard.*)

PATHOLOGIST: Gently, gently does it, don't touch the body.

SUPERINTENDENT: Rip off the entire lid.
(*The sound of the coffin lid being placed on the floor can be heard.*)

PATHOLOGIST: Carbolic acid! Pour it onto the sheet . . . remove the sawdust . . . lift up the body now . . . watch your hands . . . some more carbolic acid . . . don't be afraid of pouring it . . . that's enough . . . pull back the sheet and reveal the face.
(*The sound of an exclamation of terror from within. Didier takes a step towards them.*)

DIDIER: (*with terror*): Blood!

PATHOLOGIST:   Note that the face is covered in blood!

SUPERINTENDENT:   Perhaps it was the crowbar as they were taking the lid off.

PATHOLOGIST:   No, no, she's been struggling. Look at her hands, she's been tearing at her face with her nails.

DIDIER:   My God! My God!

PATHOLOGIST:   The poor thing was alive!

DIDIER:   Alive! She was alive!

SUPERINTENDENT:   The gentleman was right. What a terrible way to die! What agony!

PATHOLOGIST *(with fury at the Doctor)*: Now are you satisfied?!

DOCTOR *(frightened)*: But how could I have known?

PATHOLOGIST:   'How could I have known?'! But that's what you're there for! Your job is to make sure that this kind of horror never happens!

SUPERINTENDENT:   This is just absolutely horrible.

PATHOLOGIST:   She's only been dead a few hours.

SUPERINTENDENT *(to the Gravediggers)*: Reseal the coffin.

DIDIER *(coming back onto the stage, followed by the Pathologist)*: Alive! She was alive! This is appalling! Appalling! (*He stops suddenly as the door on the right opens and Philippe, mad with anguish, approaches him.*)

PHILIPPE *(in a strangled voice)*: Well? What's happened?

DIDIER:   Well . . . (*He pauses, almost imperceptibly, and glances at the Pathologist before continuing.*) She was dead when she was buried.

PATHOLOGIST:   Yes.

PHILIPPE:   Ah! (*He starts to sob.*) Can I . . . can I see her?

PATHOLOGIST:   No.

DIDIER *(taking him in his arms)*: No, my friend, there's no need, there's no need. (*Philippe rests his head on Didier's shoulder and continues mumbling between sobs.*)

PHILIPPE:   My darling! My poor darling!
(*Pale and motionless, the Pathologist, the Superintendent and the Warden watch them, whilst the Doctor stands in the corner dismayed.*)
(*The curtain falls very slowly.*)

THE END

# The Final Kiss

*(Le Baiser dans la nuit, 1912)*

*by*

MAURICE LEVEL

## Preface

Maurice Level's two-act *Le Baiser dans la nuit* premiered on 10 December 1912 and is one of the definitive plays of the Grand-Guignol, being revived in 1922 and 1938. Based on Level's short story (published in *Journal*, July 1912), it concerns Henri, hideously disfigured and blinded in a vitriol attack by his jilted lover, Jeanne. The first act involves Henri's brother, his doctor, and lawyer. Henri refuses to appear in court to testify against Jeanne (or even to prejudice the jury by simply 'showing his face') and so she is acquitted to the disgust of Henri's supporters. What seems to be an extraordinary act of altruism is in fact a careful ploy to ensure that he meets Jeanne again. In a masterful scene of cat-and-mouse, Henri coerces Jeanne into giving him a 'final kiss' and exploits the moment to exact his revenge and pour vitriol on her.

Level exploits the audience's fascination and fear of the *crime passionel* and the use of vitriol, which was a sensational and yet authenticated method of revenge attack. As Pierron reveals, the verb 'vitrioler' entered the dictionary in 1888 (Pierron 1995, 549). Henri's appearance makes him a pathetic figure, but also an image of horror. In the original production he was blindfolded, while in this adaptation his head is wrapped in bandages. Either approach makes him reminiscent of icons of horror: the man with the hidden face exploits the idea of the 'horror behind the mask', used so effectively in films like *The Invisible Man* (James Whale, 1933), *The Fly* (Kurt Neumann, 1958) and *Onibaba* (Kaneto Shindo, 1964).

In this play, though, the monster is a glamorous model: the vengeful Jeanne is a case where the beauty *is* the beast. If Level masterfully exploits the delicate balance between pity and terror, in the final violent action of the play Henri lives up to his appearance and becomes a monster. In so doing, Level shatters our sympathy for Henri, whilst at the same time presenting an Old Testament-style 'eye for an eye' morality of retributive vengeance. *The Final Kiss* is a morality tale of 'do as you would be done by'. The spectator resolves the play's horror by recognizing that Jeanne

THE FINAL KISS 181

and Henri deserve each other in their mutually created Hell. It is as if the vitriol peels away Jeanne's mask just as Henri's act of violence justifies his monstrous appearance: the curtain falls on two hideous de Lordean monsters who have risen to the surface.

The play is grotesquely erotic, as is the title of the play and Henri's last request: 'I want to kiss you. There—I've said it. One kiss. The last time.' Level uses the irony of the situation of two former lovers that will culminate not in a sexual act but in a graphically violent act. But it is fair to say that in the Grand-Guignol's *sadistic* philosophy violence, death and love are intertwined: as *The Torture Garden* makes clear 'whoever talks of death talks also of love' (Pierron 1995, 907).

Indeed, even if the symbolism of the violent spilling of liquid, by a male onto a female, were lost on the audience, which seems unlikely, then the dual meaning of the word 'baiser' in the title ('kiss' or 'fuck') removes any ambiguity. As Henri demands his final 'kiss' the request is loaded with sexual and orgasmic symbolism. In this respect the play is redolent of the widely known 'Aids Mary/Typhoid Mary' contemporary legend (Brunvand 1989, 195–202), in which an infected person takes revenge by deliberately infecting somebody else, often through an actual or symbolic sexual act. Whilst it is more likely that Level was interested in exploiting factual occurrence at the time rather than deliberately and consciously drawing upon contemporary legend, it could at least be argued that this provides further evidence of the way in which the theme taps into the communal or 'folk' subconscious.

Although not mentioning *The Final Kiss* specifically, Jean-Léo—in 'Requiem pour le Grand Guignol' (unpublished typescript in British Library Manuscript Collections, dated 1962)—describes how the effect of vitriol scarring can be achieved:

> . . .a simple recipe: the face is covered with a silk stocking onto which strips of sponge are attached. Green light is recommended. (4)

In specific relation to *The Final Kiss*, the 1913 publication of the play in *Monde Illustré* (number 31) includes an introduction, critical overview and an interview with Level compiled by H. Dupuy-Mazuel. It includes Level's description of the make-up Brizard developed for the role of Henri:

> The actor put a thin sheet of sponge over his left cheek and filled some of the holes with black or red pencil. (17)

Interestingly, in the original production no effects were used to create the wounding of Jeanne. Level says that some spectators were disappointed that 'the young woman did not appear disfigured and bleeding'. Level's response is:

> . . . I am not keen on such an extreme display of horror as I believe
> that the play relies on tension and does not need to resort to tricks
> that I would regard as facile and somewhat vulgar. (17)

However, the publicity still reproduced by Pierron (1995, plate on page
4 between 794 and 795), presumably from the 1922 or 1938 revivals,
reveals that ultimately the Grand-Guignol spectators would have it their
way: the image shows Jeanne's skin peeling away from her face in the
final tableau of the play.

This is the freest adaptation in the present collection. In producing the
adaptation, the decision was made to shorten the work into one act,
reduce the number of onstage characters, streamline the exposition, and
abridge some of the longer monologues. This allows a predominant focus
on the climactic scene of the play: Henri's ironically erotic encounter
with Jeanne. It is interesting to note that Level himself focuses on this
section in his own short story version of the play, which we will discuss
in due course.

This is one of the first adaptations we used in the Grand-Guignol
Laboratory and it has had a successful performative lifespan, including a
student performance at the 1999 Edinburgh Fringe and a professional
production by Instant Classics Theatre Company at the 2001 London
Festival of Unusual Theatre.

Aside from this adaptation, Level's masterpiece has enjoyed other
significant reincarnations. Frederick Witney wrote a one-act version of
the play for his 1947 collection *Grand Guignol* (the play was
premiered at the Granville Theatre, London on 26 October 1945).
Witney called his version *The Last Kiss*, and our title *The Final Kiss* is
partly a tribute to Witney's adaptation. Witney seems to be unaware of
Level's play as he describes his version as based on 'the short story by
Maurice Level' (Witney 1947, 111). In 1920, Alys Eyre Macklin
translated a collection of Level's stories under the title of *Crises: A
Volume of Tales of Mystery and Horror* (reprinted in 1922 in a
popular edition under the title of *Grand Guignol Stories*). Interestingly,
the programme for the fourth series of London Grand Guignol plays at
the Little Theatre (June 1921) includes an advertisement for *Crises*. It
is clear that Witney based his own version on Macklin's translation of
Level's *Journal* short story as it is also entitled 'The Last Kiss'. In
Witney's adaptation, the two central figures (the only characters in the
original story, while Witney adds Mrs Upton, the landlady) are called
Tom and Minty, while Level, in his short story, opts for an anonymous
encounter between 'He' and 'She'. Interestingly, Witney's characters
begin similarly anonymously, but their names are gradually revealed in
the dialogic exchanges. In Level's short story (or at least in Macklin's

translation) we experience a heightened narrative which has an almost operatic (even gothic) grandeur in contrast to the clinical, sub-melodrama of the play. The story concludes with the line 'And round them, as in them, was great Darkness' (Macklin 1920, 239), which Witney adapts into:

> He: And the Devil said let there be Dark—and there was Dark. (*Suddenly She screams and screams and screams and goes on screaming.*)
>
> (Witney 1947, 123)

Although the Little Theatre only sold a prose version of Level's play and Witney's play was not performed publicly until 1945, the British Grand-Guignol presented a distinctly similar if not derivative work in its second series (January 1921). In H.F. Maltby's *The Person Unknown* a hideously disfigured victim of the First World War confronts the female singer who led him and many others to enlist in jingoistic fervour. The woman dies of fright. The play definitely echoes *The Final Kiss*, but as it is primarily an example of anti-war drama it is more blatantly satirical and politicized: Level's *crime passionel* changes into crimes of the state. In his autobiography, Maltby makes no reference to Level, but explains why he wrote the piece. He despised Paul Rubens's patriotic song 'We don't want to lose you, but we think you ought to go' and the publicity stunts of young women singing it to encourage men to enlist. The bitter irony is that the stunt involved: 'Forgetting all about the promise contained in the last line of that dreadful chorus: "We will love you, hug you, kiss you, when you come back home again."' (Maltby 1950, 130).

The scenario of the play made a generic shift in the 1950s when it was used (once again, unaccredited)[1] as a cartoon strip in an American horror comic: 'The Acid Test' (written by Al Feldstein and William M. Gaines and sketched by Jack Kamen in *The Haunt of Fear*, Issue 11, EC Comics, January 1952). In this version we are told the story of Cedric and Florence Blair. Florence is driven to distraction by the obsequiousness of her husband, eventually throwing muriatic acid in his face. The disfigured Cedric continues to be deferential in court, successfully plead-ing for Florence's acquittal. As in Level, his seeming magnanimity is a ploy so that he can demand a kiss and exact his revenge (fig. 9). The most significant difference between the versions is that in Level, Jeanne's

---

[1] In a recent e-mail to the authors, however, Al Feldstein acknowledged the Grand-Guignol as a 'subconscious inspiration' for EC's horror comics (12 January 2002).

*Figure 9.* An adaptation of Maurice Level's *Le Baiser dans la nuit*: the final page of 'The Acid Test' (written by Al Feldstein and William M. Gaines and sketched by Jack Kamen in *The Haunt of Fear*, Issue 11, EC Comics, January 1952) (EC Publications, Inc/William M. Gaines, Agent, Inc.)

original action is the *crime passionel* of a thwarted mistress, while the EC version presents a failing marital relationship: Level's situation could be perceived as archetypically French, while EC reflects a major anxiety of post-war American society.

Although not quite the 'storyboard' version that EC provided in the 1950s, the 1913 publication of the play included several sketches of the production by P. Delaroche that provide an invaluable insight into Grand-Guignol performance practice. Particularly interesting, alongside the general images of all the performers in costume, is the artist's impression of the final moments of the play (see fig. 7). The positioning of Henri behind Jeanne, locking her into place with his legs and left hand while his right hand brandishes the bottle of acid, means that the audience acquire a full-frontal view of the performers. A similar positioning was used in Samouraï Films' 1997 version of the play, and the Laboratory's 1999 Edinburgh Fringe production (produced before the company had seen either the *Monde Illustré* sketches or the film version).

David Cottis of Instant Classics, reveals that:

> . . .when the actors first read the script, the thing they most enjoyed was the uncertainty as to what was going to happen. The form suggests that violence will occur, but no one is sure how, when, and to whom. A lot of the rehearsal process was concerned with recapturing the innocence of that first reading.
>
> (Letter to the authors, 23 March 2001)

This is an interesting perspective, and has implications about the effect that the Grand-Guignol hopes to exact on the audience: innocence being dragged into experience. By the same token, we have also found audience members (like good *guignoleurs*) who have said they know precisely what is going to happen, and that the formula that Cottis outlines is simplified into the pleasure of seeing *how* and *when*. The play relies on an excruciating build-up, complete with red herrings and a great deal of teasing of the audience. *The Final Kiss* culminates in a few seconds of graphic violence. This is only effective because of the subtlety of what precedes it, and much of the 'horror' inherent in the piece is contained in the detail of the actor's performance. As Chris Campbell, writing in *The Scotsman*, says of the 1999 Edinburgh production:

> Despite the liberal splashes of red liquid, the key to the night's success is its subtlety. [They] know that horror is more horrific when it is partly obscured from the audience, and the company

uses this approach for maximum effect. Andrew Pullen's Henry, for example, is bandaged for the majority of the time, so it is only his scorched voice and pained movements that communicate the alarming sight beneath the mask.

(10 August 1999, 8)

# THE FINAL KISS

*(Le Baiser dans la nuit, 1912)*

*by*

MAURICE LEVEL

---

Doctor
Nurse
Henri
Jeanne

---

*(The room is very dark. Henri sits in a dressing gown with his back to the audience. His head is wrapped in bandages. He lights up a hubble-bubble and a sickly smell of opium clouds up. The door opens very slowly and the Doctor and Nurse step in.)*

DOCTOR: You do realize, Henri, that my professional standing does not allow me to condone this.

HENRI *(after a pause)*: Hello, Doctor.

DOCTOR: I've heard of too many people getting hooked on that stuff. And opium addiction is not at all pleasant, believe me.

HENRI: But the pain . . . it never stops . . .

DOCTOR: Can't you try *aspirin?*
*(Henri glares at the Doctor who stops dead.)*

HENRI: This is all that can ease the pain. Torture. *(Silence)*

DOCTOR: So how do you find life in this halfway house? It's got to be better than the hospital. You're independent but they keep an eye on you. Make life tolerable.

HENRI: Yes—can get you *anything* you want. *(Gestures at opium.)*

DOCTOR: Mm—I'm not sure what to think of—

HENRI: Absolutely anything.

DOCTOR: Come on, sister, let's get the dressing changed.

NURSE: Right then, gentlemen—this won't take a moment.
*(Nurse and Doctor tentatively approach Henri and stand either side of him. Henri still has not moved.)*

DOCTOR *(a quake in his voice reveals his nervousness)*: Let's . . . have a look then.

NURSE:     Yes, sir. (*She unpicks the bandage and begins to coil it off. Henri tenses up, his hands gripping the arms of the chair.*)

HENRI:     Easy, easy now.
           (*The bandage is completely removed. Nurse and Doctor try to hide their grimaces. Silence.*)

NURSE     (*trembling voice*): There . . . not so bad . . . healing up . . . it's much, much better now. Good news. Yes. Definitely. We can be quite optimistic—

DOCTOR:    I know I haven't been a doctor for many years, but I've never seen anything as appalling as these injuries. And I hope I never see anything like it again. (*Henri's head lowers.*) Sulphuric acid. Vitriol. That's what caused this. An acid attack.

NURSE:     They happen too often, sir.

DOCTOR:    It's quite hideous. Thinking about a career change, sister?

NURSE     (*forced brightness*): Oh no, it's all part of a day's work . . . I suppose—

DOCTOR:    Get a nice job in an office. Or be a nanny. I wouldn't blame you. Too often we see the dark side of life. (*Doctor braces himself and goes closely to Henri's face and then acquires a consummate professionalism.*)

DOCTOR:    It's been the best part of a year since it happened. I'm afraid it will never get any better than what you see now. We've done all we can—and so has nature, I'm afraid. He was nearly blinded—his eyes are seriously damaged but mercifully he can see.

NURSE:     That's good—in fact, it's great.

HENRI     (*sullen*): But light. Light burns my eyes.

DOCTOR:    It was so calculated. Often with this kind of assault, the perpetrator throws the acid from too far away or too quickly or they lose their nerve and their hands shake. But in this case, it was done with absolute precision. Every drop hit the intended target—this face. The attacker had a very cool head. Exceptionally cool.

NURSE:     He wanted to maim him.

DOCTOR:    He? It was a lady.

NURSE:     Oh . . . a crime of passion . . . how very sad.

DOCTOR:    Our patient's 'estranged' fiancée. They should've given her the death penalty. Put a new dressing on. (*She does so.*)

NURSE:     They . . . caught her?

DOCTOR:    Oh yes, she was arrested. A great performance in court, so I hear. She got off lightly. A six-month sentence. She's probably free already.

NURSE:     And he got a life sentence. How old is he?

HENRI:     I'm twenty-five.

NURSE:     Is that all? And your life has been ruined. (*Correcting herself*) Oh well, nothing to despair about—

DOCTOR:    The annoying thing is Henri's altruism. *He forgives her.*

NURSE: No!? How could he . . . (*Checks herself*) I suppose to err is human, to forgive divine!

DOCTOR: She attacked him in a vicious fit of jealous rage—ruined him, as you put it, subjected him to indescribable agony. And he forgives her. If anything, he even helped her get a light sentence.

NURSE: He must have loved her.

DOCTOR (*wry smile*): Yes.

HENRI: I still do. (*Silence*) It was a . . . disaster. But nothing can right it now. My suffering is great. It was a terrible thing to do—she knows that. I forgive her.

DOCTOR: I will never understand.

NURSE: It's truly remarkable. *Love.* To forgive like that. No desire for revenge. Just forgiveness. Underneath the pain, you must have a great peace to forgive like that.

HENRI: Yes. Maybe. Yes. I'm tired now. Please go away now. Just leave me.

NURSE: Oh.

DOCTOR: Well, this is goodbye then, Henri. I'm sorry we were not able to do more for you. We will pop by again to see how you're settling in a week or two, maybe a month. Is that alright? (*Henri shrugs in indifference.*) I will have a word with the warden about the . . . (*Gestures towards the hubble-bubble. Henri looks plaintive.*) Oh, very well, but take it easy, old chap. Cheerio. (*He shakes Henri's hand and very subtly rubs his hand afterwards. Nurse gives a little bow and an embarrassed giggle. They exit. Henri stands up and turns and we see his bandaged face. He walks around the room somewhat impatiently, once or twice he feels something in his dressing gown pocket. He checks the time. He sits down like before. After a moment of stillness and silence, Jeanne silently enters. She stands there, Henri suddenly senses her.*)

HENRI: Who's that? Is it . . .? It is you. At last! It's you!

JEANNE: Yes, Henri, it is me.

HENRI: Are you alone?

JEANNE: Yes. (*Starts weeping*) Forgive me, forgive me.

HENRI: Stop. Don't cry. It's very difficult to *come back*. I know you didn't want to.

JEANNE: Didn't want to? When you asked me to? How can you think that? There's so much I wanted to tell you . . . but I couldn't . . . and you are so *good* . . .

HENRI: Good? It's difficult to . . .

JEANNE: No, you *are* good. I feel so guilty. I wish I was dead for all the terrible things I've done to you!

HENRI: I'm not without blame though, am I?

JEANNE: Yes, you *are*.

HENRI: No. You did . . . love me, didn't you?

JEANNE:   Yes. Of course I did.

HENRI:   Well, why did I leave you then?

JEANNE:   No excuses. There aren't any. I don't deserve any. I'm not worthy of forgiveness. If you only knew how much I've cried . . .

HENRI:   I know. Your lawyer told me . . . He told me of your suffering . . .

JEANNE:   When you said 'I'm leaving you' I thought I'd go insane . . . It was my entire life . . . I lost my head. People can become ferocious when they're . . .

HENRI:   Yes, ferocious. The remorse, the pity comes later . . . Too late . . .

JEANNE:   I have been so contemptible.

HENRI:   When I realized what you'd done to me with that sulphuric acid . . . that my whole life would be horrible and . . . finished . . . I mean I'm more reasonable now than when I first realized that.

JEANNE:   But . . . you're not bli— You can see—they told me you can see.

HENRI:   Yes. I can see. But light is agony. And it's getting worse and I may become . . . blind. Yes, blind. The doctors have done all they can to save my sight. They subjected me to days of agony. But I think it's getting worse.

JEANNE:   You must hate me. (*She turns away and starts to cry.*)

HENRI:   Me? I can hear you crying. I've cried too. And the tears caused me such pain. They came out of my eyes like molten steel. (*Silence*) When you live in the dark like I do, you have time to think, turn things over in your mind, come to terms . . . So I don't cry anymore. You can see that. Actually, having you here makes me feel better. It brings back such memories!

JEANNE:   Forgive me. I beg you to forgive me.

HENRI:   Don't cry anymore. This is the last time we'll be together.

JEANNE:   Why?

HENRI:   Because . . . (*Henri faces Jeanne head on for the first time, his eyes wide and staring between the bandages.*)

JEANNE:   Ah!

HENRI:   What is it?

JEANNE:   Nothing . . . Nothing . . .

HENRI   (*almost menacing*): I'm frightening to look at, aren't I?

JEANNE:   No.

HENRI:   Frightening. You cried out . . .

JEANNE:   No.

HENRI:   Yes you did. I want you to come nearer to me. Do you know how much I'd like to feel the touch of your hands again? Would you . . . give me your hand? Just one touch would bring back so many good memories. (*She pauses then walks over and touches his hand.*) Thank you. It feels so good . . . (*Jeanne suddenly looks uneasy for a moment.*) You're not upset?

JEANNE:   Of course not.

HENRI:   Or angry?

JEANNE:   Why are you saying that?

HENRI:   I thought you . . . pulled away. (*He sits on the chaise longue.*)

| | |
|---|---|
| JEANNE | (*kissing his hand*): No. |
| HENRI: | I think we'll always be lovers, deep down . . . but . . . where's the engagement ring? You got rid of it? |
| JEANNE: | No. |
| HENRI: | Why don't you wear it? |
| JEANNE: | Henri . . . I didn't dare to. |
| HENRI: | You must. Promise me. You must wear it. |
| JEANNE: | I promise. |
| HENRI: | I'm so cold. Frozen. Will you let me caress your skin? I feel that I've never touched anyone before . . . I feel like a child. |
| JEANNE: | Oh God, God. |
| HENRI: | I'm so happy you're here—you have no idea how happy I am! |
| JEANNE: | Me too . . . |
| HENRI: | I wish you could stay . . . but I know it's impossible. |
| JEANNE: | I'll do whatever you want. |
| HENRI: | I'm hideous, aren't I? |
| JEANNE: | No, Henri, I swear— |
| HENRI: | If you removed my bandages you'd be horrified. People shudder when they look at me. Give me your hand. I want you to touch me . . . I'm a thing without form . . . or name . . . I have suffered . . . and I'm scared . . . |
| JEANNE: | I didn't want to hurt you! |
| HENRI: | Move your fingers across there—aagh! It hurts! |
| JEANNE: | Stop . . . |
| HENRI | (*holding her hand to him*): No. Feel around my mouth . . . the scars . . . the skin is so fragile. When I eat I can sometimes taste blood in my mouth . . . |
| JEANNE: | I beg you—it's too much—I can't . . . |
| HENRI: | You understand that I've suffered. |
| JEANNE: | Yes . . . yes . . . |
| HENRI: | You're shaking. I can understand why. |
| JEANNE: | I'm shaking because of the pain I've caused you . . . because you cried out just then . . . because . . . |
| HENRI: | Don't lie! |
| JEANNE: | I'm not! |
| | (*Silence*) |
| HENRI: | Forget everything I've said to you. Just go. |
| JEANNE | (*deep sorrow*): Forget? |
| HENRI: | Yes. Look, tell me about yourself now . . . What are you going to do now you're out of prison? |
| JEANNE: | I don't know. I haven't thought about it. It's just not important now. |
| HENRI: | You must have some idea. |
| JEANNE: | I'll rest for a few days then I'll go back to work. I might do some modelling if they want me. |
| HENRI: | Why wouldn't they? You're young, pretty . . . You were always pretty . . . You still are. You're still beautiful. |

JEANNE: I don't look at myself.
(*Henri pulls her close to him.*)
HENRI: I remember this dress. Your black dress.
JEANNE: Yes.
HENRI: Don't move, don't move . . . I like your perfume . . .
JEANNE: I'm not wearing any. I haven't for weeks.
HENRI: It's the scent of your body, your skin, your hair. (*Pause*) Are you scared?
JEANNE: No.
HENRI: You're trembling. Am I so disgusting?
JEANNE: No—I'm cold.
HENRI: You're not wearing a coat! It's November! It's grey and damp. The streets are muddy.
JEANNE: I didn't think—I came here so quickly.
HENRI: You're really shaking! We must warm you up.
JEANNE: No, it's alright.
HENRI: You'll have to go soon. Get yourself home.
JEANNE: There's no rush. All the same, I'd better not be too late . . . I've got a long journey . . . I'm staying a few days with a friend— she's waiting for me.
HENRI: Downstairs? I thought you—
JEANNE: No—she's at her house. But you understand. I don't want to keep her waiting too long.
HENRI: Stay a few more minutes.
JEANNE: A few minutes.
HENRI: I feel so calm since you got here. Do you love me?
JEANNE (*with great effort*): Yes . . . But I'd really better go now. I'll come again and stay longer next time.
HENRI: No—there will never be a next time. This is all too much for you. Only . . . because it's the last time . . . I'd like . . . I daren't say it . . .
JEANNE: Do . . . tell me . . .
HENRI: I'd like . . . No. It's impossible. Just go.
JEANNE: What?
HENRI: You'd never agree. (*Silence*) I want to kiss you. There—I've said it. One kiss. The last time. I'd be so happy. Happy for a long time. I'd ask for nothing else from you. You could go. Would you?
JEANNE: Yes. (*She hesitates then sits next to him and puts her head on his shoulder and pulls close to him. Henri seizes her.*)
HENRI (*ferociously triumphant*): I've got you!
JEANNE: What!? Why are you holding me so hard!?
HENRI: I've got you! I'll never let go!
JEANNE: Look—I'm not struggling . . . hey, you're hurting me . . . let me go, please . . . I've got to go now . . .
HENRI: Leaving? Already?
JEANNE: Yes.

HENRI:   No, no.

JEANNE:   Okay . . . just don't hold me so hard. Let me go.

HENRI:   Just one kiss . . . (*He presses his face towards her and she struggles and moves her face away, her lips pressed tightly together.*) You're so beautiful . . . just let me kiss—
(*Jeanne scratches Henri's cheek and he collapses on the chaise longue in agony, deeply groaning. Jeanne stands up boldly and rearranges her dress. She looks over superciliously.*)

JEANNE:   I shouldn't have come here. The lawyer told me not to.

HENRI   (*very weak*): Just go. Go. You can see the door. Go.

JEANNE:   Such a mistake to come here. (*She adjusts her hair and touches her lips.*) You're still the same old cowardly little bastard, aren't you. Pathetic. (*Silence. Henri is completely still. Jeanne sighs as a wave of guilt runs through her.*) Henri? Are you alright. Look, I'm sorry I hurt you. There's just too much . . . I just shouldn't have come back. Look, are you okay? Henri. Should I call someone? (*Henri mumbles unintelligibly. Jeanne moves closer to him cautiously.*) Should I get one of the wardens? Henri.
(*Henri leaps and grabs her. They struggle in near-silent ferocity, Henri finally succeeding in pushing Jeanne to the floor, holding her in a firm arm lock. Both breathe heavily.*)

JEANNE:   Okay . . . let's just take it easy . . .

HENRI:   I'm going to punish you.

JEANNE:   Punish? No—help!

HENRI:   Shh!

JEANNE:   Help me!

HENRI:   *Shut up!* (*Jeanne is silent and looks mad with fear.*) Do you honestly think I got you here for a cosy little chat? To listen to you, to say nice things to you, to beg you for a final kiss? You've lost all sense of reason if you think I could ever forgive you for what you did to me. I will take my revenge.

JEANNE:   No—you won't . . . What are you going to do?

HENRI:   Simple. What you did to me. (*He pulls a glass bottle of acid from his pocket. Jeanne doesn't see this, she stares straight ahead, her eyes wide in paralysed terror.*)

JEANNE   (*a whisper growing louder*): You can't . . . You can't . . .

HENRI:   Oh, be quiet. You must be punished like I was, you bitch. (*Henri opens the bottle of vitriol with his teeth.*)

JEANNE:   No!

HENRI:   We'll be the perfect lovers . . . we'll be *made for each other!* (*He pours.*)

JEANNE   (*a terrible scream*): Aagh! (*She collapses in agony and crawls across the floor, screaming and retching. Henri goes over to her and continues pouring acid on her face.*)

HENRI:   Hurts, doesn't it.

JEANNE:   My face, my face . . .

HENRI:    Nothing can help you now . . .
JEANNE:   No, no! Aagh!
HENRI:    Shh . . . Screaming won't help . . . and I don't want to kill you
          . . . that would be too much . . .
JEANNE:   I'm burning!
HENRI:    It hurts, doesn't it. It's *Hell*.
JEANNE:   My skin! My skin! My skin!
HENRI     (*removing his bandages*): It's over . . . It's over . . . It's over . . .
          It's over . . .
JEANNE:   My skin! My skin! My skin!
HENRI:    You're like me now . . . Like me! Like me!

THE END

# The Torture Garden

## (Le Jardin des supplices, 1922)

*by*

### PIERRE CHAINE AND ANDRÉ DE LORDE

## Preface

China was commonly perceived as a land of torture in the occidental imagination for, as George Ryley Scott writes:

> Of all the countries in all the world China has perhaps acquired a reputation for being the one place in which torture is more universal and takes stranger, more cruel, and more revolting forms than it does in any other part of the civilized and uncivilized globe. Much of this reputation is due to the description, in books of fiction, of forms of torture which have originated largely in the fertile imaginations of sensational novelists.
>
> (Scott 1995, 102)

*Le Jardin des supplices* (1899), by Octave Mirbeau (1850–1917)—and the Grand-Guignol's subsequent adaptation of it—may seem, at first glance, to be good examples of fertile imaginations creating such a myth of China, but both versions are more complex than they initially seem. Mirbeau's novel was a particularly notorious work of fiction in the context of the late 1800s. It was even described as 'the most sickening work of art in the nineteenth century' (quoted in Mirbeau 1989, 7). The novel remains, to this day, an explicit and disturbing work of erotic fiction. A classic example of decadent literature, the main part of the novel is a first-person account of a journey into excess and sadomasochistic 'pleasures'. The male narrator is, significantly, anonymous. Far from being the heroic Monsieur Marchal that he will become in the 1920s dramatic version, the nameless narrator is a debauched and lethargic failure who leads us on a journey of a sexual and morbid nature. It is when he meets Miss Clara on board the *Saghalien* (the *Sphinx* in the play) that his journey of immorality and self-humiliation takes an ultimately extreme direction. The young English widow Clara leads the French narrator into a taboo world of sexual horrors and horrific sex. She wallows in a mire of sadistic, exploitative and voyeuristic excesses in a decadent quest for self-fulfilment. This reaches its zenith (or rather nadir) in the Chinese torture garden of the title.

Clara is a constantly alluring and enigmatic figure as the narrator follows her into the torture garden, and elsewhere, giving the reader a simultaneously titillating and repulsive account of the sights, sounds and smells of this journey of depravity through India and China. These include the ravages of disease and torture: the narrator (and, of course, Mirbeau) relishes the explicit details of these excesses, whether in the long descriptions of elephantiasis, or the mutilation and destruction of condemned men and women. The narrator, in his role as Clara's apprentice, sometimes cannot conceal his disgust: he describes the executioner they meet as a 'monster' (Mirbeau 1989, 86), to Clara's outrage. Clara defends the torturer as an artist and condemns her squeamish lover on imperialist grounds: for wanting, essentially, a homogeneous—and obviously bourgeois—global culture. But such reprimands soon turn into the sexual: they always send a 'thrill of desire' through the masochistic narrator's veins.

In addition to such graphic and sensual descriptions that make the novel quasi-naturalistic, another controversial and shocking aspect of the original novel is its sustained exposé of the politics and ideology of colonialism. We are told that 'the filth of (occidental) progress' (Mirbeau 1989, 83) is causing the destruction of China. Clara makes it clear that the cruellest nations are not oriental but the English and French. Moreover, in a delightfully ironic moment, we are told that the landscape artist Li-Pe-Hang, designer of the torture garden itself, had a major influence on Kew Gardens (Mirbeau 1989, 100). Early in the novel, we find arrogant European figures boasting about their violent excesses. Sometimes this takes the form of outright racism, on other occasions it is a similarly despicable patronizing attitude towards the indigenous peoples. One figure, a particularly loathsome officer (Smithson in the play is based on him), boasts of cannibalism, going so far as to describe the different flavours and textures of the European people he has devoured. He draws the line at eating 'negroes', however, because they are 'wild beasts': an attitude Clara rejects with her condescending redemption of negroes as 'gentle and gay . . . they are like children' (Mirbeau 1989, 42).

Over all, Mirbeau's erotic novel is a haunting depiction of the pitiless and self-serving excesses of colonialist and bourgeois mentality. As the narrator declares 'There is nothing real, then, except evil!' (Mirbeau 1989, 47).

Pierre Chaine and André de Lorde's adaptation of Le Jardin des supplices opened at the Grand-Guignol on 28 October 1922. The adaptation keeps a number of the central characters, incidents and speeches from the novel, although we are spared several of the more excessive moments, and neither does the play have quite the political and satirical clout of the original. All the same, it is a long and substantial play, establishing a depth of character, context and situation unusual in the Grand-Guignol repertoire. What is not unusual about the play is the fact that it is a dramatization. The Grand-Guignol, like the melodramatic tradition it emerged from, made a significant contribution to the history of theatrical adaptation. It took classics of horror and suspense by writers like Poe and Kipling; Maurice Level used his own short fictions as a starting point for his plays; and the theatre even used film as a source for its drama.

Jean Marchal, the central male character in the play, is initially established as a kind of forerunner to the James Bond-style hero. He works for the French government, actively involved in undermining subversive activity in China. When we first meet him in the play, he is about to embark on another covert mission for the government. We soon discover, however, that he has become romantically involved with Clara. The young Englishwoman is the ultimate *femme fatale*. In both the play and novel, her actions, world-view and demeanour are equivalent and recognizable. However, the play turns her into Mata Hari: not content with her being simply a pleasure-seeker, she is turned into a spy. This undoubtedly gives more drama to the piece, ensuring that the play is, at least to a certain extent, a thriller (as with so many other pieces of 'horror' drama in the Grand-Guignol, 'suspense' is probably a more appropriate generic description).[1]

Most significantly, making Clara a spy gives a reason for the horrific mutilation of her at the end of the play. She is simply receiving her retribution, and although she swears to her lover that she has not betrayed him, her answer is not guaranteed to be the truth and the audience's sympathies may lean towards the underground revolutionaries of the Scarlet Dragon. The radicals tell Marchal that Clara has betrayed him, and secure safe passage out of China for him. What we find here is an example of just retribution in the Grand-Guignol. Although this form of theatre often seems amoral it sometimes sustains the force of retribution so familiar in melodramatic theatre. Clara's long description of the demise of Annie becomes a melodramatic and sinister encounter—

---

[1] The horror potential of the play is reinforced by the fact that Clara's excesses as a *femme fatale* with a penchant for sadistic pleasure-seeking turn her into a modern vampire in her parasitic and destructive exploitation of Marchal, Annie and others. Aptly enough, her bloodlust—witnessed most explicitly during the torture of Ti-Bah—is punished in her demise wherein the gouging of her eyeballs with a needle is equivalent to the archetypal death-by-penetration in horror: the vampire's destruction by the stake.

complete with threatened blackmail—between the two women. It is in such ways that the adaptation can be seen as a melodramatization, not least—in its theatrical context—to inject more action and thrills into the play.

There are substantial changes in the process of adaptation: the poet Wang is not the political radical described in the play, but rather a tragic figure who has been tortured so long that he can only howl like an animal while Clara obscenely recites his own verses to him. Likewise, the play does not present the young woman rubbed all over with red peppers and her nipples crushed with thumbscrews (Mirbeau 1989, 100), nor several other ghastly executions and tortures dwelt on in the novel. This all seems to endorse that familiar chant in adaptation studies, namely that theatre is rarely as bold as fiction, and that even the most notorious 'Theatre of Horror' drew the line at certain spectacles. The dramatic Clara, however, does not remain untouched as she does in the novel. Mirbeau's novel ends when Clara comes to after her seizure, promising the narrator 'Never again!' although he sees this ominously mocked by the grotesque phallus of a bronze ape (Mirbeau 1989, 112). The play includes the seizure but concludes with the blinding of Clara with hot needles. This is done in political retribution, but is also a 'just desserts' for all the delight the Englishwoman took in watching the misery of others: 'let us begin with the eyes . . . those eyes which loved to feast on suffering and death', as Ti-Mao decrees. Injuries to the eye—whether through eye-gouging or vitriol attack—have a special place in the Grand-Guignol. Freud associates the deep-seated horror of eye injury or going blind with castration:

> We know from the psychoanalytic experience, however, that the fear of damaging or losing one's eyes is a terrible one in children. Many adults retain their apprehensiveness in this respect, and no physical injury is so much dreaded by them as an injury to the eye. We are accustomed to say, too, that we will treasure a thing as the apple of our eye. A study of dreams, and phantasies and myths has taught us that anxiety about one's eyes, the fear of going blind, is often enough a substitute for the dread of being castrated.
>
> (Freud 1985, 352)

Clara and other female victims of eye-gouging such as Louise in *Un crime dans une maison de fous* (de Lorde and Binet 1925) and Claudine in René Berton's *La Drogue* (1930) are all established as objects of beauty and desire. Their blinding represents the ruination of their desirability (making them abject), and therefore—in castration-complex style—the devastation of their former empowerment.

*The Torture Garden* serves as an interesting comparison to *The Ultimate Torture*. The earlier play is imbued with racism, above all with the threat of a barbaric, unseen enemy. *The Torture Garden*, in contrast, presents several Chinese characters (albeit, originally, with actors like Paulais in make-up). The first to appear is the enigmatic Prince Li-Tong. This dreamy and, so we are told, opium-addicted figure gazes at the stars and quotes Chinese poetry. The character may be enigmatic, but in comparison to the brutal westerners, he seems somewhat civilized, recommending hot tea to the loutish drunk, Muller. Similarly, some of the other Chinese characters are given depth and psychology. The exploited 'dancer' Ti-Bah springs to mind here, and there is even a level of empathy for Ti-Mao, the retired torturer, when he exacts punishment on Clara. As in Mirbeau's original, many of the decadent Europeans are far more repugnant than the Chinese they exploit and patronize for their own pleasure or gain.

Edward Said coined the word 'Orientalism' in his book of the same title (1978), his groundbreaking analysis of Occidental traditions of interpreting the Orient. Above all in French and English culture, Said identifies a tendency to see the Orient as the ultimate 'Other' standing in stark contrast to their own cultures and ideologies. Said explains that this view is predominantly racist, ethnocentric and imperialistic. In this view, the Orient is perceived as being characterized by 'its sensuality, its tendency to despotism, its aberrant mentality, its habits of inaccuracy, its backwardness' (Said 1978, 205). Said's assertion is easily applied to the Grand-Guignol's construction of the Orient: whether seen or unseen, Grand-Guignol's China is a forum for barbarism and excess. As Clara says, 'Everything is so horrific in this country: love, nature, disease, death.'

Grand-Guignol's China may serve as an antithesis to the nobler values of Europe, but we should not overlook the irony. We have already foregrounded the destabilizing irony of *The Ultimate Torture*'s finale, and although Chaine and de Lorde may not be as unremittingly radical as Mirbeau, their play nevertheless locates a great deal of horror in the desire and demand of Clara and her increasingly corrupted Marchal.

The premiere featured Paula Maxa and L. Paulais. Maxa, predictably, took the key role of Clara. This is a demanding role: Marchal may be the focalizing character, but Clara is the central figure in the play. She needs to be in part alluring and yet despicable. Paulais took the role of Han. Although appearing only in the latter half of the play, Han is a role that makes great demands on the performer. The character may not execute or endure physical violence but he needs significant gravitas: he must connote an aura of intimidation, the threat of what he *might* do. This comes into play, above all, in his relationship with, and provocation of, Marchal. This takes on an urgency towards the end of the play when he orders the Torture of the Ribbon of Flesh to be executed on Ti-Bah in front of Marchal, despite the latter's pleading for clemency. If Han will have that done to an insolent servant, what will he do to Marchal? He clearly suspects that the Frenchman is the assassin of a major noble, and audiences will remember that he has already warned that the killer of Li-Tong will be 'made an example of'.

As in other Grand-Guignol plays, especially de Lorde's, *The Torture Garden* is economical in its horrors and exemplary in its pace. There are four principal moments of onstage violence: the murder of Li-Tong; Annie's attempt to assault Clara; the punishment of Ti-Bah by the Torture of the Ribbon of Flesh; and the blinding of Clara. Apart from that, there are numerous descriptions of violent excess, such as Clara's account of the Torture of the Bell, and Marchal's post-traumatic incoherence after the torture garden. De Lorde and Chaine manipulate the audience and sustain a tension throughout the play. Part of the tension is created by the fact that the audience is never sure where the play is going: the murder of Li-Tong is a surprise; and Han's provocation of Marchal comes to nothing, contrary to expectation. The play is about the deceptive nature of appearances and is built on carefully timed revelation: Marchal is having an affair with Clara; Clara is a spy; Ti-Mao and his entourage are really members of the notorious Scarlet Dragon sect; the charming manners of characters disguise their contempt and suspicion. It is also about the volatility of emotions, not least when lust comes into play. We see military hero Marchal allow himself to be corrupted in his descent from his place of honour and duty into debauchery: deserting his post for the morally dubious charms of Clara.

In his enlightening analysis of *Thrillers*, Martin Rubin asserts that a 'key descriptive figure for the heightened world of the thriller is the *labyrinth*' (Rubin 1999, 22). The many twists and turns of the thriller plot are like a journey (for the participating characters and readers alike) through a maze until the Minotaur is confronted and destroyed, and escape is successfully achieved. This is certainly helpful in analysing thriller narratives, but it could be argued that it is also a useful metaphor for the plays of the Grand-Guignol.[2] Certainly sex farces like *Tics* lead both characters and audience on convoluted, maze-like journeys while the horror plays are structured as increasingly nerve-wracking voyages into terror until the ultimate horror is confronted. We should stress that Rubin, drawing on theorists like Pascal Bonitzer (see Rubin 1999, 22–30), is using the labyrinth strictly as a metaphor for the thriller *film*.

---

[2] Interestingly, H.P. Lovecraft also defines the plays of the Grand-Guignol as thrillers (Lovecraft 1973, 50).

Cinema can use numerous locations and tracking shots in the 'physical' construction of labyrinthine journeys; the Grand-Guignol, in contrast, may have a maze-like narrative, its claustrophobic, fixed-location stage settings representing the final chamber of the Minotaur's or Medusa's lair.

If the heroes of many thrillers may escape such lairs, the Grand-Guignol is more likely to present what we could call the triumph of the Minotaur or Medusa. The monsters of the Grand-Guignol are blood-thirsty Minotaurs or Medusas that can petrify you with a gaze, while their counterparts in the plays are more often the failed adventurers decaying in the labyrinth than Theseus or Perseus-like heroes, and the numerous violent and macabre endings to the plays emphasize this. We need only think of the unsightly 'Minotaur' Henri and his complex plan to lure Jeanne into his clutches (*The Final Kiss*), or the mortifying gaze of the mad-eyed 'Medusa' Hélène, beholding the death of Joubert (*The Kiss of Blood*). In contrast, the entrapment of the killer in *Jack* represents the death of the Minotaur as it allows present danger to become, appropriately enough, *legendary* (Violette's encounter will certainly grace the pages of the modern myth-making *faits divers* that she reads with such fascination at the beginning of the play). Marchal is permitted to be a failed hero rather than a victim at the end of *The Torture Garden* when he is dragged out of the 'labyrinth' by Li-Tchang who, like the string of Ariadne, leads Marchal to safety and freedom while the monstrous Clara is destroyed.

# THE TORTURE GARDEN

*(Le Jardin des supplices, 1922)*

*by*

PIERRE CHAINE AND ANDRÉ DE LORDE

*Based on the novel by Octave Mirbeau*

---

Muller
The Captain
Smithson
Li-Tong
Madame Lacroix
Lady Huntley
Mrs Clara Watson
Jean Marchal
Kipai
Annie
Han
Ti-Bah
Li-Tchang
Ti-Mao

---

## ACT 1

*(A corner of the bridge on board the cruiser Sphinx. Nightfall. The occasional ship bell and horn can be heard while in the distance there is music from a ballroom. Cabins are stage left. Muller, Smithson and the Captain are drinking and smoking. Li-Tong is at the side of the ship, looking at the sea and the sky.)*

MULLER *(draining his glass)*: You've certainly got some excellent whisky on board, Captain . . .

CAPTAIN: You'd probably be wiser to have something a little more thirst quenching.

MULLER: This is fine—believe me.

SMITHSON: Yeah, at the moment, but just you wait—

MULLER: I know . . . I'll regret it! But I can't help it . . . my throat's burning up . . . it's so stifling . . .

CAPTAIN: It's only thirty-eight degrees!

MULLER: That's hot enough for me . . .

LI-TONG (*approaching*): You could always have some tea, Monsieur Muller. Hot tea, like we do in China.

MULLER: Tea? In this weather!

LI-TONG: It would certainly quench your thirst.

SMITHSON: If you think this is hot, you should come on one of my trading trips to Oubanghi.

MULLER: Sure, everything's relative.

CAPTAIN: The best thing to do is not to think about it too much. It won't bother you then. Just listen to them dancing on the upper deck—they seem happy enough!

SMITHSON: They're crazy! How can anyone enjoy themselves in this—

MULLER: What? In weather like this, lust is in the air . . . All those half-naked women . . . It's not so much a ball as an orgy!

CAPTAIN: If you think that, it's probably best to keep you down here then, Monsieur Muller. (*Everyone laughs. Enter Madame Lacroix and Lady Huntley, both in evening dress.*)

MADAME LACROIX: Well, the gentlemen seem to be enjoying themselves—good evening Captain!

CAPTAIN: Madame Lacroix, Lady Huntley . . . Good evening, ladies.

MADAME LACROIX: Captain, gentlemen.

CAPTAIN: I hope you are having a wonderful time, ladies?

MADAME LACROIX: We certainly are!

LADY HUNTLEY: I don't think we have any choice! (*Captain laughs.*)

MADAME LACROIX: Captain . . . I'm saving a foxtrot for you . . .

LADY HUNTLEY: And I will settle for nothing less than a *tango*!

CAPTAIN: A tango! At my age!

MADAME LACROIX: And you as well, Prince Li-Tong!

LI-TONG: I am sorry, ladies, but I do not dance.

LADY HUNTLEY: What a shame!

MADAME LACROIX: Jilted again! (*They exit stage right, laughing.*)

CAPTAIN (*calling after them*): I'll see you presently, ladies.

MULLER: Oh no you don't—what about that game of poker you promised us?

CAPTAIN: What, without Marchal?

SMITHSON: I think Marchal's up there swapping his mutton for a bit of lamb! Haha!

CAPTAIN: No, he's packing actually. He's going to disembark at Hanoi.

MULLER: Why?

CAPTAIN: Taking up his post, I suppose.

MULLER: Oh yeah, he's a soldier isn't he? I'd forgotten. You never see him in uniform.

CAPTAIN: You will—I'm sure he'll have put it on for the party.

SMITHSON: He's part of the Hanoi garrison, is he?

MULLER: Not exactly—he's on some mission in China.

SMITHSON: What sort of mission?

CAPTAIN: I wouldn't know. There's always some trouble or other.

LI-TONG: Great danger. Everything is treacherous: the land, the paddy fields, the enemy is invisible . . .

CAPTAIN: Monsieur Marchal knows the land. It's not the first time he's been there.

LI-TONG: But Hanoi to Phnom Penh is a long way. I hope Monsieur Marchal avoids all the dangers. I hope he does. (*Walks away.*)

MULLER: When do we arrive at Hanoi?

CAPTAIN: In about six hours.

SMITHSON: Is that all? *Fantastic.*

MULLER: Can we get off the ship as soon as we get there?

CAPTAIN: Of course. We'll be docked for a couple of days, for coal and—

MULLER: Two days! Thank god! Now, what about the women in Hanoi?

LI-TONG: Ah—the phoenix desires to play with the dragon!

SMITHSON (*laughing*): Don't you just love those Chinese metaphors!

CAPTAIN: Yes, Muller, you can get anything you want . . . Annamites, Japanese, Spanish . . . whatever colour you want . . . and, er, whatever *gender* you want too. (*Smithson roars with laughter.*)

MULLER: Just make sure I've got a place on the first boat that's going ashore.

SMITHSON: Me too!

CAPTAIN: A touch of cabin fever, gentlemen?

MULLER: It's been a month since I—

CAPTAIN: Just think what's it like for me!

MULLER (*sarcastic*): Yeah, right . . .

CAPTAIN: I'm sorry?

MULLER: Oh come on, we know what's been going on—

SMITHSON: A certain attractive young English lady called Mrs Watson . . .

CAPTAIN: I assure you—

SMITHSON: Don't deny it!

CAPTAIN (*points stage left*): Ssh . . . she might hear you . . .

MULLER: Isn't she at the party?

CAPTAIN: No, she's in her cabin.

SMITHSON: You're always with her . . .

CAPTAIN: This is the fifth trip she's made on my ship, so I've come to know her—

SMITHSON: And what sort of lady is this Mrs Clara Watson?

CAPTAIN: A most extraordinary lady. Although she's barely twenty-eight, she's already been around the world . . . She actually lives in China now.

LI-TONG: Yes, Shanghai. My hometown.

CAPTAIN: Her father was a ship owner from London and settled in Canton . . .

LI-TONG: I heard he traded in opium.

SMITHSON: She's a very strange woman . . .

MULLER: Is she married?

CAPTAIN: She *was*, quite a while ago, to an elderly Chinese gentleman.

LI-TONG: The governor of Chan-Tong province.

CAPTAIN: But she was widowed soon after.

SMITHSON: Lucky her!

(*Enter Clara.*)

CAPTAIN: Here she is.

(*All stand up. Clara is wearing nothing but a simple, elegant dress made of thin, white muslin.*)

CLARA: Good evening, gentlemen. Don't get up for me . . . I've just come for a breath of air . . . It's such a balmy night. (*Looks to horizon*) Not far from land are we, Captain?

CAPTAIN: Indeed.

CLARA: Mmm. You can smell the fragrance in the air . . . A rich, alluring perfume . . . It smells like the skin of a woman beneath a mink coat . . .

LI-TONG (*approaching her*): The poet Lok-Ya said 'My true love sends me the perfume of her lips with the sweep of a fan'. It is the sacred land of my ancestors sending their breath to us!

CLARA: It's so beautiful . . . I can always feel it in my body when I get near to China . . . A magical land where you can live without restraint . . . I feel free of Europe!

SMITHSON: I'm the same, Mrs Watson, I don't like Europe either.

CLARA: I *hate* it. Europe makes me ill. I could never live there again. I'd feel trapped like an animal in a cage.

SMITHSON: Yes, it's a prison. Especially for people like me who work in the colonies. We're treated like criminals—

CAPTAIN: Really?

SMITHSON: *Really.* They always ask us how many niggers we've killed.

CAPTAIN: Good grief!

SMITHSON: Have we killed them *en masse* or one at a time with bullets, cannon balls, sticks of dynamite . . .

MULLER: Come on, Smithson, you're forgetting there's a lady present. Let's talk about . . . love and romance!

CAPTAIN: But whoever talks of death talks also of love. Wouldn't you agree, Mrs Watson?

CLARA: You're right about Europe. It's prejudiced, full of hypocrisy and narrow-mindedness . . . In China you can be totally free. Well, people of our class, anyway. Monsieur Li-Tong, accompany me to the bridge. We can talk about the spirits of the air and you can recite old Chinese poetry about the lotus, bamboo and jade!

LI-TONG: *Ouang tei thcou!*

CLARA: *Oua tchan moug.*

MULLER:   I wouldn't mind a bit of that poetry myself—

SMITHSON:   Yes . . .

CLARA:   No. Please stay here. (*Ironic*) You might frighten the spirits away. Stay here and . . . talk about Europe. (*Exits with Li-Tong. Silence.*)

SMITHSON:   She's obviously got something on with our little Chinese friend . . .

CAPTAIN:   Our 'little Chinese friend' happens to be a very important person in his country.

MULLER:   He's normally off his head on opium!

CAPTAIN:   That doesn't prevent him being—
(*Enter Marchal.*)

MARCHAL:   Evening . . .

SMITHSON:   About time too!

CAPTAIN:   Have you finished packing?

MARCHAL:   Ages ago. I've been saying my goodbyes. Most of the ladies won't be up when I leave in the morning.

CAPTAIN:   Have you said goodbye to Mrs Watson?

MARCHAL:   No, I couldn't find her. I thought she might be here . . .

SMITHSON:   She just left.

MULLER:   She's on the bridge.

MARCHAL:   Well, if you'll excuse me . . .

MULLER:   I wouldn't go there if I were you . . .

MARCHAL:   Sorry?

SMITHSON (*ironic*): She's reading the heavens with a son of the skies.

MARCHAL:   What?

CAPTAIN:   She's with Monsieur Li-Tong.

SMITHSON (*loud laugh*): I think the phoenix is playing with the dragon, as they say in China!

MARCHAL:   I'm sorry, I don't understand Chinese.

CAPTAIN:   I think the gentlemen are suggesting that Mrs Watson is otherwise engaged.

MULLER:   Our Mrs Watson is quite something!

SMITHSON:   She's going to get herself into all sorts of—

MARCHAL:   She seems rather carefree, but it's just bravado . . .

MULLER:   So if someone told you that underneath it all she's actually as pure as the driven snow you wouldn't be surprised?

MARCHAL:   Not at all. Why?

SMITHSON (*sniggering*): Pure . . . You haven't been watching, have you . . . The way she talks, smiles . . . The way she moves her body . . . Her breasts are so . . .

CAPTAIN:   Ah, Smithson, you're getting a little carried away! You really do need those two days in Hanoi!

MULLER:   She just loves to tease . . . Always naked under those dresses she wears . . .

SMITHSON:   But strictly no-go to guys like us!

MULLER:   She knows she's safe with us. Our Western inhibition. But she'd better watch out. Better not play her little game with me much longer. One of these days—

MARCHAL: What? What will you do?

MULLER: Treat her like one of those Annamite whores . . . I'll take her by force if necessary . . .

MARCHAL: You're drunk.

MULLER: She's asking for it!

SMITHSON: I know her sort of English woman. They seem like puritan angels but . . .

MARCHAL (*growing anger*): Gentlemen, I think you'd better—

CAPTAIN: Monsieur Smithson, a little more respect if you don't mind. She is a passenger on my ship and . . .

MULLER: But most passengers don't act like—

MARCHAL: *Muller.*

MULLER: What?

MARCHAL: You'd better shut up. I will not let anyone insult a woman whose conduct has been irreproachable.

MULLER: Irreproachable! A woman who hangs around in dark corners with sailors, giving them money . . . In exchange for what, I wonder!

MARCHAL: That's enough!

MULLER: What about that sleazy bar in Shanghai?

MARCHAL: Enough of this nonsense.

MULLER: One of the sailors saw her. You wouldn't *believe* what—

CAPTAIN: That'll do, Muller.

MARCHAL (*looming over Muller*): Not another word. Understand?

MULLER (*standing*): We'll see about that!

CAPTAIN: Gentlemen, please.

SMITHSON: Muller, don't . . .

MARCHAL: You're behaving like a hooligan.

MULLER: Say that again you'll get a smack in the mouth. (*Suddenly enraged. Captain and Smithson hold him.*) Yeah—a smack in the mouth! *You French pig*!

SMITHSON: Ignore him, Marchal.

CAPTAIN: It's the drink.

MULLER: Get off me!

(*Clara enters.*)

CLARA: What on earth is going on?

MARCHAL: Muller has been—

CAPTAIN: No, it's nothing, Mrs Watson.

CLARA: Is he all right?

CAPTAIN: The heat . . .

SMITHSON (*to Muller*): Come on, let's go to the bridge . . . It'll calm you down . . .

MULLER: Let go! I want to . . .

CAPTAIN: I want you to come along with us. You can't stay here. Let's go. (*Captain and Smithson escort Muller offstage left.*)

CLARA:  What happened?

MARCHAL:  Don't worry about it, Mrs Watson. It was nothing . . .
nothing at all. Monsieur Muller drinks too much . . . and in
this temperature . . . (*Suddenly*) Clara, my darling!

CLARA:  Ssh!

MARCHAL:  Your lips!

CLARA  (*pushing him away gently*): Careful . . .

MARCHAL:  *Please*. This is our last night together. (*Seeing that they are
unobserved, Clara embraces Marchal and gives him a long
kiss.*) The ship will be at Hanoi for two days, and then
you'll be so far away from me . . .

CLARA:  Yes, too far.

MARCHAL  (*depressed*): And everything will be over!

CLARA:  You'll find yourself another Clara.

MARCHAL:  No, no other woman.

CLARA:  You're talking nonsense!

MARCHAL:  But I love you.

CLARA:  Love? *Lust* more like.

MARCHAL:  No, not lust—something deeper than that . . .

CLARA:  Nothing's wrong with lust, nothing's more *powerful* . . .

MARCHAL:  The thought of leaving you makes me feel that my heart is
being ripped out of me. It's so terrible—never to see you
again! To lose you forever!

CLARA:  This time tomorrow you'll have forgotten all about me.

MARCHAL:  Clara!

CLARA:  Tomorrow you'll be in Hanoi. All those phallic temples and
gardens of love. The beautiful dancers at the pagoda of
Tchin . . . (*Marchal signals his indifference.*) They're
beautiful, voluptuous, experienced. You'll forget about me.

MARCHAL:  No. I won't. I'll never forget your kiss . . . That hot tropical
night when I held you and felt you tremble . . . Remember?

CLARA:  It's not worth thinking about it anymore.

MARCHAL  (*bitter*): *You'll* forget *me*.

CLARA:  Let's not make a scene, darling. Calm down. I will always
keep a very precious memory of what we had. We shared a
wonderful journey of discovery together . . . Without you I
would have been so *bored*! But since that night at Port Said,
the time's flown by . . .

MARCHAL:  So I was just a distraction, was I? A fling? You just don't
understand. Clara, it is so much more than that for me. I
want to share my life with you.

CLARA:  Very well. Stay with me.

MARCHAL:  Stay?

CLARA:  Yes. In China. Come and live with me. My house and
gardens are wonderful: they are designed for love and
pleasure.

MARCHAL:  If only I could . . . But it's impossible.

CLARA: Why?

MARCHAL: You know why. The mission.

CLARA: Well, don't go. Stay with me.

MARCHAL: It'd be *desertion*.

CLARA: You're such a child, so *European*. All those pathetic European scruples.

MARCHAL: Well, you're talking like a typical *woman*. You don't understand how serious it is.

CLARA: What *exactly is* your mission? Do they really need you to put down some silly little rebellion?
(*Captain enters quickly.*)

CAPTAIN: Ah, Monsieur Marchal. (*To Clara*) Sorry to disturb you, Mrs Watson, but I have an urgent message for Monsieur Marchal.

CLARA: Of course, Captain.

MARCHAL: What is it?

CAPTAIN: A telegram from Hanoi. It's in code. I can help translate it. (*Marchal takes it.*)

CLARA: Nothing serious, I hope.

CAPTAIN (*to Marchal*): Official instructions.

CLARA: Is it about the Phnom Penh rebellion?

CAPTAIN: How do you know about that?

CLARA: Monsieur Li-Tong mentioned it . . .

CAPTAIN: I see that Monsieur Li-Tong isn't just interested in Chinese poetry.

CLARA: Monsieur Li-Tong deplores the rebellion. He's very worried about the diplomatic repercussions. What about the blockaded ships? Have they been freed? Monsieur Marchal—do tell us.

CAPTAIN: Madame, messages from the Admiralty are like love letters: strictly confidential.

CLARA: Sorry! If it's *really* so important . . .

CAPTAIN: Monsieur Marchal doesn't have the right to tell you if it's important or not . . . (*To Marchal*) Do you need anything deciphered?

MARCHAL: Yes . . . there are a few details . . .

CAPTAIN: Shall we retire to my cabin?

MARCHAL: It's probably not *that* important.

CLARA: If duty calls, gentlemen, don't let me get in the way. I'll go for a walk on the bridge.

MARCHAL: Just a couple of minutes . . . You sure you don't mind?

CLARA: As it's confidential . . . One can't be too careful, can one, Captain? (*Exits stage right.*)

MARCHAL: Really, Captain, you treated Mrs Watson like a spy!

CAPTAIN: Unjustified, I suppose?

MARCHAL: Unjustified *and* insulting! Mrs Watson—

CAPTAIN: Mrs Watson is associated with some of the most important people in Chinese politics. She comes and goes freely from

Cairo to Shanghai, and those journeys often coincide with the troubles on the Tonkin frontier.

MARCHAL: And . . . you suspect her?

CAPTAIN: Influential politicians visit her all the time . . . It would seem that her house is a centre of intrigue and conspiracy . . .

MARCHAL: But everyone's divided in China—everyone's in conspiracy with each other!

CAPTAIN: I am not talking about the general mood of rebellion. I'm talking about specific underground movements acting directly against *us* . . . our territory . . . And Mrs Watson looks very suspicious to me.

MARCHAL: I don't believe it . . .

CAPTAIN: You've been warned. Be extremely cautious.

MARCHAL: Captain. We both understand the importance of my current mission. It's not the first time I've been assigned a task like this. Now, just tell me how I'll get to the gunboat that's waiting for me at Hanoi.

CAPTAIN: I've been in touch with the *Vigilance* since dusk. I'll tell you when we're near it.

MARCHAL: At what time, roughly?

CAPTAIN: About three o'clock.

MARCHAL: I'll be ready. Nothing else?

CAPTAIN: No, that's all.

MARCHAL (*nods goodbye*): Captain. (*Starts to leave in the direction Clara went.*)

CAPTAIN: Monsieur Marchal?

MARCHAL: Captain?

CAPTAIN: Would you object to a little advice from an old gentleman?

MARCHAL: About what?

CAPTAIN: Mrs Watson.

MARCHAL: Oh?

CAPTAIN: Yes. I can't let you go without a word of warning. I regard it as my duty. (*Pause*) You're young. There's a good future ahead of you. Don't throw it away.

MARCHAL: I don't understand.

CAPTAIN: What I have to say is rather delicate. I would've kept quiet, if I didn't think you were in very real danger.

MARCHAL: Danger? What do you think—

CAPTAIN: Your argument with that alcoholic Muller.

MARCHAL: Well?

CAPTAIN: You defended Mrs Watson . . .

MARCHAL: As anyone would . . .

CAPTAIN: No. Not with such passion . . . There was something unmistakable in it . . . Be honest with me. You're in love with her.

MARCHAL: And what if that was true?

CAPTAIN: You mustn't. You must avoid her like the plague.

MARCHAL: Captain . . .

CAPTAIN: You don't know her. You think she's romantic and sentimental . . .

MARCHAL: She's had plenty of lovers, I don't doubt that—

CAPTAIN: Not lovers . . . *victims*. You heard what Muller said—

MARCHAL: He lied—you said so yourself!

CAPTAIN: What else could I do? Be a drunken lout like him!? But when it comes to saving a fine young man, gallantry goes out the window . . .

MARCHAL: So what they said about her is true?

CAPTAIN: I'm sorry . . . I can see how upset you are . . .

MARCHAL: It's so hard to believe . . . And what happened in that place in Shanghai that Muller mentioned?

CAPTAIN: Last year we were reloading at Shanghai. She went to a bar and stripped naked and danced for the locals . . . They went wild . . . It ended in bloodshed—almost a lynching. She had to be rescued by force.

MARCHAL: Why tell me now? On my last night! Without you I'd have had good memories of her . . . Just let me go . . .

MULLER: I'm just scared that you *won't* go.

MARCHAL: Captain!

CAPTAIN: Or that you'll pretend to leave but go back to her.

MARCHAL: But the mission . . . It'd be desertion! You doubt me? You question my honour?

CAPTAIN: No, I don't doubt your honour . . . But that woman is dangerous. She's perverse and cruel. Go to her again and she will drag you down into the gutter with her.

MARCHAL: Don't worry, Captain. You've warned me. It was just a little episode in my life . . .

CAPTAIN: Yes, yes. I've stood here before and heard someone just like you tell me the same thing . . . He said he'd avoid her too, but he fell right into the trap!

MARCHAL: Another lover?

CAPTAIN: Yes, he was an ensign on a warship . . . He was healthy, well balanced, impeccable. She turned him into a wreck of a man. A coward. As sick as her. He gave up everything to follow her. I witnessed the whole thing from the start . . . As soon as she was done with him, she took another lover, one of my passengers. He killed himself on this very ship, over there . . . in her cabin.

MARCHAL: How can she travel on this ship!?

CAPTAIN: She even insists on the same cabin! The one spattered with the blood of that poor man.

MARCHAL: It's horrific!

CAPTAIN: That's why I've warned you.

MARCHAL: Thank you, Captain.

CAPTAIN: I hope I haven't upset you.

MARCHAL: Doesn't matter.

CAPTAIN: So can I rest assured that—

MARCHAL: I will do my duty.

CAPTAIN: I'm pleased to hear it. I'll see you—

MARCHAL: Yes.

(*Captain exits stage right. Marchal is still for a moment. Enter Clara.*)

CLARA: Has your meeting finished?

MARCHAL (*cold*): Yes. Finished.

CLARA: It interrupted our goodbye. I guess it couldn't wait.

MARCHAL: It was urgent.

CLARA: Well . . . we've got one more night.

MARCHAL: I've got things to do.

CLARA: What's wrong?

MARCHAL: Nothing.

CLARA: You're completely different.

MARCHAL: You were right. We should just say goodbye and forget each other.

CLARA: Look at me. (*She takes Marchal by the shoulders but he looks away.*) Why won't you look at me? Did the Captain say something to you?

MARCHAL: Please . . .

CLARA: Tell me what he said.

MARCHAL: You *know* what he said.

CLARA: That *swine* . . .

MARCHAL: Well? Are they true?

CLARA: Yes—I've had my share of lovers. What do you expect? I'm young . . . free . . . I've done nothing to be ashamed of!

MARCHAL: The man you deserted. Who killed himself in *your* cabin.

CLARA: Was that my fault? He followed me . . . pestered me . . . I didn't want anything to do with him . . . He disgusted me . . . But I couldn't get rid of him . . . So I gave in to him, out of pity, out of cowardice! One night he was high on cocaine and killed himself. You can't blame me for his stupidity!

MARCHAL: What about that night in Shanghai last year . . . in that bar?

CLARA: That was a stupid mistake, I admit. I went with a friend out of curiosity and I was foolish enough to wear my jewellery. We were attacked . . .

MARCHAL: They weren't after your jewellery! You stripped naked and—

CLARA: Shut up!

MARCHAL: You offered your body to them!

CLARA: Please, stop it.

MARCHAL: You gave in like a child! And you loved every minute of it! Everyone knows about you . . .

CLARA: Listen to me. Even if it was true, what does it matter when all I want right now is *you*? Don't you still want me?

MARCHAL: No, Clara, no . . .

CLARA: Are you scared?

MARCHAL: Yes, you frighten me . . .

CLARA: But I'm the woman you want . . .

MARCHAL: No!

CLARA: *Yes*. You chose me. You wouldn't have wanted some shrinking violet . . . It's me who can satisfy your desires . . .

MARCHAL: You've given yourself to everyone . . .

CLARA: So what? That was my choice! And now all I want is you!

MARCHAL: You *whore*!

CLARA (*upset*): Get away from me!

MARCHAL (*grabs hold of Clara*): Listen—I'm sorry! Forget what I said!

CLARA: Let go of me!

MARCHAL: Come on . . . It's our last night . . . Let's . . .

CLARA: No! I don't want to! You're hurting me!
(*Li-Tong rushes on.*)

LI-TONG: Please let go of her.

MARCHAL: You've been spying on us!

LI-TONG: Go to your cabin, Mrs Watson.
(*Clara exits to her cabin.*)

MARCHAL: You were going to meet her after I'd gone!

LI-TONG: I will not let you go to her cabin.

MARCHAL: Let me pass.

LI-TONG: No.

MARCHAL: I told you to step aside!

LI-TONG: The lady does not want to see you.

MARCHAL: She does—she's slept with me every night!

LI-TONG: Shut up, you dog!

MARCHAL (*approaches Li-Tong*): So you're her lover too, are you!

LI-TONG: Don't touch me with your filthy hands! (*They fight.*)

MARCHAL: I'm going to see her whether you—

LI-TONG: I'll kill you!

MARCHAL: Let go or I'll—

LI-TONG (*puts hand in his pocket as though he is going to pull out a knife*): I will kill you!
(*The men struggle violently. Marchal manages to grab Li-Tong round the neck and throttles him. Li-Tong eventually breaks free and Marchal pushes him with great force. Li-Tong struggles to keep his balance but falls over the side of the ship, emitting a loud scream. Marchal looks over the side in horror. Silence. Clara appears slowly, and immediately understands what happened.*)

CLARA: What have you done?

MARCHAL: He attacked me . . . I defended myself . . . I pushed and he fell . . . Raise the alarm, quick!

CLARA: Why? It's too dark. They'll never find him.

MARCHAL: It's horrific . . .

CLARA: No . . . it was just an accident . . . It must've been an accident . . . He was always high on cocaine . . . He lost his balance . . . and fell!

MARCHAL: What if someone heard him?

CLARA: They'd be here by now. Everyone's at the ball.

MARCHAL: Yes, that's true.

CLARA: Yes . . . No one will ever know . . . No one but me . . . but I'll never betray you . . . Never . . .
(*Clara gently leads Marchal towards her cabin.*)


## ACT 2

(*The boudoir in Clara's Shanghai villa, furnished with sumptuous Chinese furniture. Stage right a bay window opening out onto a rich, sunny garden. On the left the bedroom and a small, marble altar. At the back a curtain covers the main entrance. As the curtain rises, Clara is reclining on a divan, gently fanning herself. Annie appears at the bay window and steps in silently.*)

ANNIE (*whisper*): Clara! Clara!

CLARA (*startled*): Annie! What are you doing here?

ANNIE (*gives Clara a bunch of flowers*): I've brought you some flowers.

CLARA (*cold and serious*): Why are you here? You mustn't leave the hospital. You're not well.

ANNIE: I'm getting better—honestly. It was nothing.

CLARA: The doctors have forbidden you to leave . . .

ANNIE: I was so lonely . . . I wanted to see you, even just for a moment.

CLARA (*gentler*): You're such a child . . . So temperamental, so demanding . . .

ANNIE (*sitting*): You don't mind if I sit down for minute . . . while Monsieur Marchal's sleeping . . .

CLARA: You *mustn't* . . .

ANNIE (*pleading*): I won't be a nuisance, I promise . . . I'll leave as soon as he wakes up . . .

CLARA: No, go now.

ANNIE: Clara, why are you so mean to me? You're not the same anymore . . . What have I done to you? What have I said?

CLARA: *Don't* start crying. If you only knew how much your begging and pleading gets on my nerves. I can't stand it anymore.

ANNIE: I've been so unhappy since you got back.

CLARA: Why?

ANNIE: Because of him! Since you brought him back here I might as well not exist!

CLARA:  No, you're wrong. We'll always be friends. Nothing will change that.

ANNIE  (*reaching out to her*): Haven't I always been there for you?

CLARA  (*stepping away quickly*): Please—don't come near me. Look, I don't want to hurt you, but I can't take anymore . . . All your emotional blackmail . . . I need time to myself . . .

ANNIE  (*sad*): Yes . . . I understand . . . you can't stand me being here . . . I'll go . . . (*Pause*) Do you think he'll be asleep long?

CLARA:  Why?

ANNIE:  Aren't you sick of him yet? (*Suddenly violent*) A deserter! A waste of time—

CLARA:  Shut up! Do you understand?

ANNIE  (*resigned*): All right . . . But I'll be waiting for you . . . I won't give up . . . Come on, Clara—kiss me . . .

CLARA  (*turns away in disgust*): No—the doctor said it might be contagious.

ANNIE  (*disgusted*): The doctor!? You paid him to say I was ill, to keep me locked up . . . It wasn't disease that kept you away from me . . . it was disgust! You wanted rid of me! *But there's nothing wrong with me!* Ah . . . I can't breathe . . . oh God . . .! Help . . . (*Falls to her knees, her head falls to the divan and she clutches at her throat.*)

CLARA  (*spiteful*): Just look at you!

ANNIE:  I can't breathe . . . Don't let me die!

CLARA:  You're not dying . . . Look, Annie, I can help you . . . Calm down . . . I've got some ancient remedies given to me by a Tibetan witchdoctor . . . (*Clara goes over to a little table and takes a small bottle. She empties it into a cup.*) Drink this . . . it'll make you feel so much better . . . Drink it all down . . .

ANNIE:  No, no! I won't! It's *poison!*

CLARA:  Annie, you're being ridiculous.

ANNIE:  It's your fault I'm so ill—all those drugs—

CLARA:  You think that I'd—

ANNIE:  I wouldn't put anything past you! You're scared of me! Scared of what I might say to your precious new lover!

CLARA  (*puts cup down*): He knows everything about me. He knows me as well as you do. He loves me.

ANNIE:  He doesn't know everything! But I'll tell him . . . I'll tell him about Tao-Ming, and Wang—

CLARA:  Shut up!

ANNIE:  All the things you've done for money!

CLARA:  Shut up, you bitch!

ANNIE:  A bitch . . . yes, that's all I was to you . . . a bitch, a slave, a toy . . . But I won't be silenced!

CLARA:  Yes, you will. You're going to be confined.

ANNIE:  That's what you want, isn't it? Lock me away! Better than killing me! Better than poison!

CLARA:    You're already poisoned.

ANNIE:    What do you mean?

CLARA:    What do I mean? Nothing really. Simply that you're infected
          . . . your body's corrupted . . . And you know it is. You
          must be confined . . . Never let out . . .

ANNIE:    Yes, locked up forever! Locked up like a . . . (*she struggles
          with the word*) *leper*! (*Pause*) Oh my God, that's what I've
          got, isn't it . . .? I've contracted leprosy, haven't I!?

CLARA:    Calm down . . .

ANNIE:    I know it is . . . You're scared of me . . . You keep your
          distance . . . You refuse to touch me . . .

CLARA:    Look, we'll help you . . .

ANNIE:    No, I'm incurable . . . You'll let me rot away . . . while you
          stay beautiful and happy and loved . . . You—who made me
          like this!

CLARA:    Me?

ANNIE:    Yes—it's all your fault! All those debauched nights that
          poisoned my flesh! Well, you too must suffer! You will rot
          away with me! (*She tries to bite and scratch Clara who frees
          herself and screams in terror.*)

CLARA:    Kipai!

ANNIE:    I'm going to give you my disease!

CLARA:    Help! *Kipai*! (*Enter Kipai, Clara's manservant, who picks up
          Annie.*)

ANNIE:    Let go of me! I want to kill her! Poison her blood!

CLARA:    Take her away! Get her locked up!

ANNIE:    I hope you rot in hell!
          (*Kipai drags Annie out. Enter Marchal.*)

MARCHAL:  What on earth's happening?

CLARA:    Don't worry—it was Annie . . .

MARCHAL:  What's wrong with her . . .

CLARA:    The poor girl . . . It's terrible . . . I don't know how to tell
          you . . . Annie's very ill . . . She's caught a terrible disease!

MARCHAL:  What disease?

CLARA:    She's dying . . . of leprosy!

MARCHAL:  Leprosy?

CLARA:    A horrific type of leprosy called elephantiasis. Everything is
          so horrific in this country: love, nature, disease, death.

MARCHAL:  How awful—how on earth did she catch it?

CLARA:    Who knows? No one can explain it . . .

MARCHAL:  Poor Annie! She was so beautiful!

CLARA:    Her skin will swell up . . . horrible tumours will cover
          her . . .

MARCHAL:  Don't think about it.

CLARA:    Her face will become an enormous pouch of flesh, distorted
          and—

MARCHAL:  Clara—there's no point thinking about it.

CLARA:    She'll rot away like a living corpse . . . she'll become a disgusting, repulsive creature . . . (*Shudders.*)

MARCHAL:    The idea that someone so close to us is going to go through such suffering.

CLARA:    Now that she knows . . . I don't think she'll live long.

MARCHAL:    Poor Annie . . . such a beautiful woman . . .

CLARA:    I know it's sad, but we mustn't see her any more . . . I'll make sure she's well looked after in confinement.

MARCHAL:    Poor Annie. (*Silence*)

CLARA:    Shall we go out?

MARCHAL:    With the sun at full strength?

CLARA:    We'll take my sampan . . .

MARCHAL:    But it's so nice here . . . Besides, I wanted you all to myself today . . .

CLARA:    I want to show you something very special . . .

MARCHAL:    Tomorrow.

CLARA:    We can't do it tomorrow, darling . . . You can only feed the prisoners on Wednesdays. Tomorrow, the prison's shut— even to me.

MARCHAL:    You want to go to the prison?

CLARA:    Yes, I want to show you the prison, the convicts . . . It's truly amazing!

MARCHAL:    Really, I can't imagine why you'd like that . . . A Chinese prison—it must be horrible!

CLARA:    It's *beautiful*! I've seen prisoners hanged back in England . . . Anarchists garrotted in Spain . . . In Russia I saw a group of soldiers flog a young girl to death . . . I've even seen a beautiful young woman fed to a lion in a cage . . . But nothing is as frightening, so terribly beautiful as what they have here: the Torture Garden . . .

MARCHAL:    Clara, I beg you, don't go there . . . Resist the temptation . . . Look at yourself in the mirror . . . Look at your eyes, they're mad with cruelty!

CLARA    (*in Marchal's arms*): When I see the convicts being punished, I don't know what comes over me . . . I'm filled with such extraordinary desires, it goes so deep into my body that I would love you so intensely tonight, I would be so *wild* . . .

MARCHAL:    No, Clara, it's frightful!

CLARA:    *Yes* . . . We'll come back on the river tonight . . . We'll go and see Ti-Bah, she's so pretty and delectable . . . Don't you want to?

MARCHAL:    Have you forgotten what happened when you saw the execution at the city gates?

CLARA:    I don't remember . . .

MARCHAL:    I do . . . It was terrible . . . You collapsed. We had to carry you away . . . Your muscles were all constricted and you were trembling . . . I thought you were going to die . . .

CLARA: Really?

MARCHAL: And then suddenly you came to and burst into tears . . . You held onto me and promised me over and over again like a child: 'I won't do it again, I promise, never again!' And you've already forgotten all that! You want me to endure yet another hideous spectacle that'll be too much for you . . . that'll overwhelm you again . . .

CLARA (*resigned*): Whatever you want.

MARCHAL: Clara, when will you grow out of this madness, this degrading perversion? Why do you find such delight in suffering and death? Haven't you ever dreamed of a pure love, free of perversion and cruelty? Isn't the love we share good enough to make you happy? Let me love you . . . I can make you forget all those dangerous and horrifying desires that are tainted with bitterness and death . . .! Mixing blood and love—it's disgusting and blasphemous!

CLARA (*staring into his eyes*): And you've never mixed love and death? What about that wonderful night on the ship . . . that *last* night . . .

MARCHAL: Forget that night! You'd driven me mad, I didn't know what I was doing . . .

CLARA: You regret it, do you?

MARCHAL: Ssh, please . . . I beg you. (*Gong sounds.*) Are you expecting someone?

CLARA: Yes, someone you haven't met yet. He'll give us the warrant to visit the prison.

MARCHAL: Who is he?

CLARA: He's a very important mandarin.
(*The curtain at the back opens and in walks Han the mandarin and Ti-Mao.*)

CLARA: Greetings, venerable brother.

HAN: Little sister, please accept greetings from one so unworthy. I salute your guest, who must be a wise and learned man.

CLARA: My guest is a foreigner unfamiliar with traditional etiquette.

HAN: Each nation has its own customs. I am happy to comply with yours . . . I have travelled in England and America.

MARCHAL: Please forgive me, sir . . . I'm a barbarian when it comes to the Orient . . . I don't even know how I should address you!

HAN: Please. Let's be European! Imagine we met in a salon: you may call me Monsieur.

CLARA: Well, Monsieur Han, allow me to present Monsieur Marchal . . . Please sit down. (*Han sits on a chair while Clara and Marchal sit on a divan together.*) Have you brought what I requested?

HAN: Here is the authorization. (*He hands her a warrant. He indicates Ti-Mao who continues to stand, motionless, at the back of the room.*) And that is the head of the prison guards. He will accompany you around the prison and the garden. He understands your language very well and will be able to answer any questions you might have. (*Ti-Mao bows silently.*)

MARCHAL: I must say that I don't approve of Mrs Watson's curiosity.

HAN: You don't care for flowers, Monsieur Marchal?

MARCHAL: Flowers?

HAN: You will see the most wonderful vegetation . . . if you care for that sort of thing. The garden was created in the middle of the last century by Li-Pe-Hang, the greatest botanist who ever lived in China. The extraordinary vitality of the vegetation in the garden is complemented by the blood and bodies of the punished. It is the most beautiful garden of its kind in China.

CLARA: The Chinese are such astonishing artists. Among the flowers, among all that luscious vegetation are instruments of torture and death. My friend and I thank you for giving us the chance to . . .

HAN: Do not thank me. I wish my visit was simply for pleasure. I must apologize for what I have to ask. (*Stands*) I am truly sorry . . .

CLARA: What is it?

HAN: You've only just returned to China and I'm afraid I have to cause you some inconvenience  . . . But the provincial authorities require a statement.

CLARA (*standing*): A statement? Whatever for?

HAN: Were you not on the same ship as our venerated Prince Li-Tong? A statement from you will be most precious . . . and from you, Monsieur Marchal.

MARCHAL: Mine as well?

HAN: Was not your name on the list of passengers?

MARCHAL: Yes . . . But the Chinese police are so well informed, surely they've had access to the official inquest carried out by the naval authorities . . .

CLARA: They concluded that it was an accident.

HAN: The Chinese police consider it to be an assassination.

CLARA: Is there any proof?

HAN: Yes. The body was found washed up on the coast.

MARCHAL: Oh?

CLARA: Well?

HAN: There is evidence of strangulation on his body.

MARCHAL: Must've been one of the sailors, after the Prince's jewellery.

HAN: All of his money, his papers, and his jewellery were intact, either in his cabin or on his person.

CLARA: How strange.

HAN (*sitting*): Yes, strange. Like other things that have happened in the last few years.

CLARA:   What do you mean?

HAN:   Prince Li-Tong had many enemies. Many people wanted him dead.

CLARA   (*whisper*): You mean the Scarlet Dragon?

HAN:   Yes, maybe that's the direction we should pursue. Remember Tao-Ming? A rebel and brilliant engineer. Paid by Moscow. He invented a bomb of terrifying power. Happily the Prince evaded that particular attempt.

MARCHAL:   Why did they want to kill him?

CLARA:   He was hated for his repressive measures . . . He was ruthless—

HAN:   Not quite. He was too lenient on Wang the poet. He should have—
        (*Servant enters with tea.*)

MARCHAL:   He should have . . .?

CLARA   (*to servant*): What is it?

SERVANT:   *Out Sail* . . .

CLARA:   *Teni Kai.*
        (*Servant distributes tea and exits.*)

HAN:   You are very wise. One never knows, one never knows. Maybe that servant is part of the Scarlet Dragon. They are everywhere.

MARCHAL:   Is it some secret society?

HAN:   Yes, an abominable sect.

CLARA:   Partly political and partly religious.

HAN:   Fanatical, seditious . . . Revolutionaries who want to destroy order, tradition, empire: the whole of Chinese society. This Tao-Ming was part of it . . . and that poet Wang . . . They were captured and tortured . . . But nothing scared them . . . and their sect carried on . . . But this time, when we capture the killer of Prince Li-Tong, he will pay, pay for everything they've ever done . . . We will make an example of him. (*Drains his cup.*)

MARCHAL:   An example?

HAN:   We have amongst our torturers a remarkable man who knows everything about human anatomy. He works a body like a sculptor carves ivory or shapes a lump of clay. He knows how to cause the most indescribable pain and suffering . . . He can cause total agony in the dark, mysterious depths of the body . . . He can take just one nerve and make his victim scream for hours. I saw him cut a man into ribbons once . . . and yet the man *did not die*! (*Marchal looks unsteady.*) What's wrong, Monsieur Marchal?

MARCHAL:   The description of that butchery!

HAN:   In that case, perhaps a visit to the Torture Garden is inadvisable.

MARCHAL:   It's all right . . . If Mrs Watson wants to . . .

HAN    (*stands*): Very well. Before I go allow me to pay homage to my ancestors.

CLARA:    That'd be an honour for me and for my house.
(*Han goes over and kneels before the little marble altar. He murmurs what sounds like a prayer in Chinese. Then he turns his head towards Clara.*)

HAN:    *Hou li pe Wang.*

MARCHAL:    What's he saying?

CLARA:    Nothing . . . it's just a prayer.

HAN:    *Hou li pe Wang!*

CLARA:    You look so pale . . . (*whisper*) *You're giving yourself away!* Be careful . . . he can read your thoughts . . . you won't fool him . . . (*Pushes Marchal towards the bedroom.*)

MARCHAL    (*whisper*): I'm frightened . . . he scares me . . .

CLARA:    Go! (*Marchal exits hurriedly.*) Why did you ask me to send him out?

HAN:    I have orders to give you.

CLARA:    Very well.

HAN:    Can your 'friend' hear us?

CLARA:    No.

HAN:    He seemed somewhat nervous.

CLARA:    You don't trust him?

HAN:    How long have you known him? Were you together on the *Sphinx*?

CLARA:    Yes. There's nothing suspicious about him . . . nothing at all.

HAN:    If he's guilty, he must pay . . . We're counting on you . . .

CLARA:    On me? Impossible! What on earth can I do?

HAN    (*severe*): You will do exactly what you did to Tao-Ming and Wang. You gave them to us. You took them for a night with Ti-Bah . . .

CLARA    (*scared*): No!

HAN:    The family of Li-Tong is rich and powerful. Do you know what they have promised to the person who finds the assassin? Three hundred thousand taels. Just think of that. You will tell me who killed the Prince . . . You will tell me tonight at Ti-Bah's . . . at the third watch . . . (*Leaving*) Three hundred thousand! A fortune . . .
(*Han pulls back the curtain and exits slowly. Clara stands still, lost in thought as the curtain descends.*)

## ACT 3

(*A very elegant bedroom on board a Chinese boat. The river can be seen outside the portholes. The three entrances to the left, right and back are covered by curtains. It is nightfall and the room is illuminated with paper lanterns. A scent burner is smoking on the table. As the curtain rises we hear bizarre, voluptuous music played on plucked strings and struck blocks. Ti-Bah, nearly naked, sits on the floor filling pipes with opium. Enter Li-Tchang from the back doorway.)*

LI-TCHANG: Ti-Bah! Get upstairs and dance! There's money to be made . . .

TI-BAH: Not tonight, Li-Tchang!

LI-TCHANG: What? Some rich merchants from Han-Keou are here . . . Some mandarins as well . . . Get going!

TI-BAH: No. The master told me to wait here.

LI-TCHANG: Who for?

TI-BAH: You know . . . the *foreign woman* . . .

LI-TCHANG: That Englishwoman?

TI-BAH: Yes . . . She went to the Torture Garden today.

LI-TCHANG: And she always comes here afterwards . . .

TI-BAH: Always . . . I've got everything ready . . . lanterns, pipes, opium . . .

LI-TCHANG: She smokes opium?

TI-BAH: It's the only thing that can calm her. After she's been to that place she's possessed by evil . . .

LI-TCHANG: Nonsense! You're lucky she's coming here—she's rolling in money!

TI-BAH: I wouldn't touch her money . . . It's blood money! Didn't you know that?

LI-TCHANG: Of course I did.

TI-BAH: Why doesn't she go back to where she's come from? I'd rather put up with drunken sailors . . . or some disgusting dockside coolie . . . They're brutes but at least I know how to deal with them . . . I understand them . . . I know what they want . . . But she's like a monster from the depths . . . her kisses are deadly . . . when she touches you it's like the claws of an animal digging into your skin . . . and her eyes . . . her eyes terrify me . . .

LI-TCHANG: It's so late—maybe she won't come tonight—

TI-BAH: She will . . . she always does . . .
(*Sound of a boat approaching. The boatmen chant mournfully, the tune is like the 'Song of the Volga Boatmen'. Enter Ti-Mao.*)

TI-MAO: They're here!

TI-BAH (*at Ti-Mao's feet*): Master, have pity . . . I hate her . . . Not today! Let her have someone else!

TI-MAO: No—she wants you.

TI-BAH: Tell her I've already been taken!

TI-MAO: No. If she can't have you she'll go.

TI-BAH: Put her off until another day—

TI-MAO:  No! She must be here tonight, understand? *It is essential.*

TI-BAH:  I'm scared, Master! When she's come from the Torture Garden she's possessed by evil . . . She's going to *kill* me one day!

TI-MAO:  Kill you?

TI-BAH:  Listen . . . Last time she was here I put some opium on the end of a needle and put it in the burner . . . Suddenly, for no reason at all, she snatched the needle out of my hand . . . and jabbed it into me . . . so many times! It was red hot! It burnt me! I screamed . . . Look . . . I'm not lying. (*She pulls open her dress and reveals the scars on her breast.*)

TI-MAO:  She's paid for you.

TI-BAH:  She pays me to keep quiet. But I don't want to do it again . . . *She'll kill me!*

TI-MAO:  The life of someone like you is nothing in the eyes of those who command us.

TI-BAH:  Please, master! I'm scared!

TI-MAO:  Don't be. I won't be far away. I'll be watching. Besides, she's not alone today—she's brought someone with her.

LI-TCHANG:  The man who was on the *Sphinx* when Prince Li-Tong was killed—

TI-MAO  (*grabs Li-Tchang by throat*): Shut up or I'll cut your tongue out!

LI-TCHANG:  Sorry, master! I thought—

TI-MAO:  You don't know anything . . . Just keep quiet . . . When the moment arrives you will do the bidding of our venerable master Han . . . You must obey his every word like the slave you are, like a machine.

LI-TCHANG  (*looking down*): I will obey.

TI-MAO:  If Master Han orders you to kill your own brother, you will kill your own brother. Understand?

LI-TCHANG:  I understand.

TI-MAO:  And you?

TI-BAH:  You are my master. (*Gong sounds.*)

TI-MAO:  They are here. (*To Li-Tchang*) Go and greet them. (*Li-Tchang exits stage left.*) Go to the bedroom. (*Ti-Bah hurries off stage left. Enter Clara and Marchal.*) Come in, milady. Everything is ready for you. What do you think of the aroma? Is not the perfume intoxicating? Shall I call Ti-Bah, the most beautiful of all my flowers?

CLARA:  Leave us . . . I'll call her.

TI-MAO:  Does milady require tea?

CLARA  (*dismissive*): Later.
(*Ti-Mao exits stage right. Clara watches the river in silence as if she has forgotten the presence of Marchal.*)

MARCHAL:  Clara! (*Clara doesn't move.*) Clara, what's wrong? When we left your sampan, you started shivering, your hand was frozen . . . I couldn't recognize you . . . you haven't been the same since we left *that place* . . . Clara, what can you see on the river? And your face looks so hard . . . Clara, tell me!

CLARA: Don't speak to me . . . I have told you before, when I've been there, to the Garden . . . something comes over me . . . all my nerves are on edge.

MARCHAL: Clara!

CLARA: Don't touch me . . . Leave me alone . . . (*She is still again and continues to watch the river.*)

MARCHAL: Clara, you know that it's too much . . . There is a degree of horror that even you cannot go past . . . You should take it easy, sit down.

CLARA: Are you mad? I'm not ill . . . I feel fine. What about you? You look pale and unsteady like a drunken man.

MARCHAL (*putting his hands to his face*): Clara, it was horrible . . . I can still see that vision of hell . . . can still hear the human cries and smell that stench, warm and stagnant . . . the stench of blood . . .!

CLARA: Don't think about it . . . it's over now . . .

MARCHAL (*to himself*): And the peacocks, those disgusting peacocks, fighting over scraps of human flesh in the sand . . . and the gaps in the trees for the instruments of torture . . .

CLARA (*suddenly exalted*): We didn't even see the most beautiful thing! The Torture of the Bell! It is the most extraordinary torture! You rarely get to see it . . . they save it for criminals of distinction . . . It's an enormous bronze bell . . . the heavy beams are black, decorated with golden inscriptions and red masks, it looks like a temple . . . It's like a huge cauldron, an abyss in the air, a hanging void that seems to rise from earth to sky, the depths of which cannot be seen. The victim is put inside it, deep into that darkness. For hours, they toll the bell . . . For hours! And the vibrations penetrate the victim's body . . . they force the muscles out, make the veins burst, breaking and grinding the bones . . . Ah! What wonderful torture! When you hear the bell tolling, it's so gentle, so touching! When you hear it from a distance, it makes you think of religious ceremonies: holy mass, baptisms, weddings . . . and yet it is the most terrifying of all the tortures! And we missed it because of you!

MARCHAL: And you really wanted me to see that, Clara . . . Do you hate me?

CLARA: No, no. Only, please, keep quiet . . . I don't want to talk right now. (*She sits down on the divan.*)

MARCHAL: Clara, I'm sorry . . . I'm such a nuisance . . . always lecturing you like a priest . . . I was crazy . . . I was trying to fight against the same obsession that has you in its grip . . . but who am I trying to fool? The truth is . . . I've never

desired you like I desire you tonight . . . You are right . . .
civilization, morality, they are just words . . . The best love
is *criminal* . . . You have woken up new desires in me,
instincts that frightened me . . . but that is over now . . .
Now I will follow you anywhere . . . I will love you through
horror, pain and fear . . . I will love you in blood and death
. . . (*He tries to grab her but she pushes him away roughly.*)

CLARA: Let go of me!

MARCHAL: Clara!

CLARA: Let go! You can exercise your filthy desires on the
whores . . . I can tell you who the best ones are . . . I know
them, each and every one of them . . . (*She laughs with
contempt.*)

MARCHAL (*revolted*): Shut up! Shut up! It's disgusting! It's monstrous!
(*Clara laughs.*) Don't laugh, you bitch, or I'll kill you . . .
Yes, I will kill you and throw you in the river. (*He grabs her
round her throat.*)

CLARA: Yes, kill me, darling . . . I would love to be killed by you.
(*Marchal's aggression turns into a long kiss.*)

MARCHAL: Clara . . . I am so sorry . . . I don't know what I'm saying . . .

CLARA: You see . . . you're so pathetic and spineless, you wouldn't
have the courage . . . (*A gong sounds twice.*) Come on, get
up . . . Han has arrived . . . if he sees you like this . . .

MARCHAL: Han is here?

CLARA: Didn't you know that?

MARCHAL: Him . . . here? What does he want?

CLARA: I invited him . . . There's nothing wrong.

MARCHAL: He's watching us . . . He suspects me . . .

CLARA: All the more reason not to behave like this . . . get a grip on
yourself . . . *please* . . . (*Enter Han, Ti-Mao and Li-Tchang.*)

HAN: Please excuse me, Mrs Watson . . . and you as well,
Monsieur Marchal, I am very sorry that I was not able to
show you round the prison myself. (*To Marchal*) I am truly
sorry . . . But you had in Mrs Watson the best guide . . . and
the most agreeable.

CLARA: Don't worry about that, Monsieur Han . . . I do believe that
my friend hasn't *quite* acquired the taste for that unique
spectacle . . . he is stifled by European prejudices . . . and he
is so impressionable . . . and so sensitive!

HAN: Really? But what about the flowers? Those beautiful flowers
. . . the terrace of peonies, the lake of irises, the avenue of
tamarind trees . . .

CLARA: He couldn't see beyond the severed heads . . . the
condemned men in their cages . . . the steel pikes . . .

HAN: Is that true, Monsieur Marchal?

MARCHAL: Mrs Watson's exaggerating . . . I was perhaps a little
ill-disposed . . . the humidity . . . the weather . . .

HAN: A little bit of a fever perhaps . . . But Monsieur Marchal obviously has a very active imagination . . . He imagined what it must be like to be one of the victims, to be in the hands of our torturers . . . You forget that you are a European, Monsieur Marchal, a most respected foreigner . . . Your nationality protects you . . . and never, whatever happens, will you be put in the Torture Garden . . . only as a spectator! Well, at least if you haven't committed a crime . . . like killing some important person . . .

MARCHAL: What are you saying?

HAN: I was just giving an example . . . a simple example! (*During this time, Ti-Mao and Li-Tchang have put some trays on little tables.*)

TI-MAO: Everything is ready, milady.

HAN: Monsieur Marchal, look at the handsome face of our host . . . Can you imagine anything more tranquil . . . more inoffensive . . . and could you imagine that this pleasant gentleman is a most celebrated executioner . . . but, yes, he was . . . he was one of our most knowledgeable and experienced torturers.

CLARA: What? Ti-Mao used to work at the Torture Garden? I never knew!

TI-MAO: I have been retired for three years, milady.

HAN: The last man he executed was Wang, a notorious conspirator . . . But enough about torture . . . Now is the time for more pleasurable things. Monsieur Marchal, have you had experience of our flower boats?

MARCHAL: Yes, I have visited them in Canton.

HAN: I believe those are designed for Europeans. Here you can experience Chinese luxury, with all its secret refinements . . . its cruel and religious mystery.

CLARA: You see, my love, this is almost like a temple . . . an obscene temple, consecrated to the gods of sex . . . I will show you round . . . the dances . . . the orgies . . . the strange and barbaric rites . . .

MARCHAL: I have heard about them . . . Will we really be allowed to watch?

CLARA: Yes, tonight . . . you will see women in a state of delirium . . . you will see their frenzy as they throw themselves down before their idol and yield to sexual abandon . . . it is like a contagious madness! You will see! But where is Ti-Bah? (*To Ti-Mao*) You have saved her for me, haven't you?

TI-MAO: Of course, milady. I will go and get her for you. (*He goes to the door on the left.*) Ti-Bah! Come here!

CLARA: No one prepares opium like Ti-Bah. (*Enter Ti-Bah. She sees Clara and recoils. After a gesture from Ti-Mao, she prostrates herself.*) Ah, here is my little friend . . . stand up, my little sister . . . (*To Marchal*) Look at her bronzed skin . . . (*She opens Ti-Bah's dress, revealing her breasts to Marchal.*) Look how supple her body is! (*Ti-Bah recoils.*) What is wrong? There is nothing to be scared of. Do you dislike me?

TI-BAH (*trembling*): No!

CLARA: Well, come closer to me . . .

TI-BAH: Mistress . . . I will get the opium ready . . .

CLARA (*strictly*): No, come here, come here at once!

TI-BAH: No, leave me alone, I don't want to . . .

CLARA: I beg your pardon? *I beg your pardon?* (*She grabs her by the wrists, brutally.*) I want to . . . do you understand . . . do you hear me?

TI-BAH: Let go! You're going to hurt me! Let go of me!

MARCHAL: Leave her alone . . . (*He goes to help her, but Han intervenes, smiling.*)

CLARA: You will obey me or . . .

TI-BAH: Bitch! (*She bites Clara's hand.*)

CLARA (*releasing her*): The little bitch! She bit me!

TI-MAO: I don't know what's wrong with her this evening, milady . . .

CLARA: You can see where she bit me!

HAN: The slave has turned on her masters . . . She will be punished. Ti-Mao!

TI-MAO: Master?

HAN: You will remove a strip of skin.

TI-BAH (*utters a scream*): No, not that . . . please . . . I will obey . . . I will do anything she wants.

HAN: I have spoken.
    (*Ti-Mao gives a sign to Li-Tchang who holds the wailing Ti-Bah.*)

MARCHAL: What are you going to do? She's just a child . . . forgive her . . .

CLARA: No, she insulted me, she must be punished.

MARCHAL: You're not going to kill her, are you?

HAN: Calm yourself, she will not die. (*He takes a knife from Ti-Mao's belt.*) You see this knife, milady, this little blade. A torturer like him does not need anything other than this to put his victims through the most atrocious suffering, and yet denying them the deliverance of death. He is going to make two long incisions down the length of her back, and then slowly he is going to peel away a long strip of skin just as you would peel a piece of fruit . . .

MARCHAL: No . . . No . . . It is barbaric! I don't want to see it . . . (*He heads towards the back.*)

CLARA: No, stay here . . . stay next to me . . .

MARCHAL: Clara!

CLARA: Stay here next to me . . . don't leave me . . . I want you here . . . (*While the Torture of the Ribbon of Flesh is executed*) Look . . . how she's suffering . . . listen to her crying . . .

how she's suffering! And now the blood is running. Ah, the blood . . . the blood . . . the blood . . . (*Clara faints.*)
(*Han makes a sign and Ti-Mao and Li-Tchang carry Ti-Bah out.*)

MARCHAL (*on his knees, holding Clara in his arms*): Clara . . . are you all right?

HAN: Do not worry . . . she will come to in a moment.

MARCHAL: Her teeth are clenched . . . her body is stiff . . .

HAN: Yes, she's always like that . . . let her rest a moment . . .

MARCHAL: Shouldn't I take her home?

HAN: Only when she is better . . . Stay here . . . I will take my leave, Monsieur Marchal. Ti-Mao will keep you company—

MARCHAL: There's no need, we'll go home when—

HAN: Stay here . . . The river's not safe at this time of night. I will see you soon, Monsieur Marchal, I will see you soon. (*Exits stage left.*)

MARCHAL: Clara, my dear, are you all right?

CLARA: Nothing . . . it was nothing . . . it's over now . . . I don't know what happened . . . I'm aching all over . . .

MARCHAL: You see, every time you see something like this . . .

CLARA (*in his arms*): My darling, never again, I promise you . . . never again . . .

MARCHAL: Come on, let's go . . . The evening air will do you good . . . it will calm you down . . .

CLARA: Where are we?

MARCHAL: We are on the river . . . at Ti-Mao's—

CLARA (*as though waking from a dream*): Ah, yes . . . (*Suddenly anxious*) Where is Han?

MARCHAL: He has gone . . . (*The sound of a bell on the river.*)

CLARA: Listen . . . it's already the second watch! (*Her anxiety grows.*)

MARCHAL: Yes, it is very late . . . come on, let's go home.

CLARA (*suddenly forthright*): No . . . We must not go home . . . we must go away . . . for your sake . . .

MARCHAL: What is it, darling? You're delirious . . .

CLARA: No, I must tell you . . . you are in danger . . . they are coming for you at the third watch!

MARCHAL: How do you know?

CLARA: Jean, I am not the woman you think I am . . . I work for Han and the Neiko of Peking!

MARCHAL: A spy? You?

CLARA: Yes . . . they have me in their control, they have my life in their hands . . . I work for them, I am a cog in the machine . . .

MARCHAL: So, Tao-Ping and the poet Wang . . . it was you who . . .

CLARA: Yes . . . I received orders to trap them.

MARCHAL: Oh my God! You've betrayed me!

CLARA    (*desperately, throwing herself into his arms*): No, not you! I swear! I don't know how they worked it out . . . I didn't tell them . . . Jean, you must believe me!

MARCHAL    (*looking into her eyes*): I want to . . .

CLARA:    Jean, take me with you, save me . . . We've got my sampan . . . we can escape . . . I'll pay Ti-Mao . . . I know how much to pay him . . . I know what he's like . . . he'll let us go and we'll get on a European ship on the river . . . there is an English packboat leaving tomorrow.

MARCHAL:    Yes . . . you are right . . . We shouldn't stay here a minute longer . . . Come on . . . (*Marchal goes to the back, opens the curtain and reveals a steel cage over the door's opening.*)

CLARA:    What's wrong? Open it! Come on, open it!

MARCHAL:    I can't open it!

CLARA    (*rushing to the door on the left*): This one's caged in as well! (*Pointing at the door on the right*) What about that one?

MARCHAL:    Yes, it's locked as well . . . why have they locked us in? It's a trap . . .

CLARA:    It must be a mistake . . . I'll get them to open it . . . Ti-Mao! (*Silence. Ti-Mao appears at the left door.*)

TI-MAO:    What do you want?

CLARA:    Open the door . . . we want to leave . . . (*Ti-Mao bows and he opens the door. To Marchal*) You see, he obeys me. (*To Ti-Mao, who is standing in front of the doorway*) Come on then, let us out . . .

TI-MAO    (*his tone and expression changes subtly*): So you've seen enough suffering? You've seen enough blood, have you?

MARCHAL:    What?

CLARA:    You dare speak to me like that? A vile servant . . . a slave!

TI-MAO    (*menacing*): Shut up . . . you disgusting bitch . . . We have been watching you for a long time.

CLARA:    Jean, this man is mad!

MARCHAL:    Who are you? What do you want?

TI-MAO:    We want to avenge our master, Tao-Ming, the poet Wang, and all our brothers betrayed to Li-Tong!

CLARA:    I'd be careful if I were you! Han is there . . . Han will protect me! (*She rushes over to the left door.*) Han!

TI-MAO:    Han is far away! Every precaution has been taken . . . You will not escape the Scarlet Dragon . . .

CLARA    (*mad with fear*): The Scarlet Dragon! Jean! Help me!

TI-MAO:    No, do not help her. She has also betrayed you.

CLARA:    It's not true . . .

TI-MAO:    Yes it is! She has betrayed you to Han . . .

MARCHAL:    It's not true! I don't believe it!

CLARA:    He's lying! He's lying!

TI-MAO:    The orders have been given . . . they are coming for you at the third watch.

MARCHAL: Let us go . . . we can pay you . . .

TI-MAO: Do not worry. The murderer of Li-Tong has nothing to fear from us. (*Li-Tchang has entered silently from the right.*) Follow this man, he will lead you to the river . . . you will get on a junk.

CLARA: Jean! Don't leave me!

TI-MAO: You can leave as well . . . but not just yet!

CLARA: Jean!

MARCHAL: No. I cannot allow it . . . It would be despicable.

TI-MAO: She has been condemned . . . Do not try to save her!

CLARA (*begging*): Let me go . . . I'll pay you anything you want . . .

TI-MAO: Yes, you will pay, but not with money . . . Ti-Bah, prepare the needles . . .
(*Ti-Bah emerges from a corner of the room, and makes her way, bleeding, towards the opium burner.*)

CLARA: No . . . not that . . .

MARCHAL: What are you going to do?

TI-MAO: I am going to treat her the same way that she treated the others. (*He grabs hold of Clara with force, pushing her to her knees and then holding her arms behind her.*)

CLARA: Jean!
(*Marchal wants to go towards her, but he is grabbed by Li-Tchang and held still.*)

MARCHAL: Let go of me . . . Let go of me!

TI-MAO: Get him out of here!

MARCHAL (*as he is dragged away*): I beg you . . . release her! Cowards! Brutes! Executioners!

TI-MAO (*to Ti-Bah*): First of all, the eyes . . . let us begin with the eyes . . . those eyes which loved to feast on suffering and death.
(*Ti-Bah goes towards Clara and grabs her head with her left hand, a red-hot needle in her right hand.*)

CLARA: No! Not that! Help!

TI-MAO (*to Ti-Bah who is beginning to push the needle into Clara's eye*): Slowly, Ti-Bah! Don't press it in too fast . . . don't push it in . . .

CLARA: Ah! Ah! Ah!

TI-MAO: Not so fast . . . Twist the needle under her eyelid . . . Don't push it in too quickly . . .

CLARA: Ah! Ah! Ah! Ah!

TI-MAO: Not so fast . . .
(*The curtain descends slowly over the cries of Clara.*)

THE END

# Euthanasia

## (L'Euthanasie, ou le Devoir de tuer, 1923)

*by*

RENÉ BERTON

## Preface

*L'Euthanasie, ou le Devoir de tuer*, a one-act drama by René Berton, premiered at the Grand-Guignol on 15 May 1923. The production was never revived by the theatre, although it did cause a lively debate in the press and focused on what was, and remains to this day, a major ethical controversy: euthanasia or 'mercy killing'. In the 1925 edition of the play, the script is prefaced with A. d'Esparbès's '*L'Euthanasie* et la Critique médicale' which argues that Berton uses drama to present the debate surrounding euthanasia very clearly and proceeds to resolve the ethical dilemma unambiguously in favour (see Berton 1925, 7–8).

Doctors are the most frequently portrayed professionals in the Grand-Guignol repertoire. The infamous Doctors Frankenstein, Jekyll, Moreau, Crippen and many other factual or fictional members of the academy of mad scientists live on in various incarnations in the Grand-Guignol. Since the theatre's demise this trend has continued unabated, demonstrating that the mad scientist/doctor remains a central archetype in modern (and perhaps even postmodern) popular horror. Here we need only think of contemporary icons like Dr Hannibal Lecter (created by Thomas Harris), the body-horror explorations characteristic of the films of David Cronenberg, or the anti-Hippocratic conspiracy in the Heidelberg medical school presented in the German horror film *Anatomie* (Stefan Ruzowitzky 2000), all of which continue this aspect of the Grand-Guignol legacy. As for real-life doctors, it is very likely that the case of Dr Harold Shipman would have swiftly been exploited in the repertoire.

Berton's earlier play *Tics* delights in its portrayal of an adulterous and hypocritical member of the medical profession. *Euthanasia* is, in contrast, a Grand-Guignol drama and, despite d'Esparbès's belief that the issue is unambiguously presented and resolved, there is scope to see Berton's 1923 horror play as ironic as his 1908 sex comedy.

Dr Sergeac is representative of the old school of medicine, a sixty-year-old family doctor who has 'developed quite a close relationship' with his patient and the patient's wife (indeed, Dr Sergeac's obvious affection for Claire Montravel, and his offstage placing of her 'on the bed' when she faints, takes on an ironic parallel with Dr Martin's unethical escapades in *Tics*. This, however, is probably an inadvertent coincidence and reflects more about the strategies of Berton's stagecraft than any conscious allusion). Professor Saint-Géry, half the age of Sergeac, is the new breed of doctor. Despite his youth, he is already one of the most important doctors in Paris and something of a 'guru'. The idealism he brings to the profession is manifest when it comes to the issue of euthanasia. His passionate advocacy of the principle of 'mercy killing' outrages Sergeac as it contradicts the Hippocratic oath, the foundation of medical ethics. More than that, in a sentence that remains incomplete, Saint-Géry begins to propose that 'there'd probably be fewer lunatics and criminals' if doctors were allowed to intervene in cases of congenital defect. Berton subtly demonstrates that there is sometimes only a fine line between euthanasia and eugenics. Saint-Géry, alone with the terminally ill patient, acts on impulse to satisfy Paul's last wish and administers a lethal injection. Initially shocked at becoming a mercy killer, he soon becomes resolute in the justification of his action—despite Sergeac's threats to denounce him—and coldly asserts that it was his 'duty' to kill. Significantly, despite his threats, Sergeac does not denounce the young star of modern medicine, but rather protects him in an act of professional solidarity. Although the audience witnessed Saint-Géry's moral dilemma and knows that his account of Paul's last wishes and demise is accurate, there may be a broader cynicism: Paul may *plead* for death, and is grateful for it, but is not actually given the chance to *consent*. Similarly, Claire is kept in the dark, obviously to protect the young Professor from potential criminal proceedings, but Berton may nevertheless be exploiting the paranoia of the audience who do not know, but dread, what may go on behind the firmly closed doors of medical practice. Claire is left to believe that her husband had a heart attack and will never know that he was murdered with strychnine. Moreover, Claire is always rather unsettled by Saint-Géry, and the aloof young specialist does not speak to her at the end of the play, preferring to let Dr Sergeac conjure up an explanation. Perhaps *Euthanasia* signals the arrival of a perceived new age of medicine where cases are rationalized and doctors have the obligation to kill when necessary. As the Professor asserts, 'Any doctor who dares to judge should also have the courage to be the executioner!', Sergeac says that only a god could be 'that certain of his judgement' to make life and death decisions. Professor Saint-Géry represents the first of such self-appointed gods: *Saint*-Géry indeed.

As well as being an exploration of ethical dilemma through drama, *Euthanasia* functions primarily as a Grand-Guignol horror play and as such has an admirable structure and pace. Suspense is established from the opening moments with the boarded-up window and the man enduring obscure agonies behind the door (it is several minutes before we learn that he is dying of liver cancer). Paul does not appear until the final stage of the play and it is a role that demands virtuoso skill. It is not surprising that the play was written as a star vehicle for the celebrated Paulais. The actor has to portray a figure who is, in Saint-Géry's words, 'no longer a man or a dog (but) nothing more than an entity in atrocious agony, his nerves torn apart, crying and screaming, waiting for death as a deliverance'. The deliverance comes in the form of a graphically enacted onstage death by strychnine. The euthanasia scene itself where, due to Claire's fortuitous syncope, Professor Saint-Géry closes the door and is left alone with Paul is an excellent example of Grand-Guignol suspense-into-climax. The audience knows Saint-Géry's ideas on euthanasia and anticipates that the ethical dilemma is soon to be played out before them, and that theory will soon be put into practice (thus fulfilling another Grand-Guignol convention whereby what is suggested is ultimately enacted). The Professor's careful procedure of filling the syringe with morphine (significantly, and disconcertingly, with his back to Paul) is in stark contrast to his subsequent rejection of medicine in favour of poison, and his rapid use of it. This is a fine example of the sudden break from suspense, whereby the painstaking build-up is at last relinquished and the audience—adrenaline surging— witnesses the swift acceleration towards the enactment of climax.

# EUTHANASIA

*(L'Euthanasie, ou le Devoir de tuer, 1923)*

*by*

RENÉ BERTON

---

Victoria, maid
Claire Montravel, 35
Doctor Sergeac, 60
Professor Saint-Géry, 30
Paul Montravel, 45

---

*(1920s Paris. A simply furnished lounge with a sofa, chairs and a table. The door to a bedroom stage left. Another door stage right. It has a window next to it, boarded and padlocked, impossible to open. At the back of the stage a fireplace.*

*As the curtain rises, Victoria is dusting the furniture. The bedroom door opens gently and Claire appears. She steps in cautiously, looking back into the room. She listens carefully. Hearing nothing, she pulls the door to, without closing it completely, and walks into the room.)*

| | |
|---|---|
| VICTORIA | *(approaching Claire)*: Well, madam? |
| CLAIRE: | Shh . . . |
| VICTORIA: | Is he asleep? |
| CLAIRE: | Yes . . . if you can call it sleep. |
| VICTORIA: | Oh the poor man . . . If only he could have a good, long sleep for once. You've had another sleepless night, madam—you haven't even undressed . . . |
| CLAIRE: | No. |
| VICTORIA: | You're getting run down . . . you'll end up ill yourself . . . *(Claire shrugs.)* There's a limit to everything—including exhaustion. You're not being sensible. As you can't afford a nurse . . . Well, I know what I'd do if I were you— |
| CLAIRE | *(with disgust)*: Put him in hospital, where he'll be constantly examined, manhandled by medical students . . . No. While there's a penny to my name and breath in my |

body, my husband will stay here and I will take care of
him! Hospital? *Never.*

VICTORIA: I understand what you're saying . . . I mean if I became
seriously ill I'd . . . But never mind—I've made your
breakfast: nice fresh coffee and a croissant, I'll go and get
them . . .

CLAIRE: I'm not hungry. Perhaps later.

VICTORIA: You're exhausted. You should make the most of it while
your husband is asleep and have a little rest yourself. I've
done the cleaning; I'll stay here a while and keep an eye on
the poor man. (*Comes close to Claire and speaks with
affection*) Go and have a lie down: you'll be asleep before
your head hits the pillow.

CLAIRE: Thank you, Victoria, my dear. But I assure you I don't need
to sleep. (*Sad smile*) I've had so many sleepless nights I've
forgotten how to rest.

VICTORIA: The fact is since your husband fell ill I can count the
number of nights you've gone to bed on the fingers of one
hand.

CLAIRE: As long as it's done something to help . . .

VICTORIA: All the same, it's bizarre that the doctors haven't been able
to cure him . . .

CLAIRE: I'm afraid the disease is incurable.

VICTORIA: Those doctors don't know anything! It's tragic—a man in
the prime of life . . . he's only forty-five, isn't he? (*Claire
nods.*) To end up like this . . . such pain and suffering!

CLAIRE: Yes, pain and suffering. (*Listens*) I think he's waking up.
(*Stands, walks over to the door and listens*) No . . . he's still
asleep. (*Returns and sits.*)

VICTORIA: He was always such a healthy and active man! He can't do
anything any more—he must be in despair.

CLAIRE: Yes.

VICTORIA: By the way, have you sorted out his sick pay?

CLAIRE: No. I couldn't bring myself to do it. (*Sits*) It's the fourth
time, you see. Dr Sergeac knows Paul's boss and said he
was happy to ask on our behalf. He's going to let me know
this morning.

VICTORIA: Oh, you're bound to get it . . .

CLAIRE: I hope so. Otherwise, what will we do? (*Door bell*) That's
probably the doctor now.

VICTORIA: I'll let him in. (*Victoria exits. Dr Sergeac walks into the
room.*)

SERGEAC: Hello, my dear. (*Takes her hands with great affection.*)

CLAIRE: Hello, doctor.

SERGEAC (*turns his head back to the door*): Come in, Professor.
(*Professor Saint-Géry comes in and bows to Claire who
recoils.*) You remember Professor Saint-Géry? He's already

met your husband . . . we had a consultation with him two months ago . . .

CLAIRE (*forcing a smile*): Yes . . .

SERGEAC: I bumped into the eminent professor as I was leaving the department of toxicology. He inquired after your husband so I asked him if he'd care to join me this morning.

CLAIRE (*awkward*): But doctor, it's . . .

SAINT-GÉRY (*smiling*): Rest assured, madam, this is just an informal visit. I'm just a clinician, a consultant. Nevertheless, I'd be only too happy to help you in any way possible.

SERGEAC: The Professor is not only one of the most important doctors in Paris, he's also a truly remarkable man . . . something of a guru.

SAINT-GÉRY: Thank you, I—

SERGEAC: It's true. A *guru*. No exaggeration.

CLAIRE: I'm sorry, I'm rather confused—

SERGEAC: Never mind—how's our patient today?

CLAIRE: Oh, last night was terrible. This morning he finished off the medicine you prescribed.

SERGEAC (*to Saint-Géry*): A mixture of bromide and chloral.

SAINT-GÉRY: Good.

(*Claire goes to the bedroom door, listens and returns.*)

CLAIRE: He's still asleep . . . he'll wake up soon though. (*To Sergeac, anxiously*) Did you see Paul's boss?

SERGEAC: Yes. I went along to the head office yesterday afternoon. He's a most charming fellow.

CLAIRE (*lively*): He confirmed Paul's sick leave?

SERGEAC: Um . . . not exactly . . . You see, your husband's situation is rather delicate . . . It's nearly a year since he last went to work and the director is not entirely happy about any further extension of sick leave.

CLAIRE (*falls into a chair*): Oh my God!

SERGEAC (*sitting beside her*): Don't worry, all is not lost . . . I'm going to see him again and I am pretty certain we'll sort it all out to your advantage.

CLAIRE (*weeping*): Oh Paul . . . I beg you—*cure him*! What will I do if he . . . passes away? He's my husband—he's all that I have!

SERGEAC: Come, come . . . don't cry, my dear . . . You know you can count on us . . .

CLAIRE: Doctor, Professor—something tells me that you will save my husband . . . why else would God have brought you to us?

SAINT-GÉRY: Madam, I swear I will do everything humanly possible to save your husband's life.

CLAIRE: Oh, if you could cure him . . .! No, that's too much to ask . . . If you could only relieve him of that terrible suffering. (*Points at the door*) I'll go and wake him.

SERGEAC: Wait! Let the poor devil get some sleep. I need to discuss a few things with my colleague . . .

CLAIRE: I'll leave you to it . . . I'll go and sit with Paul a while . . . Tell me when you want me to wake him.

SERGEAC *(walks with her to the bedroom door)*: That's right my dear. *(Claire goes into the bedroom.)* Poor woman!

SAINT-GÉRY: We've given her a grain of hope. I think that's all we can do. Monsieur Montravel's condition is critical isn't it?

SERGEAC: Absolutely . . . to say the least . . . But you'll be able to reach your own conclusions soon.

SAINT-GÉRY: Well, the fact is there has never been a case of liver cancer that hasn't proved fatal. They're a brave couple, I must say.

SERGEAC: Very brave. I've developed quite a close relationship with them. Montravel worked at the post office, in administration. About a year ago he secured a three-month leave of absence to undergo treatment. Naturally the job remained open to him once his leave expired. However, he extended it by another three months, then another; and now he's asked for yet another three months. His wife begged me to go and ask on their behalf. I told her that he'll probably get another three months. The truth is, the manager refused point blank! Regulations are regulations, you see. And now we have this situation: Montravel's sick leave expires on the 15th of March—in other words, nine days' time—and if he's not back at work on that day, he's off the books.

SAINT-GÉRY: Yes, but surely he'll receive a pension proportional to his—

SERGEAC: No! According to the regulations he won't have served the required number of years. And as it will be impossible for him to go back to work in nine days, he'll find himself without a penny to his name—I mean, all they've had to live on has been that sick pay. What a way to spend the little time he's got left . . . and what will become of his wife?

SAINT-GÉRY: She'll have to find employment—

SERGEAC: Doing what? She has no qualifications or training . . . and she's not exactly in the best of health herself.

SAINT-GÉRY: I find it hard to believe that his manager is so unsympathetic despite knowing the truth of the situation.

SERGEAC: I've tried everything, believe me, there's nothing we can do—absolutely nothing.

SAINT-GÉRY: It's heartbreaking!

SERGEAC: Well, this caps it all: if he dies while still officially an employee his wife will receive compensation. In other words, the management have given him nine days to die. If he dies on the *tenth* day, his wife will starve to death.

SAINT-GÉRY: That's terrible!

SERGEAC: That's our profession for you. From time to time, we find ourselves caught up in difficult situations like this—terrible situations. (*Points at the bedroom*) In that room is a man whose days are numbered . . . we know exactly what he's contracted, and can only stand by and watch helplessly as it slowly eats away at him; we know that nothing on earth can stop its progress; that sooner or later it will end in death. And we can't even hurry things along! All we can do is watch powerlessly as the poor man endures indescribable agony, as he screams and struggles as he's put through tortures that we cannot even begin to imagine! And we can't even put him out of his misery!

SAINT-GÉRY: It's horrific! Only a miracle could save him!

SERGEAC: Unfortunately our profession doesn't allow us to believe in miracles. (*Pause*) You look distant—what are you thinking?

SAINT-GÉRY: I was just thinking that one day we in the medical profession will no longer be forced to take such an inactive and powerless role.

SERGEAC: What are you implying?

SAINT-GÉRY: (*standing*): Don't you think—I'm just talking hypothetically, of course—don't you think that a doctor should have the right to seriously consider the best interests of an individual rather than adhere to the fundamental ethical principles of medicine?

SERGEAC: But . . .

SAINT-GÉRY (*developing his thesis and growing in excitement*): Don't you ever wish that a doctor had the right to intervene—let's say, in the life of a baby that has congenital physiological defects that we know full well will inexorably deteriorate . . . (*Points at bedroom*) Or what about hastening the demise of the unfortunate victims of incurable disease? I mean if we had the right to intervene in cases of congenital defects there'd probably be fewer lunatics and criminals in the long run—

SERGEAC: Ah, yes, the famous theory of euthanasia. Mercy killing. I think, my dear friend, you're letting your ideas run away with you. Any doctor that could be that certain of his judgement, that could make a life or death decision about a child with congenital defects or a man with an incurable disease—I mean the doctor who could decide that would have to be a god! And, unfortunately, we are only human, as prone to error as anyone! Besides, between you and me, how many people have been given a terminal diagnosis only to make a full recovery?

SAINT-GÉRY (*forcefully*): But there are certain cases that are irrefutable. (*Points at bedroom*) Like the man in that room—

SERGEAC:    Well, yes, in this case I have to agree with you. There can be no doubt about the condition of Paul Montravel. It's a matter of days.

SAINT-GÉRY:    Wouldn't the most humane thing be to relieve him of his suffering?

SERGEAC:    Yes, without a shadow of doubt . . . But it is not for a doctor to meddle in Destiny!

SAINT-GÉRY:    When he has given a diagnosis that condemns another human being to death and stands there with his arms folded passively watching death do its work? I suppose you think that's noble? Noble—more like cowardice!

SERGEAC    (leaping up): Oh!

SAINT-GÉRY    (forcefully): Any doctor who dares to judge should also have the courage to be the executioner!

SERGEAC:    I've said it once and I'll say it again: *he does not have the right*!

SAINT-GÉRY:    Perhaps it's not a question of right—maybe it's a question of *duty*.

SERGEAC    (lively): The duty of a doctor is to combat illness, not be a party to it! The duty of a doctor is to prolong life by all means possible, even if it's by one day or a single hour. Because every human has an absolute right, a sacred right: the right to life! And you cannot ignore that right without committing a terrible crime!

SAINT-GÉRY:    A crime? In some cases it'd be more like committing an act of humanity. You mentioned mercy killing. If you found a dog run over by a car you'd certainly put it to sleep. What if it was a man, screaming in agony, suffering horrific injuries that are going to kill him albeit painfully slowly—why shouldn't you put him to sleep as well? Why not? Because he's a man? But in the suffering that comes before death he's no longer a man or a dog; he's nothing more than a creature in atrocious agony, his nerves torn apart, crying and screaming, waiting for death as a deliverance . . .! And the duty of any doctor is to help him to that deliverance!

SERGEAC:    It's against the law!

SAINT-GÉRY    (overexcited): You would *have* to do it! In an extremely difficult delivery, wouldn't we kill a baby to save the mother? Not long ago they used to suffocate people with rabies.

SERGEAC    (lively): We can cure that now!

SAINT-GÉRY:    Yes . . . (Points at bedroom) But until we find a cure for that horrible disease it's only right that the law should permit the medical profession to shorten the life of such unfortunate victims.

SERGEAC    (stunned): It's the first time I've heard a doctor talk like this. I'm shocked. It's monstrous!

SAINT-GÉRY    (*regaining his composure*): Do forgive me . . . I got a little carried away . . . (*Smiling*) Rest assured, I know full well that when it came to it I would just fold my arms and stand there . . . I have never made a life or death decision—and I'm not about to do so.

SERGEAC    (*relieved*): I'm pleased to hear it—you were starting to frighten me.

(*Sound of a man groaning in the bedroom.*)

VOICE OF PAUL:    The pain . . . the pain . . . No—let me out! Let go of me! (*The bedroom door is flung open and Paul appears, followed by his wife, trying to restrain him. His face is gaunt and waxy, worn out by illness and suffering. He takes a few feeble steps, his hands clutching at his chest.*)

PAUL:    The pain, the pain!

CLAIRE:    Paul, I beg you, calm down! (*Pointing at the doctors*) Look . . . here's Dr Sergeac and a Professor from the university . . . a specialist . . . they're going to cure you!

PAUL    (*collapsing on the sofa with a gesture of defeat*): Cure me?

SERGEAC:    Come now, Montravel, be brave! We'll certainly find something to ease the pain—

PAUL    (*again a gesture of defeat*): Ease the pain?

SERGEAC:    Just lie back on the sofa . . . My colleague is going to examine you.

SAINT-GÉRY    (*approaching Paul*): May I? (*He helps Paul to lie down. He kneels down and examines Paul's abdomen, tapping and listening.*)

PAUL    (*quietly*): Oh, doctor, you're hurting me . . .

SAINT-GÉRY    (*standing*): Well, as far as I can detect it looks as if the disease has not progressed in the last two months. In fact, quite the opposite: it looks as if there's some improvement.

CLAIRE    (*joyous*): You see! You're getting better! My darling!

PAUL    (*sombre*): You're just humouring me. I'm going to die. I know I am.

SERGEAC    (*aside to Saint-Géry*): Well?

SAINT-GÉRY:    Hopeless. The disease has spread—the liver, intestines, stomach, it's just one mass of cancer. Dead in one month. (*Paul suffers a spasm of pain and writhes in Claire's arms.*)

PAUL:    Let go . . . it hurts too much . . . let go! (*He staggers and falls into a chair, exhausted.*)

CLAIRE    (*distressed*): Paul . . . my darling!

SERGEAC:    Give him a dose of morphine—quick!

CLAIRE:    I'll go and get some . . . (*She stands and walks very unsteadily towards the bedroom.*)

SERGEAC    (*observing Claire*): The poor woman's not at all well . . . (*Claire enters the bedroom. We hear her cry out.*) I feared as much! (*He runs to the bedroom followed by Saint-Géry.*)

SAINT-GÉRY    (*looking into the bedroom*): She's fainted. Lie her down on the bed and keep an eye on her. I'll give her husband morphine.

VOICE OF SERGEAC:    You'll need some of the morphine—

SAINT-GÉRY:    It's okay, I've got some with me.
(*Saint-Géry closes the door. He goes over to the fireplace, pulls a syringe kit from his pocket and opens it. He takes out a syringe and a phial of morphine and begins to prepare an injection.*)

PAUL    (*desperate*): Doctor . . . doctor . . .

SAINT-GÉRY    (*with his back to Paul*): What is it?

PAUL:    Doctor . . . as you can't do anything to cure me, please, I beg you, put me out of my misery!

SAINT-GÉRY    (*continuing to prepare the injection*): But I told you I *can* cure you.

PAUL:    I know the disease . . . is incurable . . . And even if you could cure me . . . the pain is just too much—I would rather die!

SAINT-GÉRY    (*still with his back to Paul*): What a thing to say! Die? Come on now. You're not going to die. There's a very good chance that you'll pull through. There's plenty of hope—

PAUL:    Hope! You're just like all the others . . . You try to calm me down with all your lies while really you're just going to let me suffer right to the very last minute . . . Oh, the pain!
(*He stands while Saint-Géry looks at him, motionless, with a syringe in his hand.*) It feels like there's a ferocious animal inside me, ripping me to shreds with its teeth and claws . . .! Aagh! It won't let go! Ripping me to shreds! (*Writhes on the sofa, screaming*) Doctor—have mercy! Set me free! I've tried to kill myself twenty times . . . but they always stop me . . . they've hidden all the knives . . . (*Points at window*) They've padlocked the window to stop me from jumping . . .! For pity's sake—*kill me!*
(*Saint-Géry approaches with the morphine at the ready.*)

SAINT-GÉRY:    I'm going to give you a dose of morphine . . . it'll give you some relief from your suffering.

PAUL:    Morphine! It doesn't work! Give me something else— something *poisonous!* (*Ferociously*) Kill me! Kill me! I want to die! I have the *right* to die! I'm doomed—I'm going to die—why let it drag on any longer? Do it now! Haven't you got a heart? (*Falls to his knees*) Please . . . please . . . kill me . . . kill me . . .!
(*Saint-Géry is pale. A violent struggle is going on inside him. He suddenly squirts out the contents of the syringe. He goes back to the fireplace, opens the syringe kit, removes a phial of brown liquid and fills the syringe. He goes over to Paul and takes his arm.*)

PAUL:  Oh doctor, you're so cruel! I told you morphine does not work . . . (*Suddenly stares at the syringe*) But that's not morphine! It's . . . it's a different colour . . .

SAINT-GÉRY  (*staring Paul in the eyes*): Yes, yes . . . It *is* morphine! (*The two men stare at each other, fixedly.*)

PAUL:  Ah . . . if that could kill me . . .! (*Saint-Géry takes Paul's arm once again, rolls up the sleeve and injects the contents of the syringe. Silence. Paul stands up suddenly.*) What's happening . . .? Is the pain coming to an end . . .? It feels like my heart is slowing down. (*Paul takes several unsteady steps, then his arms and legs begin to stiffen.*) Ah, I understand . . . You've . . . Thank you . . . thank you . . .! (*He emits several inarticulate cries, his limbs stiffen more and more, and then he falls down dead. Saint-Géry is scared to look at Paul's body. Suddenly, Saint-Géry goes over to the bedroom and opens the door.*)

SAINT-GÉRY:  Sergeac!

SERGEAC  (*entering*): What is it? (*He sees Paul.*) Is he unconscious? (*Rushes over to Paul, kneels down and feels his chest*) He's dead . . .! You gave him morphine? (*Saint-Géry stares at Sergeac without answering. Sergeac looks around, and then goes over to the fireplace and looks at the empty phials. Reads the labels.*) Strychnine! Oh! You—

SAINT-GÉRY  (*calmly*): I killed him.

SERGEAC  (*shaking his fist*): You . . . *bastard*! You put your abominable theory into practice!

SAINT-GÉRY:  When I saw this poor wreck of a man, tortured and suffering . . . when I saw this pathetic man fall to his knees and beg me to put him out of his misery, I suddenly saw what I had to do very clearly. I knew that I must relieve him of his suffering and set him free.

SERGEAC:  Murderer!

SAINT-GÉRY:  Ah, the cry of joy he gave when he felt death overcome him . . . Ah, if only you'd seen his expression of gratitude . . . If you'd only heard him thank me when he realized I'd poisoned him . . .! No—I do not regret what I've done.

SERGEAC  (*beside himself*): Murdered! You murdered this man! It's monstrous! I'll report you—I will *denounce* you!

SAINT-GÉRY:  I accept full responsibility for my actions and I am prepared to face the consequences.

SERGEAC:  It's criminal! Criminal!

CLAIRE  (*entering*): What's going on?

SERGEAC  (*rushing towards her*): Madam, madam, listen—

CLAIRE  (*sees Paul's body*): Paul! (*She rushes over and clutches the corpse.*)

SERGEAC:  Madam . . . madam . . .

CLAIRE:     Dead? He's dead? (*The two men look at her. Saint-Géry is very calm, Sergeac trembles all over. Sergeac wants to cry out the truth, but his voice sticks in his throat and he is unable to speak.*) Tell me . . . what happened . . . How did he die?

SERGEAC     (*forcing himself to speak*): He died . . . suddenly . . . A heart attack, probably . . .

CLAIRE:     My poor husband . . .! Only death could set you free from all your pain and suffering! (*She falls onto the body in tears. After a few moments, Sergeac, very moved, goes over to Saint-Géry.*)

SERGEAC     (*aside to Saint-Géry*): Perhaps . . . perhaps you did the best thing . . .

SAINT-GÉRY   (*simply*): I have done my duty.


THE END

# The Kiss of Blood

## (Le Baiser de sang, 1929)

*by*

### Jean Aragny and Francis Neilson

## Preface

When Jean Aragny and Francis Neilson's two-act drama premiered at the rue Chaptal on 6 March 1929, it caused something of a stir on account of the gruesomeness of the opening scene. André Antoine recounts that at the premiere, 'Some fifteen members of the audience had to leave the auditorium. Two ladies were taken ill and the house-doctor was forced to enlist the help of one of his colleagues' (*L'information*, 9 March 1929, quoted in Pierron 1995, 1113).

In this respect *The Kiss of Blood* is unusual as a piece of Grand-Guignol. It is more common for any onstage violence to occur as a climactic finale to a play after a long, carefully constructed build-up. Under those circumstances the violence comes as an inevitable (and often sexually charged) release of tension. This is still the case, however, in *The Kiss of Blood* when Joubert severs his hand at the wrist in the final scene. This comes after the tension is carefully ratcheted up during the whole of the play, but in particular during the second act, climaxing in the violent act of self-mutilation, the spurt of blood and a 'post-coital' inertia (Joubert's rather abrupt death).

At a theatre that had acquired an international reputation for its onstage violence, shocking the audience must have been no mean feat, but by deliberately undermining the accepted Grand-Guignol structural formula by confronting the audience with a gruesome tableau the moment the curtain rises, it seems that the director, Jack Jouvin, achieved exactly this. Jouvin was meticulous in his research, consulting with members of the medical profession to ensure the accuracy of the finest details of the operation. The beginning of the play is almost a pastiche of the celebrated *final* tableau in one of the Grand-Guignol's most popular plays, de Lorde's *Le Laboratoire des hallucinations* (1916), which ends with de Mora exacting his revenge on the sadistic Dr Gorlitz by strapping him to an operating table and cracking open his skull with a hammer and scissors. However, far from being a (self-)parody of the Grand-Guignol form, in many respects *The Kiss of Blood* actually conforms to the conventions of the genre.

In the first instance the opening scene is a good example of what Michel Corvin calls 'une dramaturgie de la parole' (Corvin, 1998).[1] The staging of the scene requires that the patient is lying comatose on an operating table, whilst Leduc and his assistant, Volguine, perform the operation from behind the table in order that their bodies do not obscure the audience's view of the patient. Considering the audience's position in relation to the patient (on the raised stage *and* on the operating table) and the surgeons (upstage *and* behind the operating table) the audience's actual view of the operation must have been nevertheless extremely limited. They must have seen what appeared to be an exposed skull (the skilful application of make-up and the strategic positioning of numerous surgical clips would make this reasonably straightforward to the practised designers at the rue Chaptal) and plenty of stage blood (easily administered from the 'blind' area behind the operating table).

The horror of the scene relies on two distinct elements, namely a combination of the stage décor (the clinical whiteness of the entire set and the costumes, and the medical paraphernalia, from the surgical instruments—with the occasional glint of steel of the scalpel—to the proliferation of cotton wool) and the carefully constructed dialogue. It is clear from the script that every surgical procedure can be performed naturally, yet still obscured from the audience. What is important is that every procedure is announced, and even described in advance of its being performed.

At the same time we must recognize that this shocking opening to the play is not the central horror in the piece. In spite of the surgical imagery and the implications of physical violence of both the operation and the amputation of Joubert's finger in the opening act, the dramatic tension of the whole piece is engineered by the psychological horror being visited upon Joubert by his wife. In this respect the play has much in common with Patrick Hamilton's classic 1930s English melodrama *Gaslight*, whilst also remaining distinct from it through its particular grand-guignolesque concerns.

Joubert believes that he is being haunted by the vengeful ghost of his wife Hélène, whom he has murdered in a fit of jealous rage. The ghost demands that he amputates the finger that pulled the trigger (and later the hand that held the gun) and the effect of this on Joubert's psychological state is to cause him unbearable, psychosomatic pain in the offending finger/hand. It is not within the conventions of the Grand-Guignol to deal with the supernatural and it transpires that Hélène has,

---

[1] This phrase can be roughly translated as 'theatre of dialogue'.

unbeknownst to her husband, survived the attack and is now pretending to be a ghost in order to drive him to madness and suicide. In a final twist of irony, we discover that Hélène—an example of what Barbara Creed would call a *femme castratice* (Gelder 2000, 51)—has herself been driven mad, and is delusional to the point of mistakenly believing herself to be an image of abjection ravaged by gangrene.

Whilst for Pierron madness is the Grand-Guignol theme 'par excellence' (Pierron 1995, XXIII), suggesting a generic obsession with psychology, emerging undoubtedly from the development of Freudian theory around the turn of the century, for Gordon a shift from physiological to psychological horror 'within the traditional crime and laboratory formats' (Gordon 1988, 28) is the defining characteristic of Jouvin's stewardship of the theatre. *The Kiss of Blood*, with its combination of the physical and psychological, is perhaps, therefore, representative of Jouvin's reign as a whole, successfully bridging, as it does, these two sub-traditions. Fittingly, the play premiered within fourteen months of Jouvin's assuming control and was revived in November 1937, less than a year before he handed the theatre over to Eva Berkson, so neatly framing the Jouvin period.

If there is a tension between the physiological and psychological approaches to horror, which was brought into focus during the late twenties and early thirties, then it is a debate that is played out within the play itself. When Joubert enters Leduc's surgery, he presents a physical condition (pain in his finger), whilst Leduc diagnoses a psychological one. The whole of their ensuing dialogue then centres on Leduc's proposing a psychological solution while Joubert demands and threatens a physical response to his situation. Although Leduc does not give any ground, Joubert will not submit to reasoned argument and the scene culminates with a physical outcome with Joubert's self-mutilation. This pattern is repeated in Act 2. Here the dialogue centres around the same debate between Leduc and Joubert, with the latter claiming he is physically cured and the former wishing to begin a course of psychoanalytical treatment. Even when Leduc wins out and Joubert's condition is proved to have a psychological rather than a physical root, the final outcome of the piece is physical with Joubert taking an axe to his own wrist. On the evidence of this play, the tension between the two approaches to horror is a creative one and the Grand-Guignol benefits from both: psychological suspense followed by physical release and denouement.

If insanity is a key theme that runs throughout the entire life of the Grand-Guignol, then it is a topic that is closely related to the portrayal of the doctor/scientist. It is no accident, of course, that the medical and scientific professions (often these are one and the same) are portrayed as paradigms of clinical rationality, the triumph of the intellect over the emotions. This is echoed in the clinical whiteness of the operating theatre in *The Kiss of Blood* and throughout the Grand-Guignol repertoire.

Within the Grand-Guignol the consequences of the scientist's ultra-rationalism are two-fold. One possibility is that the doctor/scientist's obsession with the rational truth can lead to his becoming divorced from reality and descending into madness himself (a key modernist concern), as can be seen in plays such as de Lorde and Binet's *L'Horrible Expérience* (1909), where the doctor's crazed obsession to bring his daughter back to life leads to his own death. The second possibility is that the doctor/scientist becomes divorced from reality in a different sense, losing contact with humanity and retaining, under all circumstances, a cool and detached demeanour that manifests itself as unfeeling, uncaring, arrogant, and even, inhuman. The latter is the case in *The Kiss of Blood*. This is established within the character of Leduc in the very first instance in the way that he deals with the death of the trepanned patient under anaesthetic. The very purpose of the opening scene is, arguably, to establish Leduc's emotional detachment from the human beings he treats, above the creation of any sense of horror amongst the audience. He is only interested in his patients in the sense that they are objects to further his medical research. In spite of his pleas throughout the play of wanting to act in Joubert's best interests, he is really only investing so much time and energy in him because he represents an interesting case with the possibility of a reputation-making research paper.

In an analysis of Leduc's character we must also take close account of Volguine, who represents the more human side of science. In a sense she can be seen to represent Leduc's *alter ego*, his 'female' side, which he regularly suppresses. It is Volguine whom Leduc pacifies, after the death of the patient, with the words, 'It's a sad day, very upsetting', only to immediately reassert the authority of the detached self with the command, 'Note the time'. Likewise, it is Volguine who shrieks in horror as Joubert amputates his hand in the closing scene, whilst Leduc remains calm and in control. Leduc is only able to remain so detached because Volguine is allowed to show her emotions, albeit in a limited way. However, it is always clear which of the two is in charge.

What is particularly interesting about *The Kiss of Blood* is the many typical aspects of Grand-Guignol drama it successfully enshrines. It is a horror play but is never far from the world of farce, above all in the irony of Joubert's failed murder attempt and his attempts at self-destruction. In addition, the combination of physical and psychological horror demanded by the play, the chilling portrayal of the medical profession and the presentation of insanity all present particular challenges to the Grand-Guignol performer.

# THE KISS OF BLOOD

*(Le Baiser de sang, 1929)*

*by*

JEAN ARAGNY AND FRANCIS NEILSON

---

Professor Leduc
Dr Jeanne Volguine
Joubert
Mme Hélène Joubert
Male Nurse
Female Nurse
Patient
Maidservant

---

## ACT 1

*(The operating theatre at Professor Leduc's clinic. Everything
(doors, walls, etc.) is tiled or painted white. A door on the left
leads to the consulting room, a door on the right leads to the
wards. A large bay window is upstage left. The cabinets
upstage right contain the sorts of surgical equipment commonly
found in hospitals. All the furniture is chrome or painted in a
white metallic colour.*

*A patient lies on a high operating table. He is undressed and
covered by a sheet from his belly down to his knees. His legs
are heavily wrapped in cotton wool.*

*The opening scene could be summed up as 'an emergency case,
under chloroform, during a trepanation.'*

*Professor Leduc wears a long-sleeved coat with the sleeves
rolled up. He is wearing latex gloves, on his head a tight-fitting
white cotton cap, over which is secured an electric lamp—the
sort which focuses its beam on the area to be operated upon. A
cable runs from the lamp to a socket on the wall. Volguine and
the Male Nurse are wearing similar caps and white cotton
overshoes. The women wear surgical masks.*

*Dr Volguine, the Professor's assistant, stands to his left during the operation. Wearing latex gloves, she administers the chloroform and has a pair of tongs with which she picks up the instruments, the cotton wool swabs and the towels, as directed by the Professor.*

*Professor Leduc and Dr Volguine are wearing surgical masks as the curtain rises. Stage right, dressed head to foot in white, the Male Nurse stands next to the trolley for taking the Patient back to the wards. The Patient is a bald man. He is in pain, in spite of the chloroform, stirring and crying out from time to time.*

*A cross-shaped incision has been made on the forehead above the right eye. The flaps of skin are clipped back so that the frontal bone of the skull is exposed. Holes have been drilled in the skull with a trepanning drill. Everybody is leaning over, with outstretched necks, and attentively following the Professor's every move.)*

LEDUC (*shaking his head*): It's no good. It's not going to work. The lesion means that I'm going to have to drill here . . . and not here after all . . . there's no alternative.

VOLGUINE: That's the most resistant spot.

LEDUC: Yes. A compress . . . and another . . . and another one . . . a swab . . . how's his pulse?

VOLGUINE: Very weak.

LEDEUC: What about his legs? Are they cold?

VOLGUINE: Very cold.

LEDUC (*raising his eyelids, then raising his eyes upwards*): I only hope he's not going to give us any trouble with his circulation like the Dutchman the other day. Get the caffeine ready, a small amount. (*The Male Nurse bustles about.*) Swab! (*He begins to drill. The Patient stirs.*) Just a moment! (*The Professor stops drilling. Volguine hands him a stethoscope. He listens.*) This is bad . . . give him a jab immediately. (*He listens.*) This is bad. (*Volguine gives an injection.*) Let's do this quickly. (*He succeeds in drilling the hole. The Patient groans almost silently. The Professor hands back the stethoscope.*) All done.

VOLGUINE: I can't feel a pulse.

LEDUC: Give him cardiac massage. (*Volguine does so.*) Mouth-to-mouth resuscitation! What are you waiting for?

VOLGUINE: Adrenaline?

LEDUC: Yes, I'll give him an injection straight into the heart.

VOLGUINE: An intra-cardiac injection. Our last resort.

(*Leduc gives the injection. They wait a moment.*)

LEDUC: Too late.

VOLGUINE:   He's dead.
            (*Leduc nods.*)
LEDUC:      He was brought in to me ten minutes too late.
VOLGUINE:   Then it's not because the patient couldn't take the anaesthetic . . .
LEDUC:      Not at all! At least not the primary cause. It's only now that we can say with any certainty that he was brought to the operating theatre too late . . . Ah well, there we are. Remove the clamps and stitch him up. Clean the wound and wash down the body. Clear up and put everything into the sterilization unit. Thank you . . . it's very disppointing, most upsetting. Note the exact time. (*Volguine does so.*)
VOLGUINE:   09.57 hours.
LEDUC:      Record the time of death as 09.56 hours. Notify the office. Do the necessary paperwork and inform the family.
            (*The Male Nurse and the Female Nurse place the body on the trolley and the Male Nurse exits with it through the door stage right. Volguine picks up the instruments and the swabs bucket and exits stage right. The Female Nurse washes the operating table and sprays it with sterilizing solution and puts away the apparatus. She leaves, re-enters and pauses for a moment.*)
VOICE       (*offstage*): No, you can't go in there.
JOUBERT     (*offstage*): Well, I'm going in there whether you like it or not.
VOICE       (*offstage*): I'm sorry, Monsieur, but you're not allowed in there.
JOUBERT     (*offstage*): Well, we'll soon see about that!
FEMALE NURSE (*going to the door and opening it*): What's going on here?
            (*Joubert enters. He is about 40 years old with a severe-looking face and wild eyes. He has the look of someone suffering great pain. His right arm is in a sling.*)
JOUBERT:    Let me through, I say.
VOICE       (*offstage*): I'll call security.
FEMALE NURSE: Monsieur, you cannot come in here like this.
JOUBERT:    Professor Leduc, please.
FEMALE NURSE: Monsieur, you simply can't come barging your way in here.
JOUBERT:    I want to see Professor Leduc immediately.
FEMALE NURSE: Monsieur, please leave or I'll call security.
JOUBERT:    Call security then.
            (*Volguine enters.*)
VOLGUINE:   I heard what you said to the nurse . . . Monsieur, you are in an operating theatre. A patient was in here only ten minutes ago, another one will be brought in any minute.
JOUBERT:    I only raised my voice because they were trying to fob me off. If I've contaminated a sterilized area, then it's nothing that can't be rectified once I've left. I'll pay, of course. Now, if someone could please call Professor Leduc.
VOLGUINE:   He is very busy and, in any case, it is ten o'clock at night.
JOUBERT:    I know, but I'm in pain . . . I'm begging you, Madame.
VOLGUINE    (*to the Female Nurse*): Go and fetch the Professor.

JOUBERT:     Thank you, Madame.

VOLGUINE:    And who shall we say is waiting for him?

JOUBERT:     He doesn't know me.
             (*Female Nurse exits.*)

VOLGUINE:    Then tell me. I am his assistant, Dr Volguine.

JOUBERT:     It's him that I want to see.

VOLGUINE:    He certainly won't be able to see you right this minute. If it's an emergency, I could examine you.

JOUBERT:     He'll need to operate and I want the surgeon himself to have a look.

VOLGUINE:    Of course, Monsieur. If you would just take a seat . . .

JOUBERT:     No! Madame! Please!

VOLGUINE:    You're in pain, you say? An accident?

JOUBERT:     Yes, or rather no! Please, Madame, go and fetch Professor Leduc straight away.

VOLGUINE:    You're sure you don't want me to give you a preliminary examination?

JOUBERT:     I'm in such pain!

VOLGUINE:    Exactly. I might be able to make you more comfortable while we're waiting for the Professor to return.

JOUBERT:     Return? I've already asked, I know he's here.

VOLGUINE:    And who shall I say is here?

JOUBERT:     It doesn't matter.

VOLGUINE:    So, who sent you here, Monsieur?

JOUBERT:     What's more important is that he comes immediately.
             (*Professor Leduc enters via a different door.*)

LEDUC:       What's going on?

JOUBERT:     Professor Leduc?

LEDUC:       Monsieur.

JOUBERT:     Please excuse the interruption . . . I know it's late, but under the circumstances I was unable to make an appointment.

LEDUC:       What's this about, Monsieur?

JOUBERT:     I'm in such pain, doctor! I can't go on any more . . . I can't stand it any more . . . I'd sooner kill myself than carry on suffering like this. The agony is unbearable. You are a surgeon?

LEDUC:       Calm down, Monsieur, and I will examine you. What's your name?

JOUBERT:     Don't ask any questions, doctor, just examine me. I told you I just can't stand it . . . Look . . . Here . . . (*He takes off his jacket and tears at the bandage.*)

LEDUC        (*undoing the bandage*): Leave it . . . please . . . leave it. Let's have a look. What happened? An accident?

JOUBERT:     No. What you're about to see will surprise you.

LEDUC:       I very much doubt it. In twenty years of surgery I've seen everything, Monsieur . . . or at least almost everything.

JOUBERT      (*showing his bare arm*): Yes, but you've never seen that. Go gently now . . . (*He suppresses a cry.*) Ah!!

LEDUC:      I hardly touched you. Just here is it?

JOUBERT:    I told you the pain was unbearable, doctor!

LEDUC:      Have you injured it at all?

JOUBERT:    No.

LEDUC:      It may be an abscess or a tumour . . . well, there's no blood.

JOUBERT:    That's right, there's no blood.

LEDUC:      So . . . (*He examines the hand.*) I can't see anything. Absolutely nothing. No sign of injury, no swelling . . . Where exactly is the pain?

JOUBERT:    There . . . that's it . . . just there . . .

LEDUC:      Here?

JOUBERT     (*suppressing a cry of pain*): Ah! Ah!

LEDUC:      Let's see . . . If it wasn't for the fact you're sweating, I'd say . . . You're not having me on, are you?

JOUBERT:    I'm in agony!

LEDUC:      Wiggle your fingers.

JOUBERT:    I can't . . . I can't.

LEDUC:      And if I press here?

JOUBERT     (*in pain*): Ah!

LEDUC:      Now, Monsieur. You're going to have to tell me everything. I've examined your hand, which seems fine . . . not even a scratch . . . it isn't sprained, it isn't dislocated, it isn't infected, nothing . . . it's not your hand that's the problem. How did all this begin?

JOUBERT:    With a pain here, at the bottom of the index finger. And then it got worse, hour by hour, without any relief, for eight whole days. And now, I tell you, I can't bear it any longer . . .

LEDUC:      It's still not clear, Monsieur, your explanation . . .

JOUBERT:    Of course, but I beg you, doctor . . .

LEDUC:      For God's sake, there's nothing wrong with your hand.

JOUBERT:    As I said, doctor, if you're unable to help me, then I'd rather end it all . . . I mean it.

LEDUC:      All right, all right . . . let's have a look at the other hand.

JOUBERT:    This one's absolutely fine.

LEDUC:      Are you quite sure about that? If I press here . . . and keep pressing . . . like this . . . you should slowly start to feel a similar pain . . . yes? You see, it's hurting!

JOUBERT:    No, I can't feel a thing. It's the other one.

LEDUC:      Not at all. I can see it in your face.

JOUBERT:    I tell you it's the other one, the right hand!

LEDUC:      Now, Monsieur, a doctor can sometimes be a confessor. I can treat you and I will cure you, but you must tell me the truth.

JOUBERT:    I give you my word . . .

LEDUC:      Have you recently had a sudden setback . . . a bereavement or some other emotional or moral shock?

JOUBERT:    No, doctor.

| | |
|---|---|
| LEDUC: | Oh, but think, Monsieur! I am certain of it. And the source of your pain is not here . . . but here . . . (*He taps his forehead.*) |
| JOUBERT: | Ah! I understand now. You think I'm mad! Of course! |
| LEDUC: | No, no, not at all, but I've seen similar cases to yours. Sometimes it begins with concussion . . . |
| JOUBERT: | We're wasting time, doctor . . . You'll have to amputate the index finger . . . |
| LEDUC: | Amputate? |
| JOUBERT: | Yes, doctor, you must. |
| LEDUC: | Oh, surely not! Oh, very well. I'm not saying 'yes', but I must first observe how the pain develops. |
| JOUBERT: | I can't wait. |
| LEDUC: | Forty-eight hours! I promise I will operate if everything isn't under control within forty-eight hours. |
| JOUBERT: | I can see that I haven't convinced you of the desperate state I'm in, doctor. |
| LEDUC: | On the contrary. After all, I have promised to operate. |
| JOUBERT: | But the pain! |
| LEDUC | (*to Volguine*): Morphine will take care of that. |
| JOUBERT: | An injection! It's no good, doctor, I've tried everything. |
| LEDUC: | Quickly, Dr Volguine, quickly! |
| JOUBERT: | There's no point. I told you, you'll have to amputate sooner or later.<br>(*Volguine hands over the syringe.*) |
| LEDUC: | Sometimes I have a bit of a struggle with my patients, but once my mind is made up, I never give in to them.<br>(*Joubert resists. With authority, the doctor injects him.*) It's for your own good . . . there . . . Monsieur, in a moment your suffering will be a thing of the past, I give you my assurance. |
| JOUBERT: | But there's no option. You must operate! |
| LEDUC: | No, Monsieur, I have to be sure. |
| JOUBERT: | But why this determination to know what exactly? The cause of my pain isn't important. If you came upon an injured animal in the road, you wouldn't hesitate . . . |
| LEDUC: | Of course not, but having examined your hand, as requested, my conscience demands that I do not intervene. It's as simple as that and I won't be convinced otherwise! |
| JOUBERT: | It doesn't surprise me. That is why I have prepared a letter, which relieves you of all responsibility. Here it is. Read it. In this way you are covered. I am making a formal request and we only have to discuss the matter of your fee. |
| LEDUC: | Please, Monsieur . . . |
| JOUBERT: | Of course, doctor . . . how much? Name your price, I'll pay whatever you ask. I'll even pay in advance. How much? |
| LEDUC: | For all the money in the world, Monsieur, I would not make even the slightest incision into a healthy limb. |

JOUBERT: You're refusing? Even though you have my letter and you will be well paid? My offer still stands.

LEDUC: It's not a question of money. I'm quite sure that your pain is easing, that the morphine is already taking effect.

JOUBERT: And I tell you that I'm suffering even more. Your refusal . . . if you're not careful, I'll kill myself!

LEDUC: I will not be threatened, Monsieur. Will you please leave! Dr Volguine! Show the gentleman out.

JOUBERT: In spite of everything I've just told you, you're throwing me out? In my state?

LEDUC: Go home, Monsieur.

JOUBERT: Just a moment. I told you what would happen! I was right and still you refuse. Look, here, here . . . (*He takes out a knife.*)

LEDUC: Ah! Monsieur, be careful!

JOUBERT: I'm not threatening you. If I use this knife on myself, you will stop the bleeding. You will be obliged to dress the wound . . .

LEDUC: No, Monsieur, this is madness . . . give that to me . . . I forbid you . . .

JOUBERT: I have every right. I don't want to suffer any more . . .

LEDUC: And I will not allow an act of voluntary and savage mutilation under this roof!

JOUBERT: Well, operate on me then!

LEDUC: Very well. But give me the knife.
(*Silence. Joubert gives him the knife.*)

JOUBERT: At last. You agree?

LEDUC: Yes! That is to say, I will first make an exploratory incision.

JOUBERT: No, doctor . . . you must remove the index finger at the base. Only then will my suffering end.

LEDUC: Very well. You have an empty stomach?

JOUBERT: I've eaten nothing for two days.

LEDUC: Very well, give me your letter.

JOUBERT: Here we are. Does it cover everything?

LEDUC: Perfect. (*To Volguine*) Get everything ready for the operation.

JOUBERT: Thank you, doctor.

VOLGUINE: But, Professor . . .

LEDUC: Just do as I say.

VOLGUINE: Very well, Professor.

JOUBERT: At last. I won't be able to feel this pain that's been tormenting me for the past eight days. I haven't been able to sleep, doctor, and I have a fever.

VOLGUINE: Professor, are you sure about this?

LEDUC: Be quiet. Prepare the alcohol, the tincture of iodine and everything else that I'll need. (*He signals to Volguine and speaks to her in a low voice.*) Lay out the instruments so that he can see each and every one. There's nothing quite like it for making an impression. He'll soon change his mind, you'll see. (*He moves away from her, then loudly.*) Dr Volguine, scalpel!

|  | Clamps! (*She does so.*) The two saws! Needles! (*She lays out the instruments.*) Bowls. Swabs. Antiseptic. |
| VOLGUINE: | Here we are, Professor. |
| LEDUC: | Put your hand on the table . . . here . . . no, like this. Dr Volguine, roll up the sleeve as far as it will go. Stretch it out . . . now, don't move. (*To Volguine*) Prepare the straps! You'll have to secure them very tightly . . . |
| JOUBERT: | Are you going to tie me down? There's no need, doctor. I won't move, I give you my word. Go on then, but I want to be able to watch. |
|  | (*Leduc and Volguine exchange glances.*) |
| LEDUC: | Impossible! The mask . . . and get ready to administer the chloroform, Madame. |
| JOUBERT: | That's not necessary. I told you, I won't move a muscle. |
| LEDUC: | The pain will be so intense that I must at least take the minimum precautions. |
| JOUBERT: | I don't want to be put to sleep. I'm not a coward, you know . . . you'll see, not a word, not a cry. Go on, doctor, do it. Look, I'm not even trembling. |
| LEDUC: | I know my job, Monsieur. Without anaesthetic the pain will be unbearable and I need the patient to be completely still. |
| JOUBERT: | But you don't understand that the pain of amputation is nothing compared to the pain that's torturing me at the moment. I beg you, doctor. Disinfect, then cut away! |
| LEDUC: | Cutting a cross-section through the hand will be too painful. I am going to put you to sleep. Otherwise I'll stop right now. It's your choice! (*Another knowing nod to Volguine. She snatches hold of a mask and violently places it over Joubert's mouth.*) |
| JOUBERT | (*struggling for a moment*): No, no. (*A cry*) Ah! (*He falls unconscious.*) |
| VOLGUINE: | That's it. What do you want now, Professor? |
| LEDUC: | Carry on with the chloroform . . . very slowly. |
| VOLGUINE: | Very good, Professor. (*She administers the chloroform in short bursts.*) Are you still going to amputate? |
|  | (*Leduc winces. A silence.*) |
| VOLGUINE: | But he's mad, Professor! A poor lunatic! |
| LEDUC: | Not at all. He isn't mad. There are some things which I can't fully explain—even to myself—but this man isn't mad . . . |
| VOLGUINE: | I had the impression that he was out of control. |
| LEDUC: | Absolutely. One false move from me and he would have killed himself right in front of us. Take his hand. (*He examines it.*) There's nothing the matter with it. No swelling, some fever— just a little fever—pass me the small scalpel. |
| VOLGUINE: | This one? |
| LEDUC: | No, the other one, it's got a sharper point. |
| VOLGUINE: | Here we are, Professor. |

LEDUC:  A little more chloroform, please. I'm going to test his reflexes. (*He stabs Joubert three times, who winces slightly.*) You see, he has all his reflexes. Well, my dear partner-in-crime, I think there's only one thing to do. Only one.

VOLGUINE:  Fake the operation?

LEDUC:  Yes, and we'll hide the truth from him for three or four days, and so I'll cure him by the art of persuasion. You must bend the finger forward like that and strap it up tightly. Put on a short dressing to create the right impression. There's a groundbreaking paper in this for the Medical Academy. Do it up really tight so that it feels painful . . . and if we just splash a bit of blood around the table, the illusion will be complete. Oh, the poor fool! I've seen more cases like this in my career than you've had hot dinners, but this one . . . I just have to know what's at the root of it all. Remove the mask!

VOLGUINE:  His breathing's returning to normal.

LEDUC:  Did he notice the time?

VOLGUINE:  I don't think so.

LEDUC:  Good. If he asks how long the operation took, tell him a quarter of an hour.

VOLGUINE:  Very good, Professor.

LEDUC:  You can go now, but don't go too far. I'll call if I need you. I'm going to wake him up.

VOLGUINE:  Very good, Professor. (*She exits stage right.*)
(*Leduc lightly slaps Joubert's face until he opens his eyes.*)

LEDUC:  Excellent. Can you hear me? The operation is over.

JOUBERT  (*holding his throat*): It's burning here.

LEDUC:  Yes, that's the chloroform.

JOUBERT:  I'd like a drink.

LEDUC:  I can't give you a drink just at the moment. A little later. And your finger? Are you still in any pain?

JOUBERT:  Thank you, doctor, from the bottom of my heart. Ah, it's still hurting me, though.

LEDUC:  That's only to be expected after an operation.

JOUBERT:  Did I lose much blood?

LEDUC:  The usual amount! You must go and have a lie down now in the next room. You'll be taken there on a trolley.

JOUBERT:  But, doctor . . . I'm in pain . . . terrible pain, just like before.

LEDUC:  Not at all. Give it a few hours and it will all settle down.

JOUBERT:  But the pain is just as before, only worse. (*Sharply*) You *have* amputated the finger?

LEDUC:  Yes . . . It had to be done, you were right.

JOUBERT:  Show it to me.

LEDUC:  I beg your pardon.

JOUBERT:  My severed finger! I want to see it!

LEDUC:  But it's been disposed of.

JOUBERT:  Disposed of?

LEDUC:     Yes. It was incinerated immediately afterwards. That's normal practice.

JOUBERT:   That's not possible.

LEDUC:     I'm afraid it is. The day after tomorrow I'll change your bandage and then you can see for yourself.

JOUBERT    (*curtly*): Doctor, you're lying to me!

LEDUC:     Not at all!

JOUBERT:   Oh yes! Ah! I'm not stupid. It's hurting as if it's still there. My finger is there . . .

LEDUC:     How dare you question me. I did what had to be done . . . I did my duty.

JOUBERT:   Oh, I understand. You think I'm unbalanced! No! You didn't amputate my finger. Remove the dressing!

LEDUC:     I forbid it, it will haemorrhage.

JOUBERT:   Even so . . . I'm in too much pain. You don't want me to see, do you? Well, let's have a look then! (*He tears off the dressing with his bare teeth.*)

LEDUC:     Stop it, Monsieur, stop it! (*The dressing is removed.*) Dr Volguine!
           (*She enters.*)

JOUBERT:   There—you lied to me! Have you no pity? A man stands before you in agony and it has no effect on you? (*He cries.*) Have you nothing in there?

LEDUC:     Go and see another doctor. That's the only advice I can give you.

JOUBERT:   This is what you should have done . . . (*He grabs a scalpel and begins to viciously cut through his finger.*) . . . like this and this and this . . . Ah!

LEDUC:     Stop it, I tell you! (*He takes the scalpel from him.*)

VOLGUINE:  Oh, my God!

JOUBERT    (*laughing demonically*): Ha! Ha! Ha! Ha! Ha! It feels better already!

LEDUC:     But it's horrifically mutilated. You do realize that your finger is done for, yes, done for. You've cut right through the bone. This time it's quite beyond saving. It's nothing more than a scrap of flesh. (*To Volguine*) I'm going to have to remove it completely.

JOUBERT    (*with a nervous laugh*): That's what I wanted all along. My blood is flowing and it feels better. (*He laughs.*) Ha! Ha! Ha! Ha! Ha!

LEDUC      (*to Volguine*): Quickly! A length of elastic and the tongs!

JOUBERT:   Now watch me stay perfectly still . . .

LEDUC:     Sit down over there.

JOUBERT:   It's all right, I'll stand. Just like this!

VOLGUINE:  But the pain must be terrible!

JOUBERT:   This is nothing compared to what it was like before, Madame.

LEDUC:     There we are. Now I'll just cauterize it and then stitch it up.

JOUBERT:   Just to see my blood flowing, doctor, you have no idea what it's like. I'm not suffering any more. You'll never know just how grateful I am to you, doctor.

LEDUC:      You can go and lie down on the bed over there.

JOUBERT:    There's no need, doctor. I want to go home now.

LEDUC:      That's not wise, immediately after you've had a dressing put on.

JOUBERT:    No, no, doctor. There's somebody at home waiting for me.

LEDUC:      Somebody at home? Then it's essential that I come with you so that I can explain what has happened.

JOUBERT:    I'll see to that. You just hang on to my letter. And thank you, doctor. My car is outside with one of my servants who will help me if necessary.

LEDUC:      You're afraid that I'll find out who you are?

JOUBERT:    You asked me a question and I declined to answer it. (*The dressing is now done.*) Now, what about your fee? Just tell me the amount and I'll settle immediately.

LEDUC:      There's no rush—I'll still need to change your dressing tomorrow evening.

JOUBERT:    Can't I go to my usual doctor for that?

LEDUC:      Of course, I can't force you to come back here.

JOUBERT:    Well, that's everything then. I'll be on my way. How much do I owe you?

LEDUC:      In the circumstances I cannot accept a single penny.

JOUBERT:    I'm no longer in any pain . . . that's miraculous! Would you pass me my jacket, please? Here, look there must be 20,000 francs there. Take it and I'll still be in your debt.

LEDUC:      Keep your money, Monsieur.
            (*Volguine helps Joubert with his jacket.*)

JOUBERT:    Well, maybe you'd rather I donate the money towards the search for a cure for cancer. I'm familiar with your research and in this way . . .

LEDUC:      I could only accept if I knew the name of the person making the donation!

JOUBERT:    Not at all. Just put down 'anonymous donation'.

LEDUC       (*after a pause*): Whatever you like.

JOUBERT     (*leaving*): Doctor . . . Madame . . . (*He leaves.*)

VOLGUINE:   Well, how about that!

LEDUC:      I have to know! My car is just outside! Follow him for me! Go on! Quickly! (*She leaves.*)
            (*Curtain.*)


ACT 2


(*The living room of Joubert's private mansion. Large fireplace with a log fire. Maria puts another log on the fire. The door bell rings. Maria exits and then enters with Leduc and Volguine.*)

LEDUC: Could you give me something to write on and I'll leave him a note. (*He takes a seat.*)

MARIA: Here's some paper. Would you prefer a pencil or a fountain pen?

LEDUC: I have my own. (*He writes.*) Thank you.

VOLGUINE: When are you expecting him back?

MARIA: M. Joubert no longer has any routine. Besides he never receives visitors, not since Madame died.

LEDUC: Ah! His wife? Madame Joubert is dead?

MARIA: Yes, Monsieur. It happened two months and two days ago. Oh, what a terrible night!

LEDUC: If he knew I was here, he would receive me. Are you sure he isn't home.

MARIA: Quite sure. As I said, M. Joubert receives no visitors. The best thing is to write to him.

LEDUC: How did Madame Joubert die?

MARIA: In mysterious circumstances. Her body was fished out of the Seine. The inquest returned a verdict of suicide.

LEDUC: Were they happy?

MARIA: Happy? A marriage made in heaven! They adored each other. When her mortal remains were placed inside the family vault, Monsieur fainted during the ceremony. They had everything they could have wished for!

LEDUC: And since then?

MARIA: Since then? Life goes on, but what good are riches after such a catastrophe? I don't like to see him so upset. Everything has been so sad since she's been gone. She was so happy, so full of joy. And this house, in the middle of nowhere, now has the air of death about the place. At night, when the wind rustles the trees, it sounds like voices crying. At night I hear him walking in the garden. Well, I'm scared and tomorrow I'm leaving. I can't take it any more.

VOLGUINE: And is M. Joubert still having pain in his hand?

MARIA: In the right hand. But Monsieur had an operation the day before yesterday. I believe he had the second finger removed. He didn't want to talk about it.

LEDUC: Do you know who performed the amputation?

MARIA: No, he hasn't told anyone. Besides, there's only myself here now. The cook has gone and the chauffeur leaves this evening. He was sacked today . . .

LEDUC: Was your master suffering with his hand for a long time?

MARIA: For eight days during which I lavished care on him. He would moan and groan and there didn't seem anything wrong with his hand!

VOLGUINE: But how did this pain come about?

MARIA: That, Madame, is his little secret.

LEDUC: Has someone called in either yesterday or this morning to change the dressing?

MARIA:      This morning he went to see a doctor and he put a new
            dressing on for him.

VOLGUINE:   And he's in no more pain, as far as you're aware?

MARIA:      Not since he had the operation.

LEDUC:      What's the name of his doctor?

MARIA:      I don't know.

LEDUC:      You can tell me, I'm a doctor myself. Here's my card. It was I
            who performed the operation the day before yesterday.

MARIA:      Monsieur never tells me anything. He left after dinner—and
            when I say 'after dinner' it's only a figure of speech because he
            doesn't eat any more. He's a broken man . . . he tries as best he
            can, but he has nothing left.
            (*A noise. A voice calls out, 'Maria!'*)

MARIA:      My God, it's him!

MARIA!      What is the world and his wife doing in my living room after I
            left specific orders! (*He enters and seizes her by the collar.*) I
            expressly forbade you to let anybody in here . . .

MARIA:      But sir . . .

JOUBERT     (*his hand has a dressing on and is in a sling*): I'll send you
            packing, d'you hear, I'll send you packing, I will! Get out of
            here! (*She leaves.*) What are you doing here?

LEDUC:      Excuse me, Monsieur, but I came across your address quite by
            chance.

JOUBERT:    What do you mean, 'quite by chance'?

LEDUC:      Do you remember me?

JOUBERT:    Of course. Professor Leduc. Who told you my name? Who gave
            you my address?

LEDUC:      Your chauffeur and mine used to work together in the same
            house.

JOUBERT:    I suppose it's to be expected to find the servants plotting! I'll
            send the chauffeur packing too! Have you got something to say
            to me?

LEDUC:      I left you a note to let you know that I had called and to
            inform you of my wish to continue to treat you . . . but I have
            outstayed my welcome, I realize that. I apologize and shall
            leave now with my assistant.

JOUBERT:    It is I who should apologize, Monsieur. (*To Volguine*) Excuse
            me, Madame, I haven't even greeted you properly.

VOLGUINE:   But, Monsieur . . .

JOUBERT:    Not at all, manners cost nothing . . .

VOLGUINE:   As you know, Monsieur, I work with the professor here and it
            was I who insisted on tracking you down.

JOUBERT:    Tracking me down?

VOLGUINE:   Yes, to see how you were feeling.

JOUBERT:    But I'm much better. The wound is healing nicely and, as I told
            you, I'm in no more pain, just a slight temperature. In eight
            days' time I'll be able to take off this blasted dressing. I keep

|  | knocking things over and dropping things because of it. It's a damned nuisance. |
|---|---|
| LEDUC: | Would you like me to have a quick look? |
| JOUBERT: | There's no point, doctor, I am cured. |
| LEDUC: | Mentally as well? |
| JOUBERT: | Mentally? Ah, that's another matter entirely! |
| LEDUC: | Don't you think that the key to all this lies there? |
| JOUBERT: | There's no remedy for that, Professor. |
| LEDUC: | Perhaps, but your case fascinates me. |
| JOUBERT: | My case? But it's nothing special, and certainly nothing particularly interesting. |
| LEDUC: | In certain cases solitude is the worst possible thing and you are preparing a solitary existence, if I am to believe your servants. |
| JOUBERT: | Indeed, but there's nothing else to be done. Life is something I will just have to bear. |
| LEDUC: | That's an odd thing to hear from someone of your age. |
| JOUBERT: | I am in mourning, Monsieur. |
| LEDUC: | I know. |
| JOUBERT: | Ah, you've been told then. Of course, it's common knowledge and everyone has their own version of things! |
| VOLGUINE: | But . . . |
| JOUBERT: | Gossip spreads like wildfire until even complete strangers know all about one's own tragedy. You see, Monsieur, I loved my wife and I've been heartbroken since I lost her . . . |
| LEDUC: | Would you like to come and see me in my clinic? Tomorrow perhaps or another time? |
| JOUBERT: | There'd be no point, doctor. |
| LEDUC: | In that case, there's nothing more to be done. |
| JOUBERT: | I'm afraid I'm going to have to ask you . . . I'm expecting somebody . . . it's an appointment I cannot afford to miss. |
| LEDUC: | Of course. (*He moves towards the door.*) |
| JOUBERT: | No, wait. Wait a moment. I'm frightened. |
| LEDUC: | Frightened? |
| JOUBERT: | It's getting dark. She'll soon be here. (*At this moment Joubert is like a madman in a fit of despair.*) |
| LEDUC: | Who exactly? |
| JOUBERT: | Her . . . my wife! |
| LEDUC: | Your wife . . . is dead, Monsieur. |
| JOUBERT: | Yes, she is dead. But she keeps coming back all the same! |
| LEDUC: | Now, come, come, Monsieur. |
| JOUBERT: | You've no idea of the power that the dead can hold over the living. I never used to believe it, of course. I found it as ridiculous as everybody else. But now at night I'm frozen with fear . . . |
| LEDUC: | You must leave this house. |
| JOUBERT: | It makes no difference where I am, she comes to find me. She's taking revenge on me, she says. I try to fight it, but I'm |

powerless to escape. She puts her lips to my hand and her kisses burn. They are the kisses of a dead person . . . kisses of blood. It was these kisses that led me to you.

LEDUC: Everything you're saying about her, suggests that you're obsessed by her memory.

VOLGUINE: Take a holiday, that will be the best cure . . .

LEDUC: After a short time, you'll come home a different person.

JOUBERT: I can't. She won't let me. I had to cut off my finger because she wanted me to. You see, that's how it is! (*He shivers.*)

LEDUC: What's the matter?

JOUBERT: I'm cold.

LEDUC: You're shaking.

JOUBERT: Yes, she's coming, I tell you. I can feel it.

LEDUC: I think we should cut this interview short. I will return, with your permission, with a friend of mine, a doctor . . .

JOUBERT: Ah, yes, I see. A psychiatrist! I think perhaps you should leave. Madame! Monsieur!
(*Volguine leaves, followed by Leduc.*)

LEDUC: Goodbye, Monsieur.

JOUBERT (*alone*): She's here, she's around somewhere. Hélène, are you there? Answer me! Answer me, please! (*Apparition enters.*) What do you want of me? Why have you come? (*The apparition advances.*) Don't come any closer. Why have you come? To cause me more suffering? Your lips brushed against my hand and the pain was so terrible that I had to cut off my finger.

HÉLÈNE: Murderer!

JOUBERT: Ssh! Be quiet! Be quiet!

HÉLÈNE: Murderer!

JOUBERT: Be quiet! I was mad with jealousy. That letter that you hid and I took from you . . .

HÉLÈNE: I was innocent. I loved you so much. I begged you to believe me. But you wouldn't let it go, no matter what I said. I am going to prove my innocence to you. Ghosts don't know how to lie. The finger that pulled the trigger—that was what had to be amputated.

JOUBERT: If you only knew how I've suffered! Why have you come?

HÉLÈNE: You killed my body, but not my soul.

JOUBERT: Let me kill myself! Let me come and join you!

HÉLÈNE: No! When you have suffered, as I have suffered, only then will I call you. Until then my memory will haunt you every night. I will appear the moment you try to forget. I will never leave you! I am . . . your conscience!

JOUBERT: I'm going mad! Have pity on me?

HÉLÈNE: Pity? Did you have pity on me? You lured me out on to the water and killed me in the boat.

JOUBERT: Forgive me!

HÉLÈNE:   The bullet lodged there. Without checking to see if I was dead you brutally kicked me overboard and then you played the role of the despairing husband. But you were scared, scared of getting caught, scared of justice. So you pretended to believe that I had committed suicide and you identified as mine the body of some other poor soul fished out of the Seine . . .

JOUBERT:   That's enough . . . enough! You're only an apparition, a figment of my poor imagination.

HÉLÈNE:   I'm close enough now. So, the proof! Give me your hand!

JOUBERT:   No!

HÉLÈNE:   Give me your hand!
(*He protects himself, but still holds out his hand reluctantly.*)

JOUBERT:   Ah! No! Not that! Not that! Not that!

HÉLÈNE:   Give it to me! Can you feel how cold my hands are compared to yours?

JOUBERT:   Leave me alone! Let me be!

HÉLÈNE   (*laughing*): Ha! Ha! Ha! (*She quickly places her lips on Joubert's hand.*) There! You will feel a terrible pain, just like before . . . only much worse!

JOUBERT:   Ah!

HÉLÈNE:   The pain will just keep on relentlessly getting worse!

JOUBERT:   It's awful!

HÉLÈNE:   Your hand cannot be saved! The hand that held the gun! Ha! Ha! Ha!

JOUBERT:   I'm in agony! Agony! I can't bear it any longer! Help! Help me! (*Leduc and Volguine enter.*)

LEDUC:   Restrain her! There, that's it. Imposter!

HÉLÈNE:   Let me go! Let me go, I tell you!

LEDUC:   Who are you?

HÉLÈNE:   I am his wife!

LEDUC:   I'm in pain! Ah!

HÉLÈNE:   He tried to shoot me in the head and then throw me in the river, but I was saved by some sailors. In the hospital my face was ravaged by gangrene.

JOUBERT:   It's agony!

HÉLÈNE:   I'm taking my revenge in my own way! Ha! Ha! Ha!

LEDUC:   This is terrible!

HÉLÈNE:   The doctors at the hospital thought I was mad. They locked me up, but I escaped!

LEDUC:   Show me your face!

HÉLÈNE:   No, not that! Not that! The gangrene!

LEDUC:   Show me your face! (*He takes a step towards Hélène.*)

HÉLÈNE:   No! Wait! (*She starts to cry. With a sob in her voice*) It's horrible. My face is nothing but an open wound. Look! Look! (*Slowly she lifts her veil. Her face is undamaged. Pause. She is very pale, with mad eyes. Pause.*)

VOLGUINE:   She is mad! Poor thing!

JOUBERT:     I'm in agony! Agony! The axe! Where's the axe?! (*He rushes forward, takes the axe from the fireplace and hacks his hand off at the wrist.*)

LEDUC:       Stop him! Stop him, I say!

VOLGUINE:    My God!

JOUBERT:     No more pain! No more pain! (*He falls.*)

LEDUC        (*bending over Joubert*): Dead! He's dead!

HÉLÈNE:      Revenge! (*Manic laughter*) Ha! Ha! Ha!


THE END

# Bibliography

Antona-Traversi, Camillo, *L'Histoire du Grand Guignol* (Paris: Librairie Théâtrale, 1933)

Arrabal, Fernando (ed.), *Le Théâtre* vol. 2 (Grand Guignol special issue) (Paris: 1969)

Bakhtin, M., *Rabelais and his World* (Bloomington: Indiana University Press, 1984)

Bassnett-McGuire, Susan, 'Ways through the Labyrinth: Strategies and Methods for Translating Theatre Texts', in Theo Hermans (ed.), *The Manipulation of Literature: Studies in Literary Translation* (London: Croom Helm, 1985), pp. 87–102

Benjamin, Walter, *The Arcades Project* (translated Howard Eiland and Kevin McLaughlin, Cambridge, Massachusetts: Harvard University Press, 1999)

Berton, René, *L'Euthanasie, ou le Devoir de tuer* (Paris: Librairie Théâtrale, 1925)

Biscaia Filho, Paolo, *The Horror of the Grand Guignol* (unpublished MA thesis, Royal Holloway College, University of London, 1995)

Bloom, Clive, *Gothic Horror* (London: Methuen, 1998)

Brophy, Philip, 'Horrality—The Textuality of Contemporary Horror Films', in Ken Gelder (ed.), *A Horror Reader* (London: Routledge, 2000) pp. 276–84

Brunvand, Jan Harold, *The Mexican Pet* (New York: W.W. Norton, 1986; repr. ed. London: Penguin, 1989)

Buchan, David, 'The Modern Legend', in Green, A.E. and J.D.A. Widdowson (eds), *Language, Culture and Tradition* (Sheffield: CECTAL, 1981)

Callahan, John M., 'The Ultimate in Theater of Violence', in James Redmond (ed.), *Themes in Drama*, vol. 13 (New York: Cambridge University Press, 1991) pp. 165–75

Canetti, Elias, *Crowds and Power* (Harmondsworth: Penguin, 1973)

Carroll, Noël, *The Philosophy of Horror* (London: Routledge, 1990)

Casson, John, *Lewis and Sybil* (London: Collins, 1972)

Citti, Pierre, 'Peur sans pitié', *Europe: revue littéraire mensuelle* (835–36: November–December 1998) pp. 157–65

Clifford, James, 'On Collecting Art and Culture', in Simon During (ed.), *The Cultural Studies Reader* (London: Routledge, 1993)

Conrad, Joseph, *Selected Literary Criticism and The Shadow-Line*, ed. Allan Ingram (London: Methuen, 1986)

Cortazar, Julio, *Blow-Up and Other Stories* (New York: Pantheon, 1967)

Corvin, Michel, 'Une dramaturgie de la parole?', *Europe: revue littéraire mensuelle* (835–36: November–December 1998) pp. 150–56

Creed, Barbara, 'Kristeva, Femininity, Abjection', in Ken Gelder (ed.), *A Horror Reader* (London: Routledge, 2000) pp. 64–70

*Creepy 1993 Fearbook* (New York: Harris Publications, 1993)

Cronenberg, David, *Cronenberg on Cronenberg*, Chris Rodley (ed.) (London: Faber, 1997)

Cronin, Vincent, *Paris in the Eve 1900–1914* (London: Collins, 1989)

de Certeau, Michel, *The Practice of Everyday Life* (Berkeley: University of California Press, 1984)

de Lorde, André, *Pour Jouer la Comédie de Salon* (Paris: Hachette, 1908)

Deák, Frantisek, 'The Grand Guignol', *The Drama Review* (March 1974) pp. 34–52

Degaine, André, 'J'ai tremblé au Grand-Guignol', *Europe: revue littéraire mensuelle* (835–36, November–December 1998), pp. 194–99

Emeljanow, Victor, 'Grand-Guignol and the Orchestration of Violence', in James Redmond (ed.), *Themes in Drama*, vol. 13 (New York: Cambridge University Press, 1991) pp. 151–63

Fluger, Marty and Dawn Williams, 'Directing Grand Guignol' (www/aboutface. org)

Freud, Sigmund, *Art and Literature* (The Pelican Freud Library, Volume 14, Harmondsworth: Penguin, 1985)

Gelder, Ken (ed.), *A Horror Reader* (London: Routledge, 2000)

Gerould, Daniel, 'Oscar Méténier and the comédie rosse', *The Drama Review* (Spring 1984) pp. 15–28

Gordon, Mel, *The Grand Guignol: Theatre of Fear and Terror* (New York: Amok Press, 1988; rev. ed. New York: Da Capo Press, 1997)

Hand, Richard J. and Michael Wilson, 'The Grand-Guignol: Aspects of Theory and Practice', *Theatre Research International* (Vol. 25 No. 3, 2000) pp. 266–75

*The Haunt of Fear* (New York: EC Comics, 1952)

Hayes, Paul, 'France and Germany: Belle Époque and Kaiserzeit', in Paul Hayes (ed.), *Themes in Modern European History 1890–1945* (London: Routledge, 1992)

Homrighous, Mary, *The Grand Guignol* (unpublished Ph.D dissertation, North-western University, 1963)

Hughes, Richard, *Plays* (London: Chatto & Windus, 1924)

Innes, Christopher (ed.), *A Sourcebook on Naturalist Theatre* (London: Routledge, 2000)

Jean-Léo, 'Requiem pour le Grand Guignol' (unpublished typescript in British Library Manuscript Collections, 1962)

Jones, Stephen (comp.), *Clive Barker's A-Z of Horror* (London: BBC Books, 1997)

Kendrick, Walter, *The Thrill of Fear* (New York: Grove Press, 1991)

Kerekes, David and David Slater, *Killing for Culture* (London: Creation Books, 1995)

Kerston, Karin and Caroline Neubar, *Grand Guignol, Das Vergnügen Tausend Tode zu sterben* (Berlin: Verlag Klaus Wagenbach, 1976)

Knowles, Dorothy, *French Drama of the Interwar Years* (London: Harrap, 1967)

Krakovirch, Odile, 'Avant le Grand-Guignol: la cruauté sur le Boulevard du Crime', *Europe: revue littéraire mensuelle* (835–36: November–December 1998) pp. 123–37

Lenormand, Henri-René, *Confessions d'un auteur dramatiques* (Paris: Albin Michel, 1949)

Lovecraft, H.P., *Supernatural Horror in Literature* (New York: Dover Press, 1973)

McGrath, John, *A Good Night Out: Popular Theatre—Audience, Class and Form* (London: Methuen, 1981)

Macklin, Alys Eyre, *Crises: A Volume of Tales of Mystery and Horror* (London: Erskine MacDonald, 1920)

Maltby, H.F., *Ring Up the Curtain* (London: Hutchinson, 1950)

Mayeur, Jean-Marie and Madeleine Rebérioux, *The Third Republic from its Origins to The Great War 1871–1914*, (Cambridge: Cambridge University Press/ Paris: La Maison des Sciences de l'Homme, 1987)

Métayer, Léon, 'Une bonne affaire', *Europe: revue littéraire mensuelle* (835–36: November–December 1998) pp. 184–93

Mirbeau, Octave, *The Torture Garden* (translated A.C. Bessie, San Francisco: Re-Search Publications, 1989)

Nelson, T.G.A., *Comedy: the Theory of Comedy in Literature, Drama, and Cinema* (Oxford: Oxford University Press, 1990)

Néret, Gilles (ed.), *Erotica Universalis Volume II* (Köln: Taschen, 2000)

Paquet, Dominique, 'Fragments d'une poétique du grime, *Europe: revue littéraire mensuelle* (835–36: November–December 1998) pp. 166–71

Pavis, Patrice, 'Du butô, considéré comme du Grand-Guignol qui a mal tourné', *Europe: revue littéraire mensuelle* (835–36: November–December 1998) pp. 200–19

Pierron, Agnès, *Le Grand Guignol: Le théâtre des peurs de la belle époque* (Paris: Robert Laffont, 1995)

Pierron Agnès, 'Avorter, vomir ou s'évanouir, *Europe: revue littéraire mensuelle* (835–36: November–December 1998) pp. 101–7

Pradier, Jean-Marie, 'La Science ou la passion d'éventrer', *Europe: revue littéraire mensuelle* (835–36: November–December 1998) pp. 108–22

Pradier, Jean-Marie and Jean Marie Thomasseau, 'Bon Sang! Mais ça crève les yeux!', *Europe: revue littéraire mensuelle* (835–36: November–December 1998) pp. 98–100

Prendergast, Christopher, *Paris and the Nineteenth Century* (Oxford: Blackwell, 1992)

Richmond, Barry Alan, 'Le Grand-Guignol aux Amériques', *Europe: revue littéraire mensuelle* (835–36: November–December 1998) pp. 220–37

Rivière, François and Gabrielle Wittkop, *Grand Guignol* (Paris: Henri Veyrier, 1979)

Rubin, Martin, *Thrillers* (Cambridge: Cambridge University Press, 1999)

Sabatier, Guy, 'Idéologie et fonction sociale du Grand-Guignol à ses origines', *Europe: revue littéraire mensuelle* (835–36, November–December 1998) pp. 138–49

Said, Edward, *Orientalism* (London: Routledge, 1978)

Schechner, Richard, *Performance Theory* (London: Routledge, 1988)

Schumacher, Claude, *Alfred Jarry and Guillaume Apollinaire* (Basingstoke: Macmillan, 1984)

Scott, George Ryley, *A History of Torture* (London: Senate Publications, 1995)

Sée, Edmond, *Le Théâtre Français Contemporain* (2nd Edition, Paris: Collection Armand Colin, 1933)

Skal, David J., *The Horror Show: A Cultural History of Horror* (London: Plexus, 1993)

Skelton, Scott and Jim Benson, *Rod Serling's Night Gallery* (Syracuse: Syracuse University Press, 1999)

Stam, R., R. Burgoyne and S. Flitterman-Lewis, *New Vocabularies in Film Semiotics* (London: Routledge, 1992)

Steiner, George, *Antigones* (Oxford: Oxford University Press, 1984)

Sullivan, Jack (ed.), *The Penguin Encyclopedia of Horror and the Supernatural* (Harmondsworth: Penguin, 1986)

Thomasseau, Jean-Marie, 'Le rire assassin', *Europe: revue littéraire mensuelle* (835–36: November–December 1998) pp. 172–83

Wedekind, Frank, *The Lulu Plays*, translated by Stephen Spender (London: Calder and Boyars, 1972)

Wells, Paul, *The Horror Genre: from Beelzebub to Blair Witch* (London: Wallflower Press, 2000)

Williams, Tony, *Hearths of Darkness: the Family in the American Horror Film* (London: Associated University Press, 1996)

Witney, Frederick, *Grand Guignol* (London: Constable, 1947)

Wolf, Leonard (ed.), *The Essential Phantom of the Opera* (New York: Plume, 1996)

In addition to the books, chapters and articles listed above, the authors have also made reference to a number of reviews and short newspaper and theatre programme articles from the following publications, many of which can be found in the Archives of the Bibliothèque de l'Arsenal in Paris and the British Library (including the Lord Chamberlain's Correspondence) in London. Other references are made to personal correspondence with the authors.

*Bataille*
*Carrefour*
*Comoedia*
*Le Figaro*
*France Tireur*
*Guardian*
*L'Homme libre*
*L'information*
*Javroche*
*La Marseillaise*
*Monde Illustré*
*Oeuvre*
*Le Petit Bleu*
*Le Petit Journal*
*Le Petit Parisien*
*The Scotsman*
*Time Magazine*
*The Times*
*La Transition*

# Filmography

The relationship between Grand-Guignol and the cinema is a long and complex one. The following is not a comprehensive list of those films which could be argued to have derived from a Grand-Guignol tradition, nor is it a list of films which necessarily make direct or indirect reference to the Grand-Guignol or its repertoire; for such a list, see Pierron 1995, 1430–35. It is rather, a list, in chronological order, of those films referred to within the text of this book.

*The Lonely Villa* (D.W. Griffith 1909)
*Das Kabinett von Dr Caligari* (Robert Wiene 1919)
*Un Chien Andalou* (Luis Buñuel 1928)
*Gardiens de phare* (Jean Grémillon 1929)
*The Invisible Man* (James Whale 1933)
*Mad Love* (Karl Freund 1935)
*Dead of Night* (Robert Hamer et al. 1945)
*Les Diaboliques* (Henri-Georges Clouzot 1954)
*Attack!* (Robert Aldrich 1956)
*The Fly* (Kurt Neumann 1958)
*Les Yeux sans visage* (Georges Franju 1959)
*Peeping Tom* (Michael Powell 1960)
*Psycho* (Alfred Hitchcock 1960)
*El Angel Exterminador* (Luis Buñuel 1962)
*The Birds* (Alfred Hitchcock 1963)
*Onibaba* (Kaneto Shindo 1964)
*Ecco* (Gianni Proia 1965)
*Blow-Up* (Michelangelo Antonioni 1966)
*Night of the Living Dead* (George A. Romero 1968)
*Straw Dogs* (Sam Peckinpah 1971)
*The Exorcist* (William Friedkin 1973)
*Phase IV* (Saul Bass 1973)
*Assault on Precinct 13* (John Carpenter 1976)
*Carrie* (Brian de Palma 1976)
*Rabid* (David Cronenberg 1976)
*Evil Dead II* (Sam Raimi 1987)
*Reservoir Dogs* (Quentin Tarantino 1991)
*Le Grand Guignol: Le Baiser dans la nuit; Le Faiseur de monstres; Sous la lumière rouge; La Veuve; Vers l'au-delà; Le Baiser de sang* (Samouraï Films 1997)
*Scream* (Wes Craven 1997)
*15 Minute Tape* (Mike Tarnower 1999)

*The Blair Witch Project* (Daniel Myrick and Edouardo Sanchez 1999)
*Anatomie* (Stefan Ruzowitzky 2000)
*Vintage Erotica, anno 1930* (Cult Epics 2000)

# Index

Emboldened entries refer to illustrations